Language as
Commodity

Language as Commodity
Global Structures, Local Marketplaces

Edited by

Peter K. W. Tan and Rani Rubdy

continuum

Continuum International Publishing Group
The Tower Building   80 Maiden Lane, Suite 704
11 York Road   New York
London SE1 7NX   NY 10038

British Library Cataloguing-in-Publication Data
A catalogue record for this book is available from the British Library.

ISBN: 978-1-8470-6422-6 (hardback)
       978-1-8470-6423-3 (paperback)

Library of Congress Cataloguing-in-Publication Data
The publisher has applied for CIP data

Typeset by Newgen Imaging Systems Pvt Ltd, Chennai, India
Printed and bound in the United Kingdom by MPG Books, Cornwall

Contents

Notes on Contributors

Lubna Alsagoff is currently Associate Professor and Head of English Language and Literature at the National Institute of Education, Nanyang Technological University, Singapore. Dr Alsagoff's current research centres on the variation, status and development of language in relation to globalization, culture and identity. As a teacher educator, her research interests also extend to the development of English language teaching professionals and pedagogical grammars.

David Block is Reader in Education in the Faculty of Culture and Pedagogy at the Institute of Education, University of London. He has published articles and chapters in a range of journals and books. He is co-editor (with Deborah Cameron) of *Globalization and Language Teaching* (Routledge, 2002) and author of *The Social Turn in Second Language Acquisition* (Edinburgh University Press, 2003), *Multilingual Identities in a Global City: London Stories* (Palgrave, 2006) and *Second Language Identities* (Continuum, 2007). His main interests include the impact of globalization on language practices of all kinds, migration, multilingualism, multiculturalism and identity.

Paul Bruthiaux (PhD Linguistics, University of Southern California 1993) authored *The Discourse of Classified Advertising: Exploring the Nature of Linguistic Simplicity* (Oxford University Press, 1996) and was principal editor of *Directions in Applied Linguistics* (Multilingual Matters, 2005). He has published on applied linguistics in *Applied Linguistics*, *TESOL Quarterly*, *International Journal of the Sociology of Language*, *International Journal of Applied Linguistics*, *Language Problems & Language Planning*, *Current Issues in Language Planning*, *Journal of Asian-Pacific Communication*, *Language & Communication* and *English Today*.

Chng Huang Hoon has degrees in Philosophy (Honours, National University of Singapore) and Linguistics (MA, National University of Singapore; PhD, University of Texas at Austin) and is an Associate Professor in the Department of English Language and Literature, National University of Singapore. Her research interests include gender and identity construction. Her publications on the subject of gender include the book, *Separate and Unequal: Judicial*

Rhetoric and Women's Rights (John Benjamins, Amsterdam 2002) and various articles including '"We women aren't free to die": transacting sexualities in a feminism classroom in Singapore' (2004) in *Critical Asian Studies;* and 'The politics of representation: negotiating crisis in a feminism classroom' (2007, both with Chitra Sankaran) in *Australian Feminist Studies.* She has also written articles on identity construction, including the following: 'Celebrating Singapore's development: an analysis of the millennium stamps', in *Systemic Functional Linguistics and Critical Discourse Analysis: Studies in Social Change,* Lynne Young and Claire Harrison (eds, 2004), and '"You see me no up": Is Singlish a problem?', in *Language Problems & Language Planning* (John Benjamins, 2003).

Jinghe Han is a lecturer in English language and literacy education at Charles Sturt University, Australia. She is currently investigating the transitional experiences, pedagogic approaches and professional challenges of international university academics, as well as quality supervision for internationalizing higher education. Previously, she studied the retention of World English speaking student-teachers to meet the skills mismatch of teachers throughout Australia. She recently co-edited a special edition of the *Asia-Pacific Journal of Teacher Education* (Volume 35, Issue 2, 2007) on the theme 'robust hope in teacher education'. Her recent publications have appeared in *Foreign Languages Research;* the *Encyclopaedia of Activism and Social Justice; Transnational Curriculum Inquiry; Melbourne Studies in Education; Mosaic* and *VOCAL.*

Agnes S. L. Lam was born in Hong Kong and later studied in Singapore and America. She is now an Associate Professor at the University of Hong Kong. She has also held visitorships from Fulbright, the British Council, ASAHIL and Universitas 21. Some recent publications are: *Language education in China: Policy and experience from 1949* (Hong Kong University Press, 2005), 'The multi-agent model of language choice: National planning and individual volition in China' in *Cambridge Journal of Education* (2007), 'Language education policy in Greater China' in Springer's *Encyclopedia on Language Education* (2008). Her poetry has also been published in various parts of the world.

Ng Bee Chin (BA Hons, PhD, La Trobe University) is currently teaching linguistics in the Division of Linguistics and Multilingual Studies, Nanyang Technological University in Singapore. Her main research interests are conceptual and semantic development in Chinese children and bilingualism. She has also published in the area of interpretation and translation, language and gender, language acquisition and language attitudes. Working and living in Singapore has given her wonderful opportunities to explore the rich and complex issues of language acquisition, language attitudes, language identity and emotions in multilingual Singapore. She is the co-author of *Bilingualism: An Advanced Resource Book* published by Routledge in 2007.

Nkonko M. Kamwangamalu is a professor of Linguistics and Director of the Graduate Program in the Department of English at Howard University in Washington, DC, USA. He holds an MA and a PhD in linguistics from the University of Illinois at Urbana-Champaign and has also received a Fulbright award. Prior to joining Howard University, Professor Kamwangamalu taught linguistics at the National University of Singapore, the University of Swaziland and the University of Natal in Durban, South Africa, where he was Director of the Linguistics Programme. His research interests include multilingualism, codeswitching, language policy and planning, language and identity, New Englishes, African American English and African linguistics. He has published widely on most of these and related topics. Also, he has been an invited plenary or keynote speaker at a number of international conferences including, most recently, the 14th World Congress of Applied Linguistics (University of Wisconsin, 2005) and the Symposium in Honor of Joshua Fishman's Eightieth Birthday (University of Pennsylvania, 2006). Professor Kamwangamalu is Polity Editor for the series *Current Issues in Language Planning* (Multilingual Matters), member of the TOEFL Board, member of the editorial boards for *World Englishes* and *Language Policy* and past editor-in-chief of *Southern African Linguistics and Applied Language Studies*.

Rani Rubdy is Senior Fellow at the National Institute of Education, Nanyang Technological University, Singapore. Her research interests include second language teacher education, the management of educational innovation, ideology in language planning and policy and world Englishes. Her recent publications include the book *English in the World: Global Rules, Global Roles* (co-edited with Mario Saraceni) (Continuum, 2006) and the book chapters, 'Remaking Singapore for the New Age: official ideology and the realities of practice in language in education', in *Decolonisation, Globalisation: Language-in-Education Policy and Practice*, Angel M. Y. Lin and Peter W. Martin (eds) (Multilingual Matters, 2005), 'Language planning ideologies, communicative practices and their consequences' in Springer's *Encyclopedia on Language*

Education (2008) and 'The social and sociolingustic context of language learning and teaching' (with Sandra Lee McKay) in *Handbook of Second and Foreign Language*, Michael Long and Catherine Doughty (eds) (Blackwell, 2008).

Michael Singh is Professor of Education in the Centre for Education Research at the University of Western Sydney, Australia. He is currently investigating globalization and teacher movements into and out of multicultural Australia, and the globalization of higher education through the Bologna Process, both studies following on from research into student mobility and the globalization of higher education in Australia. He has recently studied the initial development of multi-level, large-scale education and training reforms to the senior phase of learning (Years 10–12); undertaken a meta-analysis of research into quality teaching and school leadership; and contributed a study of the motivation and engagement of rural, remote, low SES and Indigenous boys. His book, *Globalizing Education* (edited with M. Apple and J. Kenway), explores the complexities of local/global connectedness evident in policies and pedagogies governing education. In *Appropriating English* (with P. Kell and A. Pandian) he studied innovations in the local/global business of English language teaching.

Peter K. W. Tan is Senior Lecturer in the Department of English Language and Literature at the National University of Singapore. His research interests include the development of Non-Anglo Englishes in South-east Asia, including their literary and computer-mediated forms and how they have influenced naming conventions. He is author of *A Stylistics of Drama* and has published in the journals *Connotations, English Language Teaching Journal, English Today, Language Problems and Language Planning, Names: A Journal of Onomastics and World Englishes*; and in books *Advances in Corpus Linguistics* (eds Aijmer and Altenberg), *English in the World* (eds Rubdy and Saraceni), *Complicities: Connections and Divisions* (eds Sankaran *et al.*), *Evolving Identities* (ed. Ooi), *Singapore: The Encyclopedia* and *Exploring the Language of Drama* (eds Culpeper et al.) (the first two book chapters were co-authored with Vincent Ooi and Andy Chiang).

T. Ruanni F. Tupas is Lecturer with the Centre for English Language Communication, National University of Singapore. He is Chief Editor of *Reflections on English Language Teaching*, writer of *Second Language Teaching* (University of the Philippines Open University, 2004), editor of *(Re)making society: The politics of language, discourse and identity in the Philippines* (University of the Philippines Press, 2007) and co-editor of *Current Perspectives on Pedagogical Grammar* (Singapore Association for Applied Linguistics, 2007). He has published in a number of refereed journals such as *Language Problems and Language Planning, World Englishes* and *The Asia-Pacific Education Researcher*, and has likewise been invited to write referee reports for several journals, including *Southeast Asian Studies, Asia-Pacific Social Science Review* and the *Malaysian Journal of ELT Research*.

Wenfeng Wang is a doctoral student at the English Centre, the University of Hong Kong, currently working on a project that explores teacher beliefs and practices in the context of curriculum reform in China. He received a BA in English from Hebei Teachers' University and an MA in Linguistics from Beijing Foreign Studies University. His research interests are in curriculum studies and teacher education. His work has been published in *English Language Education in China, Research Studies in Education* and *English Teacher Education in China: Theory and Practice* (forthcoming by Foreign Language Teaching and Research Press).

Lionel Wee is an Associate Professor in the Department of English Language and Literature at the National University of Singapore. His research interests include New Englishes, metaphor and discourse, language ideologies, language policy and planning and general issues in pragmatics and sociolinguistics. His articles have appeared in *Applied Linguistics, Journal of Linguistics, Journal of Multilingual & Multicultural Development, Journal of Pragmatics, Journal of Sociolinguistics, Language in Society* and *World Englishes*. He is author (with Antonio Rappa) of *Language Policy and Modernity in Southeast Asia*.

Praise for *Language as Commodity:*
Global Structures, Local Marketplaces

Looking at language in relation to current conditions of globalization, this book takes up the key issue of the commodification of languages. With a focus particularly on Asian contexts (Singapore, Malaysia, China, India, the Philippines) the authors in this book ask what happens to languages (and varieties of language, and language learners and users) when languages are seen primarily in terms of their usefulness and value within commercial markets. This book does an excellent job of exploring and opening up for further discussion and investigation crucial questions about how languages are valued differently as commodities, even at times as consumer items. To view language as a commodity is to view language in instrumental, pragmatic and commercial terms, which, as this book well demonstrates, is precisely the dominant discourse on language in many contemporary contexts. The different studies in this book therefore give us ways of taking seriously notions of linguistic capital when applied to languages such as English, Chinese or Malay. For all of us involved in language education, these are highly significant questions for they go to the heart of motivations for language learning, language policy decisions, and the ways in which languages are valued.

Professor Alastair Pennycook
Faculty of Education
University of Technology Sydney
Australia

The post-colonial nation making of the 1950s and 1960s is a time of dashed dreams. In the wake of the receding colonialism that had characterised the bulk of the geo-political space of the world new nations were forged and old nations resurrected. Their common aim was to provide linguistic dignity to what their often multilingual realities. In some of these new nations English was given notice, in others it was ejected, in still others it was restricted. Such nationalist and nativist language planning affected all colonial languages but English has returned decisively to where it was distanced, denied or delimited. This is a transformation from Language of Empire to Language of Economy; a bounded commodity traded in borderless commerce, realised in education and training and authorised in official discourse. Linguistic commodification reflects the ruling rationality of markets, our time, New Times, but probably a contingency awaiting future challenge. In this significant volume educationists, socio-linguists, and sociologists subject this phenomenon of language as commodity to a multi-perspective scrutiny, especially of English as lingua mundi in its unprecedented expansion and penetration of societies in Asia and Africa and elsewhere, producing a series of sharp, critical and engaging contributions on global English and the related questions of language rights, linguistic difference, multilingualism and cross-national communication and exchange.

Professor Joseph Lo Bianco
Chair of Language and Literacy Education
University of Melbourne
Australia

Preface

In today's world, languages are frequently in competition with each other and this affects the decision-making of those in positions of power in determining language policies and planning: for example, schools boards or Ministries of Education or even governments deciding on mediums of instruction or the choice of second or foreign languages. Often decisions about language (or dialects or language varieties) are related to notions of usefulness – whether defined in terms of their pragmatic and commercial currency; or their value as symbols of sociocultural identity; or as modes of entry to coveted social hierarchies; or as strongholds of religious, historical, technological and political power bases. Languages are seen as commodities that carry different values in an era of globalization. In this volume, we seek to engage with the issue of the articulation of language policies and positions in relation to the role and function these languages have in the context of particular communities. The chapters examine how the valuing of different languages, defined in terms of the power they have in the global marketplace as much as within the complex matrices of the local sociopolitics, strongly underpin the various motivations that influence policy-making decisions. Operating in tandem or in conflictual positions, and often reinforced by the sociopolitical structures existing within these particular communities, these motivations create the tensions that characterize many language-related issues in the postcolonial, postmodern world we live in today.

Introduction[1]
Peter K. W. Tan and Rani Rubdy

Let us take you through three attested vignettes.

The first is that of a classroom of an independent college in Britain. The pupils are mainly white and they are carefully following the pronunciations of words in Mandarin Chinese. The head teacher, Richard Cairns, has recently made Mandarin Chinese a compulsory subject in this college, and he justifies his decision thus: 'We in Britain need to face up to this challenge, see it for the trading opportunity that it is, and ensure that our nation's children are well-placed to thrive in this new global reality' (BBC 16 January 2006). His is not an isolated view. Another advocate of more Chinese in British schools is Anthony Seldon, master of Wellington College, who says, 'If current and future generations of children do not have access to lessons in the main Chinese language, this will disadvantage the UK economically and culturally' (BBC 27 February 2006). This seems to be the brave new world where languages are learnt to gain economic advantage.

The next vignette is in South Korea – a camp some 40 miles from the capital Seoul, where there are many Korean middle school (lower secondary school) pupils. The buildings are an unusual mix – with European-style terraced houses and castle structures and the place is known as the English village. The children have come through a mock passport control station to enter the English village, and once in only English can emanate from their mouths (Faiola 2004). And the reason for this? More and more English is used in businesses, even within Korea: 'South Korea's top companies, Samsung and LG Philips, have begun conducting job interviews partly in English. Philips is gradually moving toward an English-only corporate e-mail policy, company officials said.'

The third vignette requires us only to cross the Sea of Japan. English has been firmly established in the Japanese school system, and pupils learn it for at least six years in middle (lower secondary) school and high (upper secondary) school, and the government has indicated that 'all Japanese [should] acquire a working knowledge of English' in a globalized world where English is a 'prerequisite for obtaining global information, expressing intentions, and sharing values' (Prime Minister's Commission 2000). And yet as we wander around the Japanese cities, we hear little English but might see what look like English words used in shop names or on commercial items. We enter a shop and might pick up a photo album that has the following emblazoned on its cover: 'The wind has shifted to the south-east. I am exposing myself comfortably to it' (McArthur 1998: 27). The English there is for decorative rather than communicative purposes. If we listen carefully to the Japanese language, we might also hear loan-words from English – manshon (like 'mansion', only it means 'apartment'). Despite the rhetoric of a globalized world, it is interesting to note that English is kept at arm's length in Japan. As Seargeant puts it, 'the English language is not imported whole as a communicative tool, but unpacked and its component parts reconfigured in unfamiliar contexts' (2005: 314).

The first two vignettes seem to show conscious decisions to devote greater attention to particular languages that seem to give the lie to the standard textbook dictum that all languages are equal. Of course, we know that this is correct at the grammatical or social level. Here, we see conscious decisions being made both by those with authority (head teachers and multinational companies) and those who vote with their feet (school pupils and their parents) to favour particular languages simply because these languages are perceived as being advantageous to other languages in the benefits that they can bring to the user – or, in Bourdieu's terms, they see linguistic capital inherent in these languages. Languages are therefore being evaluated as commodities that command an exchange value. Linguistically, we also appear to be moving into the postmodern age (as Graddol (2006) describes it in *English Next*) when multilingualism is the norm as opposed to the modernist norm of a single language identified with the nation state. These earlier-established notions and ideologies surrounding language such as national identity through language (Heller 1999) give way to complex identities through the notion of globalization because never before have there been more options in linguistic choices.

The third vignette shows a challenge to globalization: where English as the global language is accepted in Japan, but not before taming it and Japanizing it and rendering it acceptable for Japanese consumption.

More than ever, these vignettes indicate that the monolinguistic model, where a single language is deemed sufficient for all functions, is giving way to a multilinguistic model, where speakers need to be able to switch languages; and this is the sticking point: how the complementary relationship between languages can be negotiated. Should one be kept at an arm's length as in the

Japanese vignette, or be welcomed with open arms? How can the relationship between various languages be maintained, and should we or governments be concerned if a language encroaches upon the traditional space of another language? And now that there is some choice in linguistic options, what are the reasons given for preferring one language to another? Is it really true that we now treat languages like commodities that we invest in and can await capital gains in time?

The complexity of today's world and the changing needs of societies mean that individuals, communities, Ministries of Education and governments are making decisions about the merits of learning, promoting or insisting on particular languages. They need to balance the positions of various languages in multilingual contexts and to decide whether to encourage, ignore or attempt to limit the encroachment of a language into the traditional sphere of another language. Treating languages as commodities comes to a head in the context of linguistic rights and language-in-education debates.

This then is the focus of this book: it explores issues surrounding treating languages as commodities. Here languages 'constitute a saleable commodity with regard to business and marketing, whilst for the clients they represent an investment in cultural capital which can then be exchanged within the global labour market' (Rassool 2007: 148). The contexts discussed are by and large postcolonial societies such as Singapore, Malaysia, the Philippines, India and South Africa, where although local languages feature centrally in the discourse of nationhood, colonial languages, in particular English, have continued to be emphasized as key elements of modernity and have retained high exchange value. But also featured are more international settings such as the United Kingdom and Australia where immigrant populations and professionals alike must attain acceptable degrees of proficiency in English if they wish to assimilate into the global cultural economy of the host communities. The inclusion of China is timely in that it represents a unique situation where earlier preference for Russian as the most favoured foreign language has been completely supplanted by English due to its economic clout. English language teaching is a booming industry in China today, motivated by its newly acquired membership of the World Trade Organization and anticipation of the 2008 Olympics, with governments encouraging citizens to learn English and parents persuading, even forcing, their children to speak it.

Many of these countries are being affected by the changes taking place in the global labour market with language popularity closely following market trends. As the economic status of these countries improves and they come to be regarded as important trading partners within the global economy, their languages grow in value within the international language market. Thus the value profiles of languages and language varieties often reflect how they are positioned in global as well as local markets. Recall, for instance, the popularity of learning Japanese during the 1980s when Japan had assumed a leading position in the world economy. The current ascendance of Mandarin Chinese in response to China gaining importance as a world trading partner and its potentially vast but as yet untapped consumer market is a more recent example. Thus, while Singapore's education policy requires that all Singaporeans learn their ethnic 'mother tongue' as an additional language, that is, Chinese children learn Mandarin, the Malays learn Malay and the Indians choose from one of the Indian languages offered by the school curriculum (English is the first language in Singapore schools), many non-Chinese Singaporeans currently wish to learn Chinese so as to be better prepared for trade with China – subscribing to much the same rationale as the head teacher in our first vignette above.

At another level, many countries with advanced economies are increasingly 'going offshore', tapping into a vast supply of low-skilled, low-paid labour located within developing countries. A huge range of services are affected by the fact that cheap communications now allow many of them to be carried out in distant locations such as India, the Philippines, Taiwan and China. Graddol observes that

> As national education systems create suitable employees, transnational companies are shifting their research and development centres to these countries. . . . Everywhere, in both developed and developing economies, there is a new urgency to increase the educational level of the workforce to maintain a country's competitive advantage as it loses advantage in less skilled areas to countries lower in the development chain. (Graddol 2006: 36–37)

Many of the postcolonial contexts discussed in this volume are bilingual or multilingual, ethnically complex societies where policy makers often have to negotiate between competing concerns such as the need to promote an international language for the purpose of modernization, the need to develop national cohesion through a common language as well as the need to retain their indigenous languages for cultural integrity. The status accorded historically to former colonial languages, combined with contemporary changes taking place within the global cultural economy, has left an enduring dilemma with regard to language planning and policy in these countries. Catapulted into a highly competitive international financial, commodity and labour market in which they had to compete, many of these countries adopted colonial languages under the assumption that it would facilitate trade and, through this, economic development. The benefits these languages offered in terms of social mobility, economic power and societal modernization constituted a powerful rationale for their inclusion in language-in-education policies.

Policy decisions involving English in particular have led to the inevitable polarization of languages in the psyche of governments and subjects alike: English is seen as an instrument of modernization, economic progress and social, educational and occupational success; the local indigenous languages, as a repository of cultural identity and social solidarity. As Rassool observes:

> Since the global language market favours ex-colonial 'world' languages, and particularly English, they serve potentially to marginalize local/national languages by reducing their exchange, or purchasing value within formal domains. As was the case under colonialism, this shapes the language choices of people, in favour of economically powerful languages – and since language is intrinsic to culture – to some extent, also the lifestyles associated with them. (Rassool 2007: 149)

In a multilingual and multiethnic context, this is detrimental to the cultural and linguistic maintenance of people whose languages are not catered for in language-in-education policy. Indeed, because of the life chances it offers, an orientation to ex-colonial languages demarcates a power divide, not only culturally and linguistically, but also economically, socially and politically.

It will be seen that in such contexts language users and learners, like the state, do covertly or overtly ascribe value to each of the languages available to them and may sometimes differ in the values they so ascribe. Thus conflicting ideologies can often underlie the language choices apparent in the discrepancy observed between the official policy of the state and the realities on the ground within the complex dynamics of this process of trading language value by agents such as language planners, educators, parents, language learners and language users (Rubdy, 2008).

The global spread of English and its increasing socioeconomic importance in the world have made it a precious commodity hugely in demand globally. However, as some of the chapters in this volume show, this trend has the potential to create unequal relations not only between individuals and groups of individuals but between and among languages and also nations. Decolonizing efforts at promoting indigenous African languages in education in South Africa have largely failed, especially in the urban communities, owing to a shift to English and French, due to the tangible economic advantages associated with these languages and the perpetuation of the colonial myth of the formal and functional inadequacies of indigenous languages. Even in a country like Singapore which is avowedly multilingual and claims to accord equal status to all four of its official languages, English is the *de facto* working language and operates as a powerful instrument of vertical control despite the state's active promotion of its indigenous 'official' languages – Mandarin, Malay and Tamil (Rappa and Wee 2006). In neighbouring Malaysia, the realization that former language policies which sought to phase out English within the social, economic and political arena were grossly misconceived has led to restoring the role of English as a valuable economic resource. These are an indication of just some ways in which individual countries are adjusting to language market demands within the global cultural economy.

The dominant role that English has acquired within the processes of globalization has been viewed by several scholars (Phillipson 1992; 2003; Skutnaab-Kangas 2000; Lin and Martin 2005) as a continuation of the hegemony of the colonial regime. Whilst colonial language-in-education policies played a significant role in shaping colonial subjectivities, they also served to frame levels of access to the labour market. That is, those who were literate and fluent in the colonial languages, which represented the languages of power, would have had better access to jobs than those who did not meet this requirement. These scholars maintain that the long-term impact of colonialism on the socio-political, economic and cultural base of colonized polities has led to the construction of a colonial consciousness and a colonial discourse which legitimizes the idea of the inherent superiority of the colonial rulers, and the new élite who have replaced them in a decolonizing world. According to these scholars, the collective and individual beliefs, values, expectations, aspirations, dreams and desires of formerly colonized societies are dispositions derived under the influence of the colonial experience and represent the colonial *habitus* (referring once again to a concept from Bourdieu 1991) The colonial *habitus* thus shaped seems to play a central role in influencing postcolonial language-in-education policy choices when ex-colonial languages are valorized and redefined as 'world' languages. This leads to the neglect and devaluation of local languages or local varieties of the 'world' language, a process in which people seem to collude (consciously or unconsciously) in their own dispossession.

The high status accorded to English, especially Standard English, has been reinforced by the significance it has assumed in the global cultural economy. English now represents the preferred language medium in which most transactions take place within transnational business organizations, as well as in political or economic encounters such as those that characterize the World

Trade Organization, World Bank and International Monetary Fund ensembles; so much so that one consequence of its current status as a world *lingua franca* is the potential intolerance with which other varieties of World Englishes are likely to be met, resulting in the economic devaluation of these speakers of other Englishes, particularly in Anglophone Inner Circle countries such as the USA, the United Kingdom and Australia. In these settings, students as well as professionals from non-English-speaking countries who do not speak the standard variety are disadvantaged, and their knowledge and expertise routinely devalued, when competing with Anglophone speakers.

Negative attitudes towards varieties of English that do not conform to Standard English norms (usually British or American) in the Inner Circle are easily transferred to countries in the peripheries, as evidenced by the Singlish–Good English debate in Singapore. What is interesting in the Singapore context is how government leaders have appropriated much of this native speaker *v.* non-native-speaker discourse in their own English language ideological debates, which reflect a steadfast rejection of any possibility of Singaporeans taking up ownership of either Standard English or Singlish.

> English has been ideologically constructed as a purely instrumental and functional language within the context of nation building and the global economy. In this context, the officially preferred model is British RP, and the Inner Circle speakers of English continue to be regarded as the true owners of English. At the same time, speakers of the local variety of English, especially the colloquial form of Singlish, are portrayed as uneducated, uncouth, and unworldly. One of the consequences of this ideological construction is that there is no discursive space in Singapore's language ideological formation to label English as a mother tongue or to allow Singaporeans the acquisition of native speaker membership – even though more and more Singaporeans do in fact primarily use English. (Bokhorst-Heng *et al.* 2008: 2)

There are alternative viewpoints regarding the role and status of English as a global language that take a more nuanced perspective of the issues relating to language choice, language use and language learning, which suggest new possibilities for language-in-education policies. One view is that while English undoubtedly is in the ascendance as a pre-eminent 'world' language, it does not mean the situation necessarily will remain static and that its hegemony will not be contested in the future by other international languages, particularly across geopolitical regions (Graddol 1997; 2006). As Graddol states, 'English is no longer the "only show in town" . . . Mandarin and Spanish, especially have become sufficiently important to be influencing national policy priorities in some countries' (Graddol 2006: 62).

Studies of communicative practices in multilingual educational settings have shown that language use in the classroom often defies policies that are largely monolingual and purist. Code selection and code-switching become particularly prominent in contesting (or constructing) domination in schools (Heller and Martin-Jones 2001; Martin 2005). While teachers and students use the authorized language for on-task and official sites, they use the unauthorized codes in surreptitious ways in unofficial and off-task contexts. Such practices enable minority students to represent their preferred cultural identities, develop solidarity and tap into local knowledge both to facilitate their learning and to resist unfavourable policies by employing covert language acquisition and communicative practices that counteract dominant policies.

Similarly, local languages also flourish in informal markets, such as popular music, the performance arts, heritage tourism and other multiple small businesses conducted at the grassroots in many developing countries, catering for the different ethnolinguistic diasporas globally and contesting the hegemony in a bottom-up sense (Canagarajah 2005). And surveys of internet users in the USA suggest that their use of English sites decline as alternatives in their first language become available. What began as an Anglophone phenomenon has rapidly become a multilingual affair. Local languages are more likely to appear in less formal contexts such as chat rooms and in contexts where everyone shares a first language (Graddol 2006: 44–45). All this presents a challenge to globalization and to the supremacy of English.

There is also the question of whether power is inherently located in languages or in the people who use them – whether to control, to contest, to appropriate, to resist, to collude or to represent themselves and their personal interests. This brings into play the role of *human agency* and *self-definition*. Recent studies have shown how together, when mobilized constructively towards social struggle, they constitute a powerful mechanism for challenging hegemonic and exploitative structures and opening up new possibilities, for re-interpreting meanings in ways that create alternative discourses that can empower individuals and groups even as they live their everyday lives.

Those subscribing to the idea of human agency (Pennycook 1994; Canagarajah 1999; 2005) hold a less pessimistic and deterministic view, taking into account that people are agents, not merely objects, in the creation of their own meanings. From this point of view, dominant languages may well be utilized to subvert the very interests they represent. Thus, in the struggle for independence, English was used as a medium of communication to challenge the hegemony of colonialism in India, as it was to contest the mental, cultural economic and political subordination that constituted the Apartheid policy and practice in South Africa. Studies have also shown how marginalized peoples are capable of resisting established policies, constructing alternative practices that exist parallel to the dominant policies, and even initiating changes that transform unequal relationships (Canagarajah 1999; 2005). The deployment of English in creating such counter-discourses indicates that the language can be used 'to empower people in their everyday lives by enabling them to defy discrimination and exploitative practices that dehumanized them' (Rassool 2007: 143).

Empowering also are the creative strategies of multilingual speakers in Kachru's (1992) Outer and Expanding Circle countries that generate linguistic or cultural blending and hybridity as the language is appropriated and adapted to a variety of new cultural contexts. As English becomes more widely used as a global language, it will become expected that people will signal their nationality and other aspects of their identity. This is a process that fundamentally involves 'a radical act of semiotic reconstruction and reconstitution' (Kandiah 1998: 100), nativizing and localizing the global in the creation of local or new varieties of English. Thus we have Indian English, Singapore English, Filipino English, South African English, to name a few, each with their own distinctive linguistic and pragmatic features. Our third vignette above, involving Japanese speakers unpacking and then piecing together components of English with a blend of local elements, is a clear instance of such *dis-embedding* and *re-embedding* of linguistic forms in new environments. In a recent paper, Pennycook points out how, the lyrics and sleeve-notes of a Japanese hip-hop outfit, Rip Slyme, suggest an even more complex, dense and contextually grounded re-embedding process. In producing and performing the local–global raplish, through this process of unpacking and rearticulating English linguistic forms, these rappers were also simultaneously engaged in creating a new identity. The global role of hip-hop in relationship to English produced for them 'particular understandings of what it means to participate in multilayered modes of identity at global, regional, national and local levels' (Pennycook 2003: 529).

One clear disadvantage of adopting ex-colonial languages or varieties in language-in-education policy, then, is that it creates an unequal distribution of power and wealth in society, where power is constructed and reproduced by small élite groups constituted intellectually, linguistically or politically (or a combination of these). Economic globalization linked in this way to language choice is inherently asymmetrical, providing legitimacy selectively to speakers of majority languages and disenfranchising speakers of indigenous minority languages. This has practical implications as well when it translates into unequal allocation of teaching and learning resources in favour of 'world' languages at the expense of educational support for indigenous languages. A mixed language economy which promotes and supports a plurality of languages and cultures that provides a wider representation for people would seem to offer a more just and fairer alternative.

Some scholars contend, however, that more education does not automatically lead to economic development. They point out that poverty reduction in societies with severely limited resources 'is not a single factor process', and 'making it come about requires much besides literacy, including development-friendly macro-economic policies, the encouragement of a business ethic, the provision of a transparent governance and of a judicial system capable of enforcing contracts predictably and reliably, and investment in infrastructure' (Bruthiaux 2002: 287). Bruthiaux goes on to argue that what providers of English language education should agonize about is less the notion of linguistic imperialism propagated through English language education than the likely diversion of scarce resources in the direction of English at the expense of vernacular language education. He maintains that

> literacy constitutes both a practical tool for handling the increasing complexities of economic transactions and a conceptual tool for visualizing hitherto inaccessible opportunities. Given that a key objective of economic development policy is poverty reduction in societies with severely limited resources, the overall objective must be to deliver basic literacy as efficiently as possible. In practice, this objective points to language education in a local vernacular rather than one of the languages of wider communication on offer, including former colonial languages such as English or French. (Bruthiaux 2002: 288)

This of course flies in the face of the intense parental demand for English language education to be provided for their children in countries like India, China, Singapore, Malaysia, the Philippines and many more worldwide.

The centrality of language and communication to economic and political life cannot be sufficiently emphasized. There is after all an organic relationship between language, literacies, knowledge acquisition and human resource development – and ultimately – the labour market. As Rassool rightly comments,

> The complexity in linguistic needs and demands within the economic terrain, and their association with human resource development, is often not considered in language-in-education policy. This is regrettable because a strategic multilingual education policy is likely to boost literacy levels in different languages, and thus

provide access to knowledge. Together, this has the potential to contribute significantly to human resource development which, in turn, would facilitate access to the labour market. (Rassool 2007: 251–53)

In line with the aims of UNESCO, she proposes a language-in-education policy that orients itself towards differential language markets nationally and internationally, aimed at improving the quality of life of all peoples within society.

What is required, therefore, in order to redress the imbalances created by the tendency to construct majority languages as instruments of modernity and economic progress and minority languages as (merely) carriers of 'tradition' or 'cultural identity' is the creation of a mixed language economy so as not to privilege any one language group at the expense of the others. Rassool (citing Graddol 1997; 2006) notes that

> The importance of pursuing multilingual language-in-education policies is supported by the fact that in practice, a mixed language economy generally prevails in the labour market, regionally and nationally in most societies. While international business and trade would rely on multilingual (including English) and high skilled labour, other sectors of the economy would continue to depend on skilled and unskilled labour fluent in regional and/or local languages. (Rassool 2007: 251)

In this case, language-in-education policy will need to take into account the specific needs of learner groups in diverse contexts in ways that grant them greater representation while being mindful of the differentiated linguistic landscapes within society. In addition, it needs to be grounded in pedagogies that empower learners, providing them with skills for negotiating multiple language relationships within the global cultural economy. These and related issues as they operate in particular contexts are explored by the authors of the various chapters.

Paul Bruthiaux's Chapter 1 attempts to come to grips with the notion of globalization together with allied notions such as trade, competition and the market by closely examining the work done within applied linguistics. Although there is a range of views and attitudes towards globalization, the consensus is that it cannot be ignored and its influence on language is profound.

The next four chapters by *Lionel Wee, Lubna Alsagoff, Chng Huang Hoon* and *Ng Bee Chin* (Chapters 2–5) focus their discussion on the Singaporean context. The Singaporean context is pertinent to the discussion about commodification because of the state-sponsored multilingualism in the form of the Bilingual Policy that promotes a specific kind of bilingualism, christened the English-knowing bilingualism by Pakir (1991). This policy supports officially recognized languages and varieties and discourages non-official languages;

it also gives rise to internal competition between the official languages: all of which generate public and private debates.

Wee's chapter discusses in particular English and Mandarin, and points out changes in the government's rhetoric in advocating Mandarin to the population leading ultimately to a reconstruction of the value of the language.

Alsagoff discusses the Malay language which has served a *lingua franca* function in the South-east Asian region, but has in the recent past served ceremonial and ethnic-identity functions in Singapore; she also focuses on how the discourse of commodification has entered the discussion about the Malay language and the tensions that this generates.

Chng appeals for language planners to allow instrumental reasons to coexist with non-instrumental ones and focuses on the tension between Standard English and the non-standard variety of English used in Singapore, Singlish. The state's promotion of English has traditionally been based on instrumentalist reasons and although support for Singlish cannot easily be tied to linguistic instrumentalism, it can be supported if one considers its role as a *lingua franca*, as an identity marker and if one sees it from the point of view of linguistic human rights.

Ng's chapter focuses the reader's attention on parents as micro-language planners and examines the choices made by parents in the languages they use with their children, as a pragmatic, and therefore instrumentalist, response to the state's bilingual language policy.

In the next four chapters by *T. Ruanni F. Tupas, Peter K. W. Tan, Rani Rubdy* and *Agnes S. L. Lam and Wenfeng Wang* (Chapters 6–9), the position of English as a language allied with the globalization enterprise in other parts of Asia is made clear.

Tupas's chapter considers how the Filipino state policy of exporting labour has, among other things, given prominence to English in the education system although this exacerbates social division in the Philippines.

Tan's chapter examines the Malaysian context and analyses the debate in relation to the use of English for teaching science and maths and discusses the prominence given to instrumentalist reasons although other reasons for advocating English are also available.

Rubdy examines the complex linguistic landscape in India and in particular how English has historically been a class marker and how it continues to perpetuate and widen the social divisions.

Lam and Wang suggest, through an examination of linguistic case histories of six people in China, that the motivations for learning any language or dialect can be very complex and that public policies about language can sometimes hide some of the complexities at the level of educators, parents or individuals.

Nkonko Kamwangamalu (Chapter 10) moves the discussion to the African continent and looks at the ideological assumptions made by postcolonial governments in their language-in-education policies which overwhelmingly favour former colonial languages and English in particular, in the light of globalization. He argues for prominence given for vernacular languages in the African education system.

Finally, *David Block,* and *Michael Singh and Jinghe Han* (Chapters 11 and 12) take us to the world of immigrants and émigrés. Block examines the issue of language loss and language shift and invites readers to consider the rights of individuals and communities to make decisions, in the light of globalization and linguistic commoditization, to spurn languages and varieties supposed to be associated with their identity

Han and Singh discuss how globalization has led to people movements and examine how, in the Australian context, different values are accorded to different varieties of English brought in by recent immigrants.

In his paper, 'Introduction: Sociolinguistics and globalisation', in a recent issue of the *Journal of Sociolinguistics*, Nikolas Coupland states, 'The qualities of linguistically mediated social experience that define 'local' – inhabitation of social networks, social identities, sense of intimacy and community, differentials of power and control – all potentially carry an imprint from shifting global structures and relationships' (Coupland 2003: 466). He further comments, 'It would be naïve to assume that the linguascapes of globalised societies will be less unequal. We can be sure they will be more complex' (ibid. 470). In characterizing the tensions between the local and the global, the authors in this volume attempt to do so in a way that acknowledges the complexities, contradictions and ambiguities that surround the use of English as an international language and its relation to other languages within the global, political and cultural economy. It is hoped, that the contributions will generate further dialogue and debate on issues that remain so central to language-in-education policy and practice.

Note

1. It is relevant to note that this volume began life as a forum organized by the Singapore Association for Applied Linguistics (SAAL); the idea arose from some of the original papers, although the majority of the chapters were commissioned later. We wish to acknowledge the support from the Association.

References

BBC (16 January 2006), 'College makes Chinese compulsory'. Retrieved 23 February 2007. http://news. bbc.co.uk/2/hi/uk_news/england/southern_counties/4616640.stm

BBC (27 February 2006), 'Call for easier Chinese exams'. Retrieved 23 February 2007. http://news.bbc. co.uk/2/hi/uk_news/education/4756886.stm

Bokhorst-Heng, Wendy D., Rani Rubdy, Sandra Lee McKay and Lubna Alsagoff (2008), 'Whose English? Language ownership in Singapore's English language debates' in Lisa Lim, Anne Pakir and Lionel Wee (eds), *English in Singapore: Unity and Utility* (Hong Kong: Hong Kong University Press).

Bourdieu, Pierre (1991), *Language and Symbolic Power*, translated by G. Raymond and M. Adamson (Cambridge: Polity Press).

Bruthiaux, Paul (2002), 'Hold your courses: Language education, language choice and economic development', *Teachers of English to Speakers of Other Languages Quarterly* 36(3): 275–96.

Canagarajah, A. Suresh (1999), *Resisting Linguistic Imperialism in English Teaching* (Oxford: Oxford University Press).

Canagarajah, A. Suresh (2005), *Reclaiming the Local in Language Policy and Practice* (Mahwah, NJ: Lawrence Erlbaum Associates).

Coupland, Nikolas (2003), 'Introduction: Sociolinguistics and globalisation', *Journal of Sociolinguistics* 7(4): 465–72.

Faiola, Anthony (2004), 'English camp reflects S. Korean ambitions', *Washington Post* (17 November 2004). Retrieved 23 February 2007. http://www.washingtonpost.com/wp-dyn/articles/A58633-2004 Nov17.html

Graddol, David (1997), *The Future of English* (London: The British Council).

Graddol, David (2006), *English Next* (London: The British Council).

Heller, Monica (1999), 'Alternative ideologies of *la francophonie*', *Journal of Sociolinguistics* 3(3): 336–59.

Heller, Monica and Marylin Martin-Jones (2001), *Voices of Authority: Education and Linguistic Difference.* (London: Ablex Publishing).

Kandiah, Thiru (1998), 'Epiphanies of the deathless native users' manifold avatars: A post-colonial perspective on the native speaker' in Rajendra Singh (ed.) *The Native Speaker: Multilingual Perspectives* (New Delhi: Sage Publications), pp. 79–110.

Kachru, Braj B. (1992), Models in non-native English. in Braj Kachru (ed.) *The Other Tongue: English Across Cultures.* (2nd edition) (Urbana: University of Illinois Press), pp. 48–74.

Lin, Angel M.Y. and Peter Martin (2005), 'From a critical deconstruction paradigm to a critical construction paradigm: An introduction to decolonisation, globalisation and language-in-education policy and practice' in Angel M. Y. Lin and Peter Martin (eds), *Decolonisation, Globalisation: Language-in-education Policy and Practice* (Clevedon: Multilingual Matters), pp. 1–19.

Martin, Peter (2005), ' "Safe" language practices in two rural schools in Malaysia: Tensions between policy and practice' in Angel M. Y. Lin and Peter Martin (eds), *Decolonisation, Globalisation and Language-in-Education Policy and Practice* (Clevedon: Multilingual Matters), pp. 74–97.

McArthur, Tom (1998), *The English Languages* (Cambridge: Cambridge University Press).

Pakir, Anne (1991), 'The range and depth of English-knowing bilinguals in Singapore', *World Englishes* 10(2): 167–79.

Pennycook, Alastair (1994), *The Cultural Politics of English as an International Language* (Harlow, Essex: Longman).

Pennycook, Alastair (2003), 'Global Englishes, Rip Slyme, and performativity', *Journal of Sociolinguistics* 7(4): 513–33.

Phillipson, Robert (1992), *Linguistic Imperialism* (Oxford: Oxford University Press).

Phillipson, Robert (2001), 'English for Globalisation or for the World's People?', *International Review of Education* 47 (3–4): 185–200.

Prime Minister's Commission (2000), 'Japan's goals in the 21st century'. Retrieved 20 February 2000. http://www.kantei.go.jp/jp/21century/report/pdfs/index.html

Rappa, Antonio and Lionel Wee (2006), *Language Policy and Modernity in Southeast Asia* (New York: Springer).

Rassool, Naz (2007), *Global Issues in Language, Education and Development: Perspectives from Postcolonial Countries* (Clevedon: Multilingual Matters).

Rubdy, Rani (2008), 'Language Planning Ideologies, Communication Practices and their Consequences' in Marylin Martin-Jones and Anne-Marie de Meija (eds.) *Encyclopedia of Language and Education, Vol. 3: Discourse and Education*, 2nd edn (New York: Springer), pp. 211–23.

Seargeant, Philip (2005), 'Globalisation and reconfigured English in Japan', *World Englishes* 24(3): 309–19.

Skutnaab-Kangas, Tove (2000), *Linguistic Genocide in Education or Worldwide Diversity and Human Rights?* (Mahwah, NJ: Lawrence Erlbaum).

1 Dimensions of Globalization and Applied Linguistics

Paul Bruthiaux

Chapter Outline

This chapter reviews a selection of papers published in 2001–2004 in applied linguistics journals for evidence of beliefs regarding globalization. It notes that few writers specify their understanding of globalization before discussing its consequences for language, language education or language policy. The chapter shows that few sources analyse the economics of globalization and that those that do represent it in largely negative terms. Applied linguists view the effect of globalization on language equally negatively, with many stressing the detrimental effect of the spread of English on local languages, though some note that resistance to that spread can result in strengthened local languages. Applied linguists also discuss the risk that globalization will weaken local cultures or at least homogenize them, with Western values as the dominant ingredient. In contrast, some note that globalization-driven hybridity provides many with a chance to break from traditional social structures that are directly responsible for many of the injustices that applied linguists rightly deplore.

Introduction

Few contemporary discussions of language in society take place without reference to globalization. This is true even when the focus is on local practices since few are assumed to be immune from global forces. Among applied linguists, key concepts regarding globalization are expressed in ways that would be entirely appropriate in studies of globalization in business or marketing as well as language contexts. For example, in the call for chapters for the present volume, key terms include *competition, power, usefulness, commerce, currency, commodities, valuations, marketplaces* and so on. In brief, language – and by extension language education and language policy – is seen as one of the myriad human activities being pulled into a seamless world by the forces of globalization. But what exactly is globalization, and how does it relate to language, language education and language policy?

Perspectives on globalization

Not surprisingly, recent publications on the topic abound. Though their focus is mainly on the economic dimension of globalization, many are highly accessible to lay readers. Weinstein (2005) and Friedman (2005) offer balanced introductions. Among advocates of globalization, Stiglitz (2002) and Wolf (2004) both examine globalization in terms of historical as well as contemporary economic exchanges. Kitching (2001) and Bhagwati (2004) outline ways to minimize the negative consequences of globalization while boosting its benefits. Even Singer (2002), a philosopher, discusses the economics of globalization at length while expressing doubts about its ethics (or lack thereof). Among the critics, Ritzer (2003) denounces the profit motive and the impending cultural homogenization he sees as resulting from globalization. Fox (2001) and Cavanagh and Mander (2004) argue that globalization reinforces injustices because it only serves the interests of the corporate West.

Despite major ideological differences, all of these writers see globalization as consisting of interrelated factors that include investment, industrialization, sustainability, colonialism, nationalism, human rights and culture. But they also make it clear that to be fruitful, discussions of globalization must refer to economics.

In contrast, a scan through recent papers (2001–2004) with globalization as a main theme published in major applied linguistics journals shows that applied linguists focus mainly on sociological perspectives for background information on the phenomenon. Among these, three authors stand out: McGrew (1992), a political analyst, examines the interaction of globalizing forces and democratic governance in a range of settings; Robertson (1992), a sociologist, brings cultural and social theory to bear on his analysis of changing relations between the local and the global; but the analyst most widely cited by applied linguists is Giddens (1990; for an update, see 2003). Primarily a sociologist, Giddens shows how growing interdependence among societies has repercussions that are not only economic but also personal, cultural and political. But how do applied linguists themselves see globalization?

Curiously, discussions of the nature of globalization itself are rare in the applied linguistics literature, a somewhat alarming observation given that applied linguists are not shy of discussing its consequences and offering solutions for the globalization-related ills they identify. Many merely skim over the nature of the phenomenon (e.g. Eichinger 2002; Horner and Trimbur 2002; Kamwangamalu 2003). Among those that pause to consider the nature and mechanisms of globalization, Zhu (2003) proposes that more people are connecting with other people more often, more broadly, and faster than ever before. To Stroud (2003), this implies major differences in social, economic and political configurations. Neustupný (2004) sees globalization resulting in growing economic development, shifting power relationships, reduced social variation and greater contact. Heller (2003), Li (2003) and Pennycook (2003) also see globalization as the interaction of economic, social, political, cultural and technological factors. Luke (2002: 98) suggests that globalization has contributed to the emergence of 'semiotic economies . . . where means of production and means of information become intertwined in analytically complex ways.' Gaudio (2003) broadly concurs before going on to discuss the impact of these factors on verbal interactions specifically.

Probably the most comprehensive review of the nature of globalization in the recent applied linguistics literature comes from Flowerdew (2002), who stresses that since societies are impacted by globalization, so is culture and, therefore, language. To Flowerdew, moreover, the localization of global forces is an inconsistent and unstable process experienced in very different ways across and within societies, a view he shares with Lo Bianco (2004), Pardo (2001) and Singh and Doherty (2004). Stroud (2003) also discusses the localization of global processes and their integration into local multilingual practices, while Blommaert (2004) warns that global perceptions of globalization (especially those of academics writing on the subject) may substantially differ from local ones.

Some applied linguists counter the widespread notion that globalization is a novel phenomenon. Some note that it can be traced to early human history (Flowerdew 2002; Sifakis and Sougari 2003) while others link it to language contact resulting from trade (Bolton 2002) or colonial expansion (Pardo 2001

Singh and Doherty 2004). Clearly, many applied linguists take an in-depth look at the phenomenon and are prepared to explore its complexities as a basis for further discussions of its implications. So what are these implications in the eyes of applied linguists? What major dimensions of globalization do they explore, and which do they play down or even ignore?

Dimensions of globalization: economics

Scanning the recent applied linguistics literature on globalization shows that most applied linguists have little to say regarding its economic dimension. This is despite the fact that, as Teubert (2001) shows, globalization is linked primarily to economic factors in an overwhelming majority of journalistic sources. This suggests a worrying reluctance among applied linguists to examine the practical basis of the debate they wish to participate in. One explanation may be that most applied linguists assume a knowledgeable audience for whom the basics need not be restated. But this assumption of consensus on the economic nature of globalization also suggests that an orthodoxy of globalization may be at play. Certainly, among those that do address the economic dimension of the phenomenon, there is little doubt that globalization is profoundly unjust because it serves the interests of one side at the expense of the other and that it must therefore be resisted, by applied linguists among others. Applied linguists who express this uniformly negative view in recently published papers include Berardi (2001), Pardo (2001), Pomerantz (2002) and Rymes (2002), to mention a few. Just as problematically, some of those who venture beyond stating their criticisms of globalization occasionally reveal gaps in their grasp of introductory economics that invalidate much of their discussion (e.g. Punchi 2001; Hasan 2003). But the most vocal of critics of globalization are Phillipson (2001) and Skutnabb-Kangas (2001), who by turning up the rhetoric at the expense of prior and comprehensive analysis of the practical basis of globalization, make it all the more unlikely that a critical examination of the arguments – on both sides – will take place, in applied linguistics at least.

One issue related to the economics of globalization that is often mentioned in the recent literature but rarely explored is the ability of multinational corporations to dictate to sovereign nation states and to weaken their ability to serve their own people's interests. While many applied linguists appear to share this view (e.g. Flowerdew 2002; Sifakis and Sougari 2003; Smolicz and Secombe 2003; Lo Bianco 2004), few elaborate or consider the mechanisms of such a shift. Among the few that do, Walter (2002) argues that the government of Thailand is gradually losing control of its educational goals and increasingly allowing these to be dictated by market forces and the economic aims of multinational corporations and their local consumers.

While any reorientation of education away from personal and collective growth towards purely utilitarian preoccupations should indeed be resisted, this concern with preserving the power of the nation state is puzzling given that its track record is hardly benign. Over its relatively short history, the nation state has repeatedly exhibited a capacity for constructing self-serving and often aggressive myths and for destroying key societal assets, be it wealth, languages, even entire populations, untroubled by outside opinion and safe in the knowledge that its monopoly of power would not be challenged. Presumably, those applied linguists who deplore the alleged weakening of the nation state are not motivated by illiberal instincts but by a sense that compared with multinationals and other globalizing agents, the nation state is the least of two evils. But if true, this is hardly a ringing endorsement of the nation state as the proper agent for the resolution of social injustices.

In brief, the reluctance of many applied linguists to consider the economic dimension of globalization and the tendency for discussions of that dimension to be cursory and one-sided severely limit the contribution the field might make to a key contemporary debate. Lack of familiarity with economics is a problem that can be remedied. But the apparent unwillingness among many applied linguists to consider alternative views is more problematic because it is attitudinal. In the end, it undermines the credibility of applied linguists and makes it unlikely they will play a significant role in solving the social injustices they so rightly deplore.

Dimensions of globalization: language

Not surprisingly, applied linguists have a great deal more to say about links globalization may have with language than with economics. One especially insightful paper discusses major similarities between economic exchanges and language contact (Meyerhoff and Niedzielski 2003). Others consider the impact of globalization on language practices from the perspective of a specific locus of social interaction such as business (Harris and Bargiela-Chiappini 2003) or a specific geographic setting such as Southern Africa (Stroud 2003). Many focus on the European context, discussing the impact of information technology on the languages of small nations (Holmarsdottir 2001), the shifting identities of bilingual populations (Eichinger 2002), the growing role of English as the *lingua franca* of European multinationals (McArthur 2003), or the power of supranational institutions to reshape perceptions of identities and language practices in ethnically complex societies (McEntee-Atalianis 2004).

Most, however, focus on the relationship between globalization and the spread of English. Many assume – with little analysis – that globalization and the spread of English are closely connected (e.g. Hu 2004). In contrast, the case for that connection is convincingly argued by Lo Bianco (2004), for example, when he notes that 19th-century political globalization was quickly followed by economic globalization, with English (British at first, then American) as a major element in both processes.

As with discussions of the economics of globalization, many applied linguists see the phenomenon as having few or no positive linguistic consequences. Moreover, since English is seen as a key factor in the process of globalization, it follows that English must be complicit in these outcomes. Here too, vocal advocates of this view are Phillipson (2001) and Skutnabb-Kangas (2001), who see in an alliance of Western corporations and transnational institutions the source of policies – including English-favouring linguistic ones – that benefit their own commercial interests exclusively through the economic exploitation and cultural weakening of weaker societies.

This is a view that resonates broadly among applied linguists. The damaging influence of English and the cultural values it embodies is noted by Punchi (2001), who regrets the tendency for countries such as Sri Lanka to reward English speakers at the expense of those schooled in vernacular languages. Concerns regarding this imbalance are also expressed in relation to languages with few speakers, whether in wealthy Northern Europe (Holmarsdottir 2001; House 2003) or in developing countries such as Papua New Guinea (Nagai and Lister 2003). According to Elkhafaifi (2002), even a vibrant language such as Arabic is at risk of losing its transnational role to English. Nor is the USA immune to these linguistic and cultural perils, as noted by Rymes (2002) in relation to immigrants and by McCarty (2003) as regards speakers of indigenous languages.

Yet some applied linguists take a more nuanced view of the spread of English and its effect on local cultures and languages. Both Luke (2002) and Pennycook (2003) reject the reduction of the issue to simplistic oppositions between oppressor and oppressed or homogeneity and heterogeneity. Others, such as Martin (2002) and Machin and Thornborrow (2003), argue that large corporations in fact have more to gain from adapting to local conditions than by imposing their own home-grown cultural values and practices. Li (2003) suggests that most learners of English are more concerned with its economic potential than its historical connection with Western colonialism. Stroud (2003) sees the spread of English in Southern Africa as giving form to localized debates over human rights and social justice. Smolicz and Secombe (2003) argue that the much-predicted homogenization of world cultures has not occurred and note instead that local languages and cultures are being revitalized, ironically as a result of resistance to the spread of English.

Overall, the positions taken by applied linguists regarding the relationship between globalization and language spread reflect greater plurality than is suggested by widespread representations of globalization and language exclusively in terms of inequality and domination. On this evidence, many applied linguists are not willing to follow the oversimplifications that sustain much of conventional wisdom. Almost certainly, the mechanisms connecting globalizing forces and language are complex and cannot be reduced to Manichean oppositions.

As expected, recent writings on globalization in applied linguistics journals also make frequent reference to language teaching. Though, as noted earlier, the mechanisms linking globalization and language education are rarely examined in depth, the connection is frequently noted, whether neutrally (Sonaiya 2003), critically (Punchi 2001; Walter 2002), or more positively, as in the positions taken by Stroud (2003) and King (2004), who both argue that language education in developing societies can help turn multilingualism into an asset provided local communities are involved at all stages of language policy making.

Focusing specifically on English language teaching, some applied linguists discuss the impact of globalization in specific domains such as air travel (Tajima 2004) or computer-assisted instruction (Tokuda 2002), or in specific countries such as Pakistan (Sarwar 2001), Hungary (Dörnyei and Csizér 2002) or Japan (Hart 2002). Others call for greater tolerance of linguistic variation in academic writing whether in the USA (Horner and Trimbur 2002) or internationally (Neustupný 2004). In contrast, Shi (2003) sees little difficulty in the simultaneous adoption – here, by Chinese scholars – of Anglo-American academic standards and the parallel retention of local linguistic and cultural practices. Indeed, several applied linguists such as Bamgbose (2001) and Gupta (2001) stress that a key development in the teaching of English has been the gradual disconnection of English from specific cultural entities, especially those that have dominated it for so long.

The increasingly hybrid identities of a growing number of learners is noted by many applied linguists, whether in the use of relatively culturally neutral

English as a European lingua franca (Modiano 2001; Llurda 2004), on Australian campuses (Singh and Doherty 2004), and in a wide range of countries including Israel (Baumel 2003), Malaysia (Nair-Venugopal 2003), Indonesia (Lamb 2004) and Cyprus (McEntee-Atalianis 2004). Broadly speaking, these writers play down fears of cultural hegemony and in seeing in globalization an opportunity for societies and individuals to become aware of their distinctive sociocultural makeup while taking part in enriching crosscultural exchanges.

Dimensions of globalization: culture

The relationship between globalization and culture is clearly of great interest to applied linguists beyond English language teaching. Some see cultural blending occurring as a result of growth in commerce (Harris and Bargiela-Chiappini 2003; Gimenez 2002), information technology (Reeves 2002; Zhu 2003) or travel (Holmarsdottir 2001; Heller 2003). A methodology for analysing processes of cultural evolution is offered by Dhir and Savage (2002) in a hypothetical corporate context.

Many applied linguists focus on the impact rather than the causes of this evolution. Some simply note that the penetration of local languages by English is often associated locally with notions of modernity and progress. Studies of specific adaptations of local languages to linguistic and cultural import – in Japan (Pennycook 2003; Piller 2003) and Korea (Lee 2004) – also show that local speakers are not passive recipients of cultural and linguistic imports but skilful blenders of both and the creators of uniquely local discourses.

Many, however, express concerns about the process. Sonaiya (2003) argues that some discourses may initially be too alien to blend seamlessly into local practices. Le (2002) sees local cultural practices as threatened by powerful Western media with the power to change these practices in ways that only benefit Western viewpoints. Economic globalization and accompanying neo-liberal values are attacked even more directly by Berardi (2001) for leading to growing inequality and the erosion of local identities. For her, social progress is only possible through resistance to the onslaught and the anchoring of progress in local values. In contrast, some linguists see the blending of cultures as unavoidable and therefore to be welcomed for its potential benefits provided cultural continuity can be safeguarded, as in the case of a small and potentially vulnerable community in Papua New Guinea (Nagai and Lister 2003).

As noted above, not all applied linguists accept that globalization leads inexorably to the homogenization of cultures. A frequently expressed view (see, for example, Le 2002; Singh and Doherty 2004) is that as imported cultural elements meet local ones, both adapt and cultural imports become localized. This view is corroborated by evidence from the corporate world showing that even powerful organizations serve their commercial self-interest best by adapting their strategies and messages to local practices (Martin 2002; Machin and Thornborrow 2003). Harris and Bargiela-Chiappini (2003) also show that English language corporate discourse is increasingly detached from specific cultures, a view that echoes that of many applied linguists working in English language teaching. Though highly critical of media practices, Fayard (2003) concedes that their globalization facilitates comparisons and a critical interrogation of identities.

Overall, the recent writings of applied linguists suggest that they take a broad and generally positive view of the cultural dimension of globalization. While keenly aware of the risks involved, many welcome its impact because it offers a chance of greater hybridity. Lo Bianco (2004), for example, comments that new identities emerge and disappear continuously and that identity is increasingly difficult to tie to location or nationality. As a result, many applied linguists argue, new models of identity stressing overlaps and frequent shifts are needed. Crucially, this encourages a sense among individuals and analysts alike that culture – and the languages that give it social form – is increasingly a kind of cultural capital, a fungible commodity to be modified, emphasized or played down, or even traded as social circumstances require. As Heller (2003) observes, this is fundamental a departure from earlier perceptions of culture and language as inherent, immutable components of identity.

Some applied linguists view this shift somewhat guardedly. Atkinson (2004) notes that change, discontinuity, inequality, hybridity and delocalization are part and parcel of modern culture, though he also notes that not all of these aspects are equally beneficial. Le (2002) warns that greater cultural hybridity may damage less powerful cultures unless both sides make the effort to analyse the values they are transmitting or holding on to. While not especially opposed to cultural diffusion, Blommaert (2004) even suggests that the process may occur more in the eye of analysts than in the daily experiences of the subjects of their inquiries, as noted above.

Others see cultural hybridity as a largely positive development. Reeves (2002) sees the phenomenon as a force for good in that it fosters greater openness and tolerance among groups as well as in individuals. But overall, the most powerful argument in favour of the intensified blending of cultures is the fact that it implies greater hybridity and new identities based in pragmatic considerations rather than in heritage and tradition. A concrete example of this beneficial development is provided by McEntee-Atalianis (2004), who describes how a reorientation of identities has the potential for defusing conflict in Cyprus, an island long prone to ethnic strife. Seen from this perspective as a process of cultural transformation, globalization can have the effect of raising individuals and groups out of limiting mindsets and reorienting them in novel and potentially beneficial directions. Though controversial, this view of globalization as a liberating force is an asset to applied linguistics that should be welcomed partly because it invigorates the debate but mostly because of its potential for contributing to tangible social change.

Globalization and applied linguistics: an overview

In this chapter, I reviewed perspectives on globalization as represented in the recent writings of applied linguists. One alarming finding of this brief survey is that few applied linguists find it necessary to specify their take on such a complex issue before discussing what they see as its causes or consequences. While this reluctance to go into the specifics may be in part due to the spatial confines of the conventional academic paper, it may also indicate a lack of familiarity with the specifics themselves, especially in the area of economics, a field discussed in depth in mainstream writings on globalization but generally ignored by applied linguists. In addition, most of the applied linguists that address this dimension of globalization do this in uniformly negative terms, in the process revealing rudimentary understanding of the subject and often offering the sovereign nation state the unequivocal support it hardly deserves. More worryingly, this dismissive approach to the specifics – and especially the economics – of globalization suggests that the factual basis of the phenomenon is seen as self-evident. Evidently, given the breadth of viewpoints represented in this review of the recent literature, no such consensus exists. In fact, the field of applied linguistics is overall very catholic in its perceptions of what matters about globalization.

This is especially apparent in the range of approaches taken by applied linguists to globalization as it relates to language spread and language teaching, two areas where, naturally, they are more convincing than when discussing (or avoiding) economics. Here, the coverage ranges from fears of linguistic hegemony and the downgrading of local vernaculars to a view of English as having a positive influence on local settings because – ironically – this very influence generates resistance and may in fact work towards revitalizing at-risk cultures and languages.

Another area where the recent writings of applied linguists demonstrate both vitality and breadth is that of the impact of globalization on culture. Though the theme of cultural homogenization preoccupies many, others question the widespread view that it is invariably in the interest of corporate forces to impose their cultural practices on less powerful societies. Instead, they argue, cultures – corporate or otherwise – will inevitably adapt as they come into contact with other cultures and will be best served by modifying their practices to suit local preferences, even if their ultimate motivation is purely commercial.

Related to the theme of adaptation is the notion of cultural hybridity, a process by which the identities of groups as well as individuals gradually become detached from ethnicity, geographic location or nationality and are able to shift across overlapping cultural territories in an effort to adapt optimally to shifting social conditions and opportunities. While the dislocation involved in these shifts creates undeniable tensions and difficulties, this loosening of traditional links between culture and identity also has liberating potential because it offers a hitherto remote chance of imagining existence in ways less tightly connected with the past. Given that for many in developing societies that past was often cruel, applied linguists concerned with redressing social injustices and contributing to raising living standards among the poorest should welcome – as many do in their writings – the role of globalization in this liberation.

References

Atkinson, D. (2004), 'Contrasting rhetorics/contrasting cultures: Why contrastive rhetoric needs a better conceptualization of culture', *Journal of English for Academic Purposes* 3: 277–89.

Bamgbose, A. (2001), 'World Englishes and globalization', *World Englishes* 20: 357–63.

Baumel, S. D. (2003), 'Teaching English in Israeli Haredi Schools', *Language Policy* 2: 47–67.

Berardi, L. (2001), 'Globalization and poverty in Chile', *Discourse and Society* 12: 47–58.

Bhagwati, J. (2004), *In Defense of Globalization* (New York: Oxford University Press).

Blommaert, J. (2004), 'Writing as a problem: African grassroots writing, economies of literacy, and globalization', *Language in Society* 33: 643–71.

Bolton, K. (2002), 'Chinese Englishes: From Canton jargon to global English', *World Englishes* 21: 181–99.

Cavanagh, J. and Mander, J. (2004), *Alternatives to Economic Globalization: A Better World is Possible* (San Francisco, CA: Berrett-Koehler).

Dhir, K. S. and Savage, T. (2002), 'The value of a working language', *International Journal of the Sociology of Language* 158: 1–35.

Dörnyei, Z. and Csizér, K. (2002), 'Some dynamics of language attitudes and motivation: Results of a longitudinal nationwide survey', *Applied Linguistics* 23: 421–62.

Eichinger, L. (2002), 'South Tyrol: German and Italian in a changing world', Journal of *Multilingual and Multicultural Development* 23: 137–49.

Elkhafaifi, H. M. (2002), 'Arabic language planning in the age of globalization', *Language Problems and Language Planning* 26: 253–69.

Fayard, N. (2003), 'Loft story in the French language class: Mapping out the perverse discourse of globalisation', *Language and Intercultural Communication* 3: 48–-63.

Flowerdew, J. (2002), 'Globalization discourse: A view from the East', *Discourse and Society* 13: 209–25.

Fox, J. (2001), *Chomsky and Globalisation* (Cambridge: Icon Books).

Friedman, T. L. (2005), *The World is Flat: A Brief History of the Twenty-first Century* (New York: Farrar, Straus, and Giroux).

Gaudio, R. P. (2003), 'Coffeetalk: Starbucks™ and the commercialization of casual conversation', *Language in Society* 32: 659–91.

Giddens, A. (1990), *The Consequences of Modernity* (Cambridge: Polity Press).

Giddens, A. (2003), *Runaway World: How Globalization is Reshaping Our Lives* (New York: Routledge).

Gimenez, J. C. (2002), 'New media and conflicting realities in multinational corporate communication: A case study', *International Review of Applied Linguistics in Language Teaching* 40: 323–43.

Gupta, A. F. (2001), 'Realism and imagination in the teaching of English', *World Englishes* 20: 365–81.

Harris, S. and Bargiela-Chiappini, F. (2003), 'Business as a site of language contact', *Annual Review of Applied Linguistics* 23: 155–69.

Hart, N. (2002), 'Intra-group autonomy and authentic materials: A different approach to ELT in Japanese colleges and universities', *System* 30: 33–46.

Hasan, R. (2003), 'Globalization, literacy and ideology', *World Englishes*, 22: 433–48.

Heller, M. (2003), 'Globalization, the new economy, and the commodification of language and identity', *Journal of Sociolinguistics* 7: 473–92.

Holmarsdottir, H. B. (2001), 'Icelandic: A lesser-used language in the global community', *International Review of Education* 47: 379–94.

Horner, B. and Trimbur, J. (2002), 'English Only and US college composition', *College Composition and Communication* 53: 594–630.

House, J. (2003), 'English as a lingua franca: A threat to multilingualism?', *Journal of Sociolinguistics* 7: 556–78.

Hu, X. Q. (2004), 'Why China English should stand alongside British, American, and the other "World Englishes."', *English Today* 20: 26–33.

Kamwangamalu, N. M. (2003), 'Globalization of English, and language maintenance and shift in South Africa', *International Journal of the Sociology of Language* 164: 65–81.

King, K. (2004), 'Language policy and local planning in South America: New directions for enrichment bilingual education in the Andes', *International Journal of Bilingual Education and Bilingualism* 7: 334–47.

Kitching, G. (2001), *Seeking Social Justice through Globalization: Escaping a Nationalist Perspective* (University Park, PA: Pennsylvania State University Press).

Lamb, M. (2004), 'Integrative motivation in a globalizing world', *System* 32: 3–19.

Le, E. (2002), 'Human rights discourse and international relations: Le Monde's editorials on Russia', *Discourse and Society* 13: 373–408.

Lee, J. S. (2004), 'Linguistic hybridization in K-pop: Discourse of self-assertion and resistance', *World Englishes* 23: 429–50.

Li, D. C. S. (2003), 'Between English and Esperanto: What does it take to be a world language?', *International Journal of the Sociology of Language* 164: 33–63.

Llurda, E. (2004), 'Non-native-speaker teachers and English as an international language', *International Journal of Applied Linguistics* 14: 314–23.

Lo Bianco, J. (2004), 'Invented languages and new worlds', *English Today* 20: 8–18.

Luke, A. (2002), 'Beyond science and ideology critique: Developments in critical discourse analysis', *Annual Review of Applied Linguistics* 22: 96–110.

Machin, D. and Thornborrow, J. (2003), 'Branding and discourse: The case of Cosmopolitan', *Discourse and Society* 14: 453–71.

Martin, E. (2002), 'Cultural images and different varieties of English in French television commercials', *English Today* 18: 8–20.

McArthur, T. (2003), 'World English, Euro-English, Nordic English?', *English Today* 19: 54–58.

McCarty, T. L. (2003), 'Revitalising indigenous languages in homogenising times', *Comparative Education* 39: 147–63.

McEntee-Atalianis, L. J. (2004) 'The impact of English in postcolonial, postmodern Cyprus', *International Journal of the Sociology of Language* 168: 77–90.

McGrew, A. G. (1992), 'Conceptualizing global politics' in A. G. McGrew and P. G. Lewis (eds) *Global Politics: Globalisation and the Nation State* (Cambridge: Polity Press) pp. 1–28.

Meyerhoff, M. and Niedzielski, N. (2003), 'The globalisation of vernacular variation', *Journal of Sociolinguistics* 7: 534–55.

Modiano, M. (2001), 'Ideology and the ELT practitioner', *International Journal of Applied Linguistics* 11: 159–73.

Nagai, Y. and Lister, R. (2003), 'What is our culture? What is our language? Dialogue towards the maintenance of indigenous culture and language in Papua New Guinea', *Language and Education* 17: 87–104.

Nair-Venugopal, S. (2003), 'Intelligibility in English: Of what relevance today to intercultural communication?', *Language and Intercultural Communication* 3: 36–47.

Neustupný, J. V. (2004), 'A theory of contact situations and the study of academic interaction', *Journal of Asian Pacific Communication* 14: 3–31.

Pardo, M. L. (2001), 'Linguistic persuasion as an essential political factor in current democracies: Critical analysis of the globalization discourse in Argentina at the turn and at the end of the century', *Discourse and Society* 12: 91–118.

Pennycook, A. (2003), 'Global Englishes, rip slyme, and perfomativity', *Journal of Sociolinguistics* 7: 513–33.

Phillipson, R. (2001), 'English for globalisation or for the worlds' people?', *International Review of Education* 47: 185–200.

Piller, I. (2003), 'Advertising as a site of language contact', *Annual Review of Applied Linguistics* 23: 170–83.

Pomerantz, A. (2002), 'Language ideologies and the production of identities: Spanish as a resource for participation in a multilingual marketplace', *Multilingua* 21: 275–302.

Punchi, L. (2001), 'Resistance towards the language of globalisation: The case of Sri Lanka', *International Review of Education* 47: 361–78.

Reeves, N. (2002), 'Translation, international English, and the planet of Babel', *English Today* 18: 21–28.

Ritzer, G. (2003), *The Globalization of Nothing* (Thousand Oaks, CA: Pine Forge Press).

Robertson, R. (1992), *Globalization: Social Theory and Global Culture* (London: Sage).

Rymes, B. (2002), 'Language in development in the United States: Supervising adult ESOL preservice teachers in an immigrant community', *Teachers of English to Speakers of Other Languages Quarterly* 36: 431–52.

Sarwar, Z. (2001), 'Innovations in large classes in Pakistan', *Teachers of English to Speakers of Other Languages Quarterly* 35: 497–500.

Shi, L. (2003), 'Writing in two cultures: Chinese professors return from the West', *Canadian Modern Language Review* 59: 369–91.

Sifakis, N. C. and Sougari, A. M. (2003), 'Facing the globalisation challenge in the realm of English language teaching', *Language and Education* 17: 59–71.

Singer, P. (2002), *One World: The Ethics of Globalization* (New Haven, CT: Yale University Press).

Singh, P. and Doherty, C. (2004), 'Global cultural flows and pedagogic dilemmas: Teaching in the global university contact zone', *Teachers of English to Speakers of Other Languages Quarterly* 38: 9–42.

Skutnabb-Kangas, T. (2001), 'The globalisation of (educational) language rights', *International Review of Education* 47: 201–19.

Smolicz, J. J. and Secombe, M. J. (2003), 'Assimilation or pluralism? Changing policies for minority languages education in Australia', *Language Policy* 2: 3–25.

Sonaiya, R. (2003), 'The globalisation of communication and the African foreign language user', *Language, Culture, and Curriculum* 16: 146–54.

Stiglitz, J. E. (2002), *Globalization and Its Discontents* (New York: Norton).

Stroud, C. (2003), 'Postmodernist perspectives on local languages: African mother-tongue education in times of globalisation', *International Journal of Bilingual Education and Bilingualism* 6: 17–36.

Tajima, A. (2004), 'Fatal miscommunication: English in aviation safety', *World Englishes* 23: 451–70.

Teubert, W. (2001), 'Corpus linguistics and lexicography', *International Journal of Corpus Linguistics* 6: 125–53.

Tokuda, N. (2002), 'New developments in intelligent CALL systems in a rapidly internationalized information age', *Computer Assisted Language Learning* 15: 319–27.

Walter, P. (2002), 'Adult literacy education and development in Thailand: An historical analysis of policies and programmes from the 1930s to the present', *International Journal of Lifelong Education* 21: 79–98.

Weinstein M. M. (2005), *Globalization: What's New?* (New York: Columbia University Press).

Wolf, M. (2004), *Why Globalization Works* (New Haven, CT: Yale University Press).

Zhu, H. (2003), 'Globalization and new ELT challenges in China', *English Today* 19: 36–41.

Linguistic Instrumentalism in Singapore[1]

2

Lionel Wee

Chapter Outline

In Singapore, the need to participate in a globalized economy has prompted a move towards a more pragmatic view of language. This can be seen in the government's attempt to assert the economic value of the local languages, officially known as 'mother tongues'. The mother tongues originally contrast with English in a narrative where they are treated primarily as repositories of cultural values and thus assigned to a domain (the traditional and cultural) that is distinct from that assigned to the latter (the economic and technological). This chapter explores the factors motivating the government's shift towards a discourse of linguistic instrumentalism, as well as its consequences, and ends by suggesting some possible general features of linguistic instrumentalism.

Introduction

According to Heller (1999a: 5), the need to participate in a globalized economy creates a situation where 'the ability to cross boundaries' and the 'construction of new global, international norms' are especially important, and this has led to the 'old politics of identity' being increasingly abandoned 'in favour of a new pragmatic position' where language and culture are valued as commodifiable resources. In Singapore, this move towards a more pragmatic view of language can be seen in how the relationship between the endogenous Asian languages and English is constructed. The former, officially known as the 'mother tongues', are tasked with preserving ethnic cultural traditions while the latter is presented as the language of economic development. Singapore's narrative, then, is fairly typical of how other languages tend to be viewed with respect to the English language. English is often seen as a world language, providing access to economic development and social mobility while other languages are seen as either hindering such access, or to the extent that they are considered important, are treated mainly as repositories of ancient knowledge or cultural heritage (e.g. Phillipson 1992; Pennycook 1994; May, 2001).

Recent changes to the narrative, however, have attempted to emphasize the economic value of the mother tongues. This emphasis on the economic value of a language is part of what I call 'linguistic instrumentalism', which is a view of language that justifies its existence in a community in terms of its usefulness in achieving specific utilitarian goals such as access to economic development or social mobility. In contrast, a language is viewed non-instrumentally to the extent that it is seen as forming an integral part of one's ethnic or cultural identity, and if its existence in a community is justified in terms of its symbolic value in allowing the community members to maintain a sense of identity. It is obviously possible for one and the same language to be seen as having both instrumentalist and non-instrumentalist functions, but it is also important to keep the functions distinct. As pointed out by Edwards in his discussion of Irish (1985: 61), it is possible for a language to be valued as a symbol of national or ethnic identity and still be accompanied by decreasing usage and general pessimism about the language's survivability. In particular, Edwards (1985: 85, 92) suggests that rather than sentimental attachments, a practical concern with social mobility and access to economic goods may be more important in determining whether or not a language survives. Edwards' observations coheres with the Singapore situation, as I show below, since there is general dissatisfaction with and insecurity about the status of the mother tongues, in particular, Mandarin, as mere cultural repositories, despite strong official support. The Chinese community tends to feel that unless there are pragmatic (i.e. economic) motivations for learning Mandarin, the survival of the language is still a matter of concern.

Three questions can therefore be asked concerning linguistic instrumentalism in Singapore. One, what are the factors responsible for this shift towards linguistic instrumentalism, and how well motivated are they? In a multilingual society like Singapore, we need to look at linguistic instrumentalism separately for each mother tongue. In the case of Mandarin, the Singapore government has argued that there is a strong motivating factor, namely, the economic development of China. But having made the case for Mandarin's economic value, the government is obliged, in the name of multiracial equality, to assert that the other mother tongues, Malay and Tamil, also have strong economic values. However, I suggest that arguments for Malay and Tamil are difficult to sustain, especially if they are motivated more by a political desire to maintain linguistic parity than by actual economic considerations. Two, what are the consequences of this shift towards linguistic instrumentalism? Here, I argue that linguistic instrumentalism tends to lead to a situation of exonormativity so that there is a tension between the role of the mother tongue as a bearer of local cultural values and its role in facilitating international trade. And finally, what are some properties of this linguistic instrumentalism? By drawing on Heller's own work and on Pomerantz's (2002) recent application of Heller, I suggest that (i) the discourse of linguistic instrumentalism is often a later addition to an earlier discourse where the language is viewed as an identity marker; (ii) it leads to a devaluing of local vernaculars; and (iii) rather than displacing the English language, it is aimed at creating bilingual individuals who are also proficient in English.

The language policy of Singapore

The successes of various Asian economies such as Hong Kong, Japan, Korea, Malaysia, Singapore and Taiwan have given rise to narratives of Asian modernity (Ong 1999) characterized primarily by a rethinking of the place of endogenous cultural elements vis-à-vis Western modernity. But as Singapore seeks to maintain its economic competitiveness, its narrative has had to change so that newer 'modes of ideological repositioning' begin to emerge. One such repositioning noted by Heller to be a general consequence of adopting a globalizing orientation is the framing of languages as forms of economic capital rather than repositories of cultural values. But to better appreciate the specific problems created by the particularities of Singapore's situation, it is useful for us to briefly discuss how its history has influenced its language policy.

Singapore is a linguistically and racially diverse country with a population of about 3.2 million (Census of Population 2000), comprising 76.8 per cent Chinese, 13.9 per cent Malay, and 7.9 per cent Indian. The remaining 1.4 per cent, officially referred to as 'Others', is a miscellaneous category comprising mainly Eurasians and Europeans. Singapore reluctantly became independent in 1965 after being ejected from the Federation of Malaysia, due to political differences with the central government. Because Singapore has no natural resources of its own, its leaders were convinced that economic survival was possible only as part of the Federation, and had worked hard to bring that about. Singapore's subsequent departure from the Federation meant that its leaders were faced, quite suddenly, with the task of building a nation out of a racially diverse population, and with developing the nation's economy without access to any natural resources. In this Singaporean narrative of Asian modernity, two major problems need to be addressed: economic development and the management of racial diversity.

Where language policy is concerned, this emphasis on economic development treats English language proficiency as necessary for attracting foreign investment and providing access to scientific and technological know-how (Chua 1995: 65). But the government also fears that exposure to English can lead Singaporeans to become 'Westernized' or 'decadent'. Thus, the government claims that knowledge of English must be balanced by knowledge of one's mother tongue. The latter supposedly counters the effects of Westernization by providing Singaporeans with a link to their traditional cultures and values.

Because of the country's racial and linguistic diversity, the government has emphasized that there must be respect and equal treatment accorded to each ethnic group and its associated mother tongue. This policy of 'multiracialism' (Benjamin 1976) is seen as crucial to maintaining racial harmony. The government recognizes three major ethnic groups, assigning each an official mother tongue. Mandarin is the mother tongue of the Chinese community, while Malay and Tamil are, respectively, the mother tongues of the Malay and Indian communities. And just as Mandarin is expected to provide the Chinese with an 'emotionally acceptable mother tongue' (Bokhorst-Heng 1998: 252), so, too, are Malay and Tamil expected to provide their respective communities with anchors to traditional cultural values. However, the official notion of mother tongue is problematic since, with the possible exception of the Malays, it does not reflect the language actually spoken at home,[2] English being a home language for a significant portion of the population (Census of Population 2000). In any case, the government's multiracial stance officially requires a demonstration of equal commitment to all the mother tongues, as seen from the following statement by Prime Minister in his 1991 Speak Mandarin Campaign speech:

> Let me assure non-Chinese Singaporeans that the government is not promoting the Chinese language or culture at the expense of the others. In fact, the Ministry

of Information and the Arts is working together with the Malay Language Committee to promote standard Malay. The Ministry has also asked the Indian community if it needs help to promote the use of Tamil. We want all the ethnic communities to preserve their language, culture and values. We aim to be a harmonious multi-racial nation.

The government's attempt to accommodate the presence of English alongside the mother tongues has therefore led to a relationship of complementarity being constructed in sense that English and the mother tongues are assigned to separate and non-competing domains. English is the language of access to Western science and technology while the mother tongues are supposed to provide links to ancient cultures and values.

Linguistic instrumentalism in Singapore

In recent years, however, there has been a shift towards emphasizing the economic value of the mother tongues as well as their role in preserving traditional values. This shift was motivated by the anticipated economic development of China, and in 1985, Ong Teng Cheong, then Second Deputy Prime Minister, suggested that:

> The Chinese learn and speak Mandarin not only because it is the common spoken language of the Chinese community, representing our roots, but also because the economic value of Mandarin is increasing, particularly after China has started its economic transformation and adopted the open-door policy. . . . We shall no doubt face competition in our trade and economic activities with China, but we have an edge over others in our bilingual ability . . . Recently, an American computer company has arranged for China's computer personnel to receive training in Singapore because our computer experts can speak both Mandarin and English. They are able to explain to the Chinese in Mandarin. (Bokhorst-Heng 1998: 254)

Notice that the rationale for being bilingual in English and Mandarin is no longer simply because Mandarin provides the 'emotionally acceptable mother tongue' that counters Western decadence; rather, being bilingual in English and Mandarin provides a strong economic advantage in the context of China's open-door policy. This emphasis on the economic value of Mandarin is clearly an appeal to linguistic instrumentalism, and undermines the strict complementarity between English and the mother tongues since Mandarin no longer functions only as a transmitter of traditional Chinese values, but, like English, is seen to have a strong economic value. Recent ministerial statements still continue the arguments made by Ong. For example, the Prime Minister Goh Chok Tong describes a knowledge of Mandarin as 'a valuable asset' as China becomes 'a major global player in the 21st century' (*The Straits Times* 21 January 1999), and in his 2002 National Day Rally Speech points out that 'if we neglect the Chinese language, while others are picking it up, very soon, we will have no edge over them in doing business with China.'

This move towards linguistic instrumentalism has had a number of important effects. For one, the Chinese community 'no longer fears the declining market value of the Chinese language' (*The Straits Times* 1 December 2001). Members of the community have always been concerned that merely having Mandarin as the vehicle of traditional Chinese culture and emblem of Chinese identity does not guarantee its survival. The younger generation may learn Mandarin in schools because the bilingual policy requires that students be taught their mother tongue. But whether the language continues to be used in a variety of domains outside the education system is much more important in ensuring that it flourishes. Drawing attention to the language's utilitarian value, 'has made more parents pay attention to the learning of the language by their children' (*The Straits Times* 16 March 1994). The other effect is that Mandarin has now become so popular that a growing number of non-Chinese parents want the schools to allow their children to study the language (*The Straits Times* 30 April 1994). Members of the Malay and Indian communities were asking for greater flexibility regarding the government's bilingual policy, with some wanting their children to be allowed to learn Mandarin as a third language, in addition to English and their mother tongue, while others, recognizing that three languages might pose difficulties for their children, wanted to be able to 'pick Chinese as their children's second language.' The primary reason for this desire to learn Mandarin was 'strictly business: facility with the language is seen as a economic asset', both internal to Singapore and in relation to China. This desire on the part of minority parents for their children to learn Mandarin continues unabated (*The Straits Times* 25 August 2002), and is a sensitive matter because if the government allows too many minority parents to replace Malay or Tamil with Mandarin, it might be criticized for encouraging Mandarin at the expense of the other mother tongues. But at the same time, to deny the learning of a language that is seen as having economic value might also be construed as holding back the development of the minority communities. One way out of this dilemma is to play up the economic values of Malay and Tamil so that these other mother tongues might be considered as attractive as Mandarin. This might then stem any desire on the part of minority parents for their children to learn Mandarin instead of Malay or Tamil. This move is advantageous because, by aiming to equalize the value of all three mother tongues, it is consistent with the spirit of multiracialism. The difficulty lies in its plausibility, that is, whether Malay and Tamil can be argued to have the same kind of economic value as Mandarin.

Consider Malay. Arguments for the economic value of Malay tend to originate from the government and are often greeted with scepticism by the general public. For example, the Home Affairs Minister suggested that 'the rapid economic growth of Southeast Asian countries such as Indonesia, Malaysia and Brunei, would place Malay in a more important position' (*The Straits Times* 4 July 1994). Letters to the press from the public, however, rejected this view, pointing out that more Malays were in fact switching to English, and the press itself supported the public, citing data from the 1990 census which indicated that the number of Malay families speaking English at home had increased from 2.3 per cent in 1980 to 5.7 per cent in 1990 (*The Straits Times* 9 April 1994). One reason for this scepticism is that Singaporeans have tended to be less impressed with the economic potential of Indonesia, Malaysia or Brunei than with that of China. Another reason is that unlike China, where Mandarin does provide a distinct advantage, it seems quite possible for business transactions in Malaysia, for example, to be conducted in English so that the economic imperative to learn Malay is weakened. Similar arguments have, as far as I can tell, not been made for Tamil, perhaps because the government realizes that if it is difficult to argue for the economic value of Malay, then there is little point in attempting the same with Tamil. Tamil poses greater difficulties because, internal to Singapore, it is not really required for conducting business especially since the Tamil elite have traditionally focused more on the literary variety, often discouraging their children from speaking the colloquial language at home (Riney 1998: 8). Externally, business with India, for example, is more likely to be carried out in English than Tamil. And in any case, the Indian community also consists of a number of non-Tamil Indian groups whose allegiance is to other Indian languages such as Bengali, Hindi or Punjabi (Riney 1998: 7).

It is therefore rather difficult to argue that Malay and Tamil have the same kind of economic cachet as Mandarin. This is problematic for the Singapore government's commitment towards multiracialism. As mentioned, under the earlier narrative of strict complementarity where only English was presented as the language of economic development, all the three mother tongues – Mandarin, Malay and Tamil – were of equal importance as languages emblematic of different ethnic identities and different kinds of cultural heritage. As languages associated with the identities and values of different and equal ethnic communities, the mother tongues were not in competition with each other. However, linguistic instrumentalism threatens the relationship of equivalence among the mother tongues since economic considerations cut across ethnic boundaries. By asserting the economic value of Mandarin, the spectre of competition between the mother tongues is raised. Especially if less economically valuable mother tongues start losing speakers to more economically valuable ones, this may create concern that ethnic identities are being threatened. For example, losing Malay speakers to an exogenous language such as English does not threaten national unity and in fact, it may facilitate such unity by invoking a discourse of Western imperialism, a discourse that is already often present in narratives of Asian modernity. But losing Malay speakers to Mandarin might threaten national unity since it could well lead to inter-ethnic friction within Singapore itself. Expressions of such fears are already in evidence. Although some Malays feel a sense of pride in hearing about other Malays learning Mandarin, there is also concern that this is being done at the expense of learning the Malay language. According to a worried Malay grassroots leader, if more young Malays go on to learn Mandarin, 'Next time, they'll be using Chinese names!' (*The Straits Times* 30 April 1994). In a sense, a Pandora's box has been opened but there was never really any choice about the matter. It would have been foolish of the Singapore government not to have exploited the economic advantages that Mandarin-speaking Singaporeans have in dealing with China. However, doing so raises corresponding questions about the economic values of Malay and Tamil. Thus, the twin demands of economic development and managing racial diversity were more easily dealt with in the previous narrative structure, where the mother tongues were only expected to act as transmitters of cultural knowledge. In contrast, the shift towards linguistic instrumentalism creates a new situation where ethnic sensitivities are intertwined with, rather than separated from, economic gains.

I want to now focus on an important consequence of linguistic instrumentalism in Singapore, namely, the tension between endo- and exonormative standards. In arguing for the economic value of Mandarin, and to a lesser extent, Malay, reference is made to external economies such as China, Malaysia, Indonesia and Brunei. In other words, it is the ability to use these languages in order to interact and communicate with individuals in these external economies that gives the languages their instrumentalist value. Thus, if dialectal differences between the kind of Mandarin spoken in Singapore and that in China are too great, this may impede communication. As such, it seems likely that this shift towards linguistic instrumentalism will lead to a greater emphasis on exonormative standards of what is considered acceptable Mandarin since there is no point in having a variety of Mandarin that the Chinese may find unintelligible. However, if Mandarin is to be a marker of a Singaporean Chinese identity, the language must be allowed, or even encouraged, to adapt to local norms so as to reflect more authentically a particularly Singaporean Chinese ethos. This would require a greater willingness to embrace a more endonormative perspective on the use of Mandarin. This tension between endo- and exonormativity has yet to be fully debated or explored. For example, in the very same speech, a government minister, George Yeo, highlights the use of Mandarin as marker of local identity and its use in dealing with China, without addressing the question of what kind(s) of Mandarin is at stake here (*The Straits Times* 14 April 1994). Yeo points out that the focus on the instrumentalist value of Mandarin should not obscure the importance of Mandarin as a reflection of local identity:

> The position we are taking is a long-term position. It doesn't mean that if there are no economic incentives, then we stop promoting Mandarin.
>
> We should promote it nonetheless, to make a part of us, a part of our own social cultural instinct. That's the objective. It's not merely to chase the dollar. I mean, chasing a dollar is important, but it is not just to chase a dollar. . . .

But then, in talking about standards of Mandarin, he describes how students are sent overseas in order to improve their command of the language:

> In the polytechnics and universities now, you find interest in Chinese Language courses growing year by year. We are also sending students for attachment to China and Taiwan middle schools and universities.
>
> Increasing numbers of our undergraduate and graduate students want to spend a period of time in the Chinese universities in order to improve their Mandarin.

And he implies that it is only by looking exonormatively that proper standards can be attained:

> It is important to give Mandarin a high standard because otherwise the people who make the effort will be demoralised. . . . The mass knows that not everyone can master the language and culture. But it's always a pleasure, let us say, when you visit China, that you lead a delegation with some members who have a good hand, who have a good brush, and everyone is proud because of that. . . . Without the standard bearers, we will have no replacement for the Nantah generation.[3]

But he then comes back to a more endonormative position when he claims that to express local culture, local forms of writing must prevail:

> But especially in the cultural field, we must have local groups, because it is not the same. If you are from China, from America, but you come here for only a few months or a year, what you write does not express fully, cannot express fully the inner feelings of Singaporeans.

This speech makes clear that the government is keen to emphasize the economic value of Mandarin without sacrificing its role as a mother tongue, but a number of questions remain unresolved. For example, how should differences between the Singapore and Chinese varieties be dealt with? What variety of Mandarin should be taught in Singapore schools? In particular, is there a problem in suggesting that a high standard of Mandarin can only be attained by going overseas and in also claiming that Mandarin must be used for expressing local culture? Until these questions are systematically dealt with, we might expect a certain degree of ambivalence in the attitudes of Singaporean Chinese towards Mandarin: while ostensibly an expression of their own culture, it only attains its 'highest standards' by looking outwards towards China.

Some features of linguistic instrumentalism

I mentioned above Monica Heller's work (1999a,b) on the impact of globalization on language and identity. Heller's work is an ethnographic study of the language practices of a French-language minority school in predominantly English-speaking Ontario, and she suggests (1999b: 336), following Giddens (1990) that as part of current processes of globalization, the following phenomena can be observed:

- the commodification of language
- pressures towards standardization for international communication; and
- the opposite, the valuing of local characteristics in order to legitimate local control over markets, and in order to attach a value of distinction to linguistic commodities in world markets of culture and tourism.

A recent application of Heller's ideas to the status of the Spanish language in the USA (Pomerantz 2002) also shows that while proficiency in Spanish is seen as a resource for the English-speaking elite, it is a detriment to the social mobility of working class US Latinos for whom the language is simply a 'heritage' marker (Pomerantz 2002: 281). Given Pomerantz's analysis of the language ideologies surrounding Spanish in the USA, Heller's work on French in Canada and the discussion of Singapore presented above, I would like to tentatively suggest some possible features of linguistic instrumentalism.

One feature of linguistic instrumentalism is that 'the question of norms is subject to different, and sometimes countervailing, tendencies' (Heller 1999b: 343). For example, there is a tension between the representations of French or Spanish as markers of cultural authenticity and integrity and the emerging globalizing orientation which treats these languages as economic resources (Heller 1999b: 336; Pomerantz 2002: 276). Similarly, in Singapore, as the government aims, in the case of Mandarin at least, to take advantage of China's open-door policy, its earlier emphasis on the mother tongues as markers of cultural identities has had to accommodate the shift towards a more instrumentalist orientation, resulting in a tension that has yet to be fully resolved. Another feature is that the vernaculars are 'the simultaneous source of stigmatization and authenticity' (Heller 1999b: 343). Speakers from working-class French Canadian families tend to 'feel that the linguistic resources they possess are devalued by the school' (Heller 1999b: 353). Similar observations obtain in the case of Latino families in the USA. (Pomerantz 2002: 281). And in Singapore, while the mother tongues are still considered important for local cultural expressions, there is a danger that, in time, local varieties will also no longer be as valued. We saw an indication of this in the speech by George Yeo, where, despite the claim that Mandarin is important for expressing 'our own social cultural instinct', there is also the suggestion that for standards of Mandarin to improve, students must travel overseas to China or Taiwan. A final feature is that the value of French or Spanish in the marketplace is based on the assumption that these languages adding to an existing English language proficiency so that the speakers are aiming for an English–French or English–Spanish bilingualism. The goal is not to displace English, whose importance remains undisputed. In Canada, speakers aim for the construction of a specific type of bilingualism, a bilingualism which is essentially two unilingualisms, one French and the other English, stuck together (as opposed to a code-switched or mixed variety)' (Heller 1999b: 353). Likewise, in Pomerantz's study (2002), Spanish is valued mainly as an added resource for the English-speaking elite. This is similar to Singapore where the goal is not to promote Mandarin at the expense of English, but to maximize the chances of social mobility or economic success by attaining an English–Mandarin bilingualism.

The Canada, USA and Singapore situations should therefore be seen as part of general picture of change where perceptions of what it means to be globally competitive have led to particular languages being reconstructed on instrumentalist grounds. And here, the particular context of Singapore, with its commitment to a policy of multiracialism, presents an interesting challenge since intra-linguistic considerations (reconciling a language's function as bearer of authenticity with its economic value) need to be dealt with alongside inter-linguistic ones (the desire to maintain parity or equal status among the official mother tongues). Important similarities, however, are discernible, which I summarize below:

1. Linguistic instrumentalism is a later addition to a previously existing view that treats the language as a marker of cultural identity and authenticity, resulting in a tension that is not yet reconciled.
2. One consequence, though, is the tendency to devalue or marginalize local vernaculars.
3. Linguistic instrumentalism assumes the continued importance of multi-/bilingualism, so that the language whose economic value is being championed is acquired in addition to English, never in place of it.

Conclusion

A prominent feature of the narratives of Asian modernity is the repositioning of endogenous cultural elements with respect to Western modernity. The primary change has been to assert that endogenous elements are not only compatible with Western modernity, but rather, in concert can act as the main engines of social and economic development. In Singapore, this attempt to accommodate the presence of both the mother tongues and English has led to a policy where the former are primarily expected to function as markers of cultural identity while the latter is expected to provide access to Western science and technology, and economic competitiveness. However, the need to adopt a more global outlook, and in particular, the developments in China, have led the Singapore government to assert the linguistic instrumentalism of Mandarin, opening the way for an even more radical rethinking of the narrative of Asian modernity, one where a mother tongue such as Mandarin is treated, like the English language, as also having a strong economic value. But the price to be paid for this move may be that it compromises the carefully laid policy of multiracialism that has been so fundamental to way in which Singapore manages its ethnically diverse population, since the question is then raised concerning the economic values of Malay and Tamil. Finally, while these reflect problems peculiar to Singapore, it has also been possible, by comparisons with Canada and the USA, to suggest a number of general features of the discourse of linguistic instrumentalism.

Notes

1 An extended version of this chapter was first published in 2003, in the *Journal of Multilingual and Multilingual Development* 24(3). I thank Multilingual Matters for permission to reproduce the article.

2 For a detailed discussion of these problems, see Gupta (1994), PuruShotam (1998) and Siddique (1990).

3 The 'Nantah generation' refers to the Chinese-educated elites, who were graduates from the Chinese language Nanyang University. In 1980, the Singapore government merged Nanyang University with the University of Singapore to form the National University of Singapore. This move upset a large portion of the Chinese community who felt that the government was not truly supportive of the Chinese language and culture.

References

Benjamin, Geoffrey (1976), 'The cultural logic of Singapore's "multiracialism"' in Riaz Hassan (ed) *Singapore: Society in Transition* (Kuala Lumpur: Oxford University Press), pp. 115–33.

Bokhorst-Heng, Wendy (1998), *Language and imagining the nation in Singapore*. PhD dissertation, University of Toronto.

Chua, Beng Huat (1995), *Communitarian Ideology and Democracy in Singapore* (London: Routledge).

Edwards, John (1985), *Language, Society and Identity* (London: Blackwell).

Giddens, Anthony (1990), *The Consequences of Modernity* (Stanford: Stanford University Press).

Gupta, Anthea F. (1994), *The Step-tongue: Children's English in Singapore* (Clevedon: Multilingual Matters).

Heller, Monica (1999a), *Linguistic Minorities and Modernity: A Sociolinguistic Ethnography* (London: Longman).

Heller, Monica (1999b), 'Alternative ideologies of la francophonie', *Journal of Sociolinguistics* 3(3): 336–59.

May, Stephen (2001), *Language and Minority Rights* (London: Longman).

Ong, Aihwa. (1999), *Flexible Citizenship: The Cultural Logic of Transnationality* (USA: Duke University Press).

Pennycook, Alistair (1994), *The Cultural Politics of English as an International Language* (London: Longman).

Phillipson, Robert (1992), *Linguistic Imperialism* (Oxford: Oxford University Press).

Pomerantz, Anita (2002), 'Language ideologies and the production of identities: Spanish as resource for participation in a multilingual marketplace', *Multilingua* 21(2/3), 275–302.

PuruShotam, Nirmala (1998), *Negotiating Language, Constructing Race* (Berlin: Mouton de Gruyter).

Riney, Timothy (1998), 'Toward more homogeneous bilingualisms: Shift phenomena in Singapore', *Multilingua* 17(1): 1–23.

Siddique, Sharon (1990), 'The phenomenology of ethnicity: A Singapore case study', *Sojourn: Social Issues in Southeast Asia* 5(1): 35–62.

3 The Commodification of Malay: Trading in Futures

Lubna Alsagoff

Chapter Outline

This chapter traces the historical development behind Malay's special status in Singapore as its national language. It examines the ideological debates surrounding the status of Malay as one of the three ethnic mother tongues in Singapore and forwards a stand that Malay does in fact continue to occupy a special place in Singapore policy, despite shifts in the politics of Singapore. It argues against a simplistic evaluation, in the commodification framework, of the three mother tongues as having equal status as cultural repositories of the different races, and argues that Malay holds a special significance for Singapore, both historically, as well as in the present day, in relation to its political value for ensuring the future of Singapore's political stability.

Introduction

In speaking of the commodification of language in Singapore, the issue that is most often raised is the contrast between English as a language valued for its economic worth and the mother tongues, Malay, Mandarin and Tamil, as languages valued for their cultural worth (Wee, Chapter 2 this volume, Silver, 2005). We begin our discussion with such a contrast in mind, although at a later stage, we see how this contrast is slowly being eroded as Singapore becomes more mindful of regional geopolitical and economic pressures. Thus, we begin with the premise that the three local languages Chinese (Mandarin), Tamil and Malay are cultural commodities, while English is one that is economic in value.

Commodification is a concept that can be applied quite aptly to the Singapore language situation particularly because of the overarching economic pragmatism that motivates the Singapore government (Wee, Chapter 2 this volume). Developed and applied to the study of language by a number of researchers (e.g. Bourdieu (1986), Phillipson (1992) and Heller (1999)), commodification draws on a larger theory of the political economics of language, which basically objectifies and evaluates languages in relation to the goods that they can be exchanged for. In other words, the measure of languages is essentially derived from an association of the language with any of a number of 'goods' which are of value to the society. For example, a language can be valued for its economic capital, in the sense that it is connected, or essential for material gain and the economic well-being of the community it serves. It is in this respect that English is viewed in Singapore. It is the language of trade, commerce, banking, finance, science and technology, what Pakir (1991) correctly calls a powerful and high-status language.

Languages can also be valued in other ways – socially, as well as culturally. These relate to the function that languages play in fostering social networks, promoting nationalism, through preserving cultural roots, tradition or ethnic identity. It is in these respects that the mother tongue languages are characterized in Singapore. Thus, it is not simply material gain that gives a language its value and that enables us to talk of it as being commodified. Rather, a language is commodified in the sense that it is given a value based on its association with some form of benefit or 'goods' of worth to the society. For Malay, we see that although its value is currently in cultural terms, this historically derived from socio-political factors, where Malay was prized not so much as a language symbolizing Malay-ness, but a language symbolizing Malayan-ness. We demonstrate how commodification when combined with a historical perspective provides an interesting sociolinguistic profile of Malay because it enables us to understand the subtle shift in the ways in which the value of Malay is derived.

Malay as the national language

Although Malay is one of the three mother tongue languages, it is given a symbolic status that is not shared by Chinese (Mandarin) and Tamil. This singling out of Malay as Singapore's national language is evident in the descriptions found in all of Singapore's official websites – from the Singapore Ministry of Foreign Affair's website, to the Singapore Tourism Board's *Visit Singapore* website, to the Singapore Infomap.

> The official languages in Singapore are Malay, Chinese (Mandarin), Tamil and English. Malay is the national language and English is the language of administration. (http://www.mfa.gov.sg)

> There are four official languages in Singapore: Malay, Mandarin, Tamil and English. English is the language of business and administration, and is widely spoken and understood. Most Singaporeans are bilingual, and speak their mother tongue as well as English. Malay is the national language. (http://www.visitsingapore.com)

> Official languages:
> English (language of administration), Chinese (Mandarin), Malay (National language) & Tamil. (http://www.sg)

In addition, other official international websites such as the US State Department's website, as well as reference sites such as the much-cited Wikipedia also confer a special status on Malay as Singapore's national language, showing that the difference between Malay and the other two mother tongue languages is also internationally recognized.

> Singapore has a varied linguistic, cultural, and religious heritage. Malay is the national language, but Chinese, English, and Tamil also are official languages. (http://www.state.gov)

> The official languages of Singapore are English, Mandarin Chinese, Malay and Tamil. English has been promoted as the country's *lingua franca* since independence, and it is spoken by the majority of the population. Malay remains Singapore's national language for historical reasons and it is used in the national anthem. (http://www.wikipedia.org)

Thus, while Malay is one of the three mother tongues, along with Mandarin, and Tamil, it has a special status, and given symbolic significance as the national language of Singapore.

Malay as a language of the nation

To understand this special status of Malay, as these websites suggest it has, a historical perspective is necessary – we need to go back to the late 1950s – to the time of self-autonomy, of 'separation' from the British, the time of merger with Malaysia and to the time of Independence. It is widely agreed in historical texts that Singapore desired a merger with the Federation to form Malaysia. The reasons are complex – the formation of the Federation of Malaysia was a pre-condition for British decolonization, and it was also seen as a means of staving off the perceived threat of Communism. It might also perhaps have been because Singapore saw the rich economic potential of access to the Malaysian common market (Lee 1959b; Oh 1967; Bokhorst-Heng 1998). To this end, the People's Action Party (PAP), which in 1959 became the ruling party of the Singapore government, argued for a special status for Malay in predominantly Chinese Singapore. Lee Kuan Yew, then leader of the PAP, and later Prime Minister, stressed that Malay should 'enjoy undisputed priority over any other language as the compulsory second language to be taught in all schools, be they English, Chinese or Indian schools' (cited in Bokhorst-Heng 1998). Bokhorst-Heng highlights the PAP's recognition that the successful merger of Singapore and the Federation of Malay required that importance of Malay as 'a common national language' be emphasized, referring to a number of speeches and statements made by the PAP and its political party members.

Bokhorst-Heng notes that as the national language, Malay would perform two functions. First, it was to be a common language that was to foster national unity and understanding among the races. Second, as a national language, it was to express a distinct and unique national identity. The political rhetoric at that time clearly indicated that the adoption of Malay as the national language was motivated by an understanding of the value of the language as a political commodity – clearly, Malay was necessary for the merger that would unite Malaya, Sarawak and Sabah. What is significant, therefore, is that Malay's worth lay in its association with the nation state – that of the Federation of Malaysia. This associative value was especially important because of concerns in Malaya that Singapore was predominantly Chinese. As the language that would represent the Federation of Malaysia, Malay took on considerable polit-ical significance and capital in Singapore. It was therefore no surprise that it was designated as the national language. This status was legislated in the Singapore Constitution, which crucially also promoted equality for all races in the recognition of the other two languages – Chinese and Tamil – as official languages:

153 A.
(1) Malay, Mandarin, Tamil and English shall be the 4 official languages in Singapore.
(2) The national language shall be the Malay language and shall be in the Roman script.

Let us first look at how Malay, as the national language, would function as a common language to foster national unity in a multiracial Singapore that was to be part of what the PAP ideologized as a similarly multiracial Federation. Malay was obviously the most suitable candidate. The only other possible candidate, English, was clearly too closely associated with the former British colonial masters to have gained favour among the Singapore citizens (or the Malayan people). With the need to 'Malayanise' (Lee 1959a) in order to accomplish a successful merger with the Federation of Malaya, Malay was, from a strategic point of view, the most logical choice. In these arguments, Malay was crucially framed and constructed as the language of a nation, rather than the language of a race. Note that even in the first argument, where the contrast between Malay and English is drawn – it is a contrast between Malay as the language of the Federation of Malaysia, and English as the language of the British Empire. Thus, Lee's (1965, quoted in Oh 1967) concept of a Malaysian Malaysia was not contradicted because Malay as a national language was constructed and represented as the nation's language, rather than the language of the Malay race.

In fostering national unity, Malay was also seen as crucially being able to diffuse Chinese chauvinism. Chinese chauvinism was seen as detrimental to the Singapore government's goal of successfully merging with the Federation of Malaya, and an obstacle to building a Malaysian nation and a Malaysian consciousness' (Lee 1959c; Oh 1967). But what is interesting is that in order to address the concerns of the Chinese community, it was not Malay as the language of the Malays that was to do this work, but Malay as the language of the 'nation' of Malaysia, of Malaysian consciousness that was to do it. Malay was, at that time, therefore not seen as a vehicle of cultural identity – as an icon for the Malay community; but rather, its value was in relation to a political identity – aligned with that of the neighbour Singapore was courting.

Next, as a national language, Malay was to express a distinct and unique national identity. Here, Bokhorst-Heng (1998) claimed that Malay failed: instead of building a unique identity, Malay actually had the reverse effect – that of de-emphasizing the uniqueness of Singapore to promote its merger to be part of Malaysia. My perspective is slightly different. Here, I believe that we need to understand which nation was supposed to have been represented. It was not so much Singapore, by itself, that was the nation in question; rather, it was the already imagined, the desired, merged nation that I believe Malay was to have served as a national language of. It is a complex issue, given the political intricacies at that time, but I feel that there was no failure. Rather, there was a subtle yet clear shift in the imagining of the nation. From this perspective, we can see Malay as an expression of a distinct identity for Singapore in the sense that it set Singapore apart from its British colonial past, and also served to obviate Singapore becoming the 'Third China'.

The legislation of Malay as the national language of Singapore was in keeping with Lee Kuan Yew's conviction that the merger to form the Federation of Malaysia should represent a Malaysian Malaysia with equality for all races, rather than a Malay Malaysia (Lee 1965, cited in Oh 1967). The message implicit in this was that nation and race were separate, and that nation should take precedence over race. Thus, Malay as the national language was conceptualized to serve the merged multiracial nation, rather than one racial group, although, in reality, it was clearly to show the willingness of the predominantly Chinese Singapore to successfully merge with the predominantly Malay Malaysia, and that issues and problems relating to racial tensions could be resolved through this constructed view of language and identity. This view – of a Malaysian Malaysia, of a secular nation – as we know from history, was not shared by Tunku Abdul Rahman and the Federal Government of Malaysia. The United Malay National Organization, the dominant political party of the Malaysian government, feared that as long as Singapore remained in the Federation, their agenda of positive racial discrimination of the Malays would be undermined. The idea of the inseparability of nation and race is also evident in the morphological constitution of the Malay word for 'national', which is *kebangsaan* – its root word *bangsa* is the Malay word for 'race' – for the Malaysian Federation, there could perhaps be no separation between nation and race. These were congruent notions for them, one and the same. Thus, it was not so much that Malay failed as a national language (*bahasa kebangsaan*), but that it fell with the demise of the imagined Malaysian Malaysia. Since it derived value from its association with this imagined nation, Malay could obviously no longer maintain its political capital.

Malay as the language of ethnic identity

Thus, like all commodities, the Malay language fell in value because of changes in the politico-economic climate. During the period around the merger, Malay's value was clearly high – it was a prized commodity primarily because of its political capital. However, with the failure of the merger, this political value was not sustainable. No longer the centre of political strategies after Singapore's independence, Malay was gradually but surely disassociated from its earlier role as an articulation of Malaysian political identity. From the perspective of many Malays, 'the period after separation was a set-back in the development of the Malay language; some regard this the lowest point in the recent history of Malays in Singapore' (Abdullah and Ayyub 1998). However, Malay, perhaps in its less-valued Bazaar Malay vernacular form, was still recognized as a common language, and it continued to be the local lingua franca for some time after Independence. In sharp contrast to the lament on the decline and eventual closure of Malay-medium schools and the abolition of the Malay language requirement for the education service, Patrick Ho's (2005) article in of *Today Online*, a local Singapore newspaper, reminisces in a sentimental vein, painting a different picture of the status of Malay:

> In my primary-school days in the '70s, Malay was taught as the national language to non-Malay students. It was the language of interaction between the races, because English was still in its infancy.

Despite the failure of the merger, the value of Malay continued to hold strong, although, as Bokhorst-Heng (1998) points out, the discourse narrowed. In a sense, Malay continued its role as Singapore's national language probably because more people spoke Malay than English. The years before and during the merger with the Federation of Malaya had inevitably led to a more widespread use of Malay as a lingua franca. However, an equally likely reason might have been that the Singapore government was still mindful that Singapore was, after all, a 'Chinese island in a Malay Sea' (Lee 1998 cited in Wikipedia.org). Flanked by behemoth Indonesia and Malaysia, and politically vulnerable especially after the withdrawal of British troops in 1971 (National Heritage Board 2000), Singapore needed to be prudent in its policies. Malay as a national language thus served as Singapore's badge of caution – an overt gesture of Singapore's awareness of and respect for geopolitical forces in the region.

However, the economic evaluation of Malay shifted – instead of being the language of the 'imagined' nation, it was now the language of Malay and Muslim ethnicity in the region. Malay was the common language of both the Malay Muslim nations of Indonesia and Malaysia (even though the two varieties took on different names: *Bahasa Malaysia* and *Bahasa Indonesia*). The continued status of Malay as a national language was necessary to stand as testimonial to the Singapore government's recognition of the importance of the Malays as the island's indigenous race, as did other pro-Malay policies, which included among others, free education for all Malays – thereby 'assuaging concerns amongst its Malay-Muslim neighbours that Singapore might become a Chinese state' (Wee 2003). And perhaps it was also this reason that led to the removal of Malay as the de jure national language from the Singapore Constitution in 1979 without fanfare or public notice (Bokhorst-Heng 1998).[1]

Thus, in a way, even before Malay became 'designated' as a mother tongue (in contrast to English, the working language), it was already quietly serving as a symbol of Malay ethnic consciousness, although this role was rooted more in a politically than culturally oriented motivation – Malay was still needed diplomatically as part of a lifeline for 'a Chinese island in a Malay sea'. Malay's fortunes continued to evolve, as the political and economic climate changed. In the 1980s, perhaps on surer footing, and with multiculturalism and multilingualism already successful demonstrations of the PAP manifesto, and with Singapore achieving success against all odds, there needed to be more emphasis on the equal treatment of the three main ethnic groups. In addition, with the rise of English as a global language, and the need for Singapore to modernize and industrialize, the Ministry of Education implemented an 'English-knowing' bilingualism policy that would ultimately lead to English eventually replacing Malay as the local *lingua franca*.

Malay then became re-articulated and reified as the language of Singapore Malay ethnic identity. As Bokhorst-Heng (1998) points out, '[t]he March 1982 Malay language campaign demonstrates very clearly the shift in language ideology. It was to be a Malay language campaign, not a *national language* campaign.' With the passing of time, there were fewer and fewer initiatives to promote Malay as a compulsory third language in school or at work, as a national language. The Malay language campaign, for example, was organized by Malay cultural organizations rather than the government. The dissociation of Malay from nation saw the tandem association of Malay with race. Malay began to be promoted, equally with the other two local languages, Mandarin and Tamil, simply as a mother tongue tied to ethnicity, as 'an important element of

Malay identity and . . . the dominant language used in cultural and social net-working' (Abdullah and Ayyub 1998). Malay, therefore, as with Chinese and Tamil, came to be valued as cultural commodities.

It would then appear from this that Malay no longer holds a unique status in Singapore, and must now be categorized together as a mother tongue together with Chinese and Tamil. But what of the Singapore statutes' and the official website pronouncements that Malay is Singapore's national language? While we will not debate on the apparent changes in the legal status of Malay as a national language,[2] we should discuss its de facto status. As a national language, Malay has been relegated to a primarily ceremonial role – as the language of the National Anthem, and that of military parade ground commands. However, as an ethnically defined language, Malay, in fact, holds a special status. In Singapore, Malay is secured of a significant political place in modern times because Malay is the language of Islam in South-East Asia; this is primarily because language, religion and culture are inextricably linked for the Malay communities in this region.

The link between being Malay and being Muslim is clear – an overwhelm-ing percentage, 99.6 per cent, of Malays are Muslims, something not seen in the other ethnic groups in Singapore. And the fact that that converting to Islam is commonly referred to as 'masuk Melayu', that is, 'entering or becoming Malay' is also indicative of the equation of race and religion for the Malay community (Ismail and Shaw 2006). Abdullah and Ayyub's (1998) observa-tion of the central role of the mosques or *madrasahs* (Muslim religious schools) in promoting Malay traditions and cultures through Malay language educa-tion augments the equation that ties language, religion and race for the Malay community. With the religious and political tensions arising from '9/11', polit-ical instability and strife in the Middle East, Malay has taken on a renewed political significance and value in recent times. Interestingly, in Malaysia, there have been attempts to revive the use of the term *Bahasa Melayu* to refer to Malay, emphasizing Malay as a language of the Malay race (in contrast with *Bahasa Malaysia*, where Malay is referred to as the language of Malaysia).

Lee Kuan Yew (2005), now Minister Mentor, in his characteristically prag-matic political outlook, has recently suggested however that Malay's role should not diminish, but continue in the light of regional and global threats and challenges. Remarking on the importance for key officers in government agencies to be competent in Malay, the Minister Mentor declared:

> The Ministry of Education is considering a third language option learning Bahasa (Malay) to listen, to speak and to read basic Bahasa for those who can cope with

a third language. It will not be of the standard that we teach our Malay students, because they will not need to write Bahasa, just listen, speak and read as in basic Chinese. We must get some 10–15% of our non-Malay population fluent in Bahasa. (Lee 2005)

While strong in his advocacy of Malay, Lee's 2005 pronouncement pales in comparison with his statement in pre-merger Singapore that Malay should 'enjoy undisputed priority over any other language as the compulsory second language to be taught in all schools, be they English, Chinese or Indian schools' (Legislative Assembly, 1956 cited in Bokhorst-Heng (1998)). Unlike the economically motivated call for Chinese to become more widely used because of the business opportunities in China,[3] the government's call for the increased role of Malay is clearly motivated by political rather than economic capital. Thus, Malay's status as a politically valued commodity appears to have come full circle, in a manner of speaking.

Conclusion

The discourse on the commodification of languages in Singapore has often led to a perspective where the 'more useful' triumphs over the 'less useful', and where the exigencies of politics and economics play a crucial role in determining the fate and fortune of languages. Wee (2003) discusses the language situation in Singapore in similar terms through the concept of 'linguistic instrumentalism', where the existence of a language is justified in terms of its usefulness in achieving specific utilitarian goals, such as access to economic development or social mobility. Wee concludes in a similar vein that it is economic gain and social mobility that are stronger motivations for the maintenance of a language rather than cultural or symbolic ones. Specifically, he makes the claim that 'there is general dissatisfaction, with, and insecurity about, the status of the mother tongues . . . as mere cultural repositories – despite strong official support' (p. 32). Wee (Chapter 2 this volume) remarks that because the Singapore Government has made 'a case for Mandarin's economic value, that the government is obliged, in the name of multiracial equality, to assert that the other mother tongues, Malay and Tamil, also have strong economic values' (p. 33).

The brief account of Malay given here demonstrates that Wee's point is perhaps made a little too generally. The broad strokes of commodification as a framework of analysis in understanding the sociology of language can often overlook the possibility of multi-discursive frames, and favour the representation of the dominant voice and perspective. While it was politically necessary to shift Malay to a different role because there was now no necessity to 'maintain a path across the causeway' (Abdullah and Ayyub 1998) – meaning that Malay therefore ceased to be as politically significant and valued as a linguistic commodity the way it was right before and during the merger – commodification as a perspective, as explained by Wee (this volume), does not clearly represent the uniqueness of Malay over the other two ethnic mother tongues.

I agree with Wee in that the value of Malay cannot be convincingly made in terms of economic capital – Wee cites the scepticism of the general public when the Home Affairs Minister attempted to exhort the promotion of Malay because of the rapid economic growth in Indonesia, Malaysia and Brunei (*The Straits Times* 4 July 1994, cited in Wee (2003)). However, as can be most aptly seen in Lee Kuan Yew's (2005) speech, this does not mean that Malay is to be treated as a mere cultural repository, or that it should be treated as the same as the other two ethnic mother tongues. First, there is a more obvious economic value in the Chinese and Indian ethnic mother tongues because of the vast economic markets of China and India. Second, Malay's historical status as a language of the nation, albeit the 'imagined' one, meant it was endowed with a symbolic status derived from its political value as a result of its association with the Federation. Third, Malay is singled out, and remains so in the Singapore Constitution, as Singapore's national language. Last and most important, the close links that the Malay language has with Malay ethnicity and Islam has meant that it has special religious and political significance in the post '9/11' world, in which the government must manage 'the competing ethno-religious identity pulls of the Muslim minority, and channelling such emotions and energies towards the forging of a Singaporean national consciousness' (Mutalib 2005).

Notes

1 Interestingly, while the printed version of the 1979 Singapore Constitution does not contain Article 153A (Bokhorst-Heng 1998), this very same article appears in the current online version of the Singapore Constitution, which also states that Article 153A has been in effect since 9 August 1965 (Singapore Statutes Online). This, of course, bears some investigation – it would be interesting, for example, to find out when the article resurfaced, and what the trigger was that prompted it.

2 Ibid.

3 To a lesser extent, Tamil has been also claimed to have economic significance in order to tap into the economic opportunities in India.

References

Abdullah, Kamsiah and Ayyub, Bibi Jan Mohd (1998), 'Malay language issues and trends' in S. Gopinathan, A. Pakir, W. K.Ho, V. Saravanan (eds), *Language Society and Education in Singapore: Issues and Trends* (Singapore: Times Academic Press, 2nd edition), pp. 179–90.

Bokhorst-Heng, Wendy D. (1998), 'Language and imagining the nation in Singapore', unpublished PhD Dissertation, University of Toronto.

Bourdieu, Pierre. (1986), 'The forms of capital' in John G. Richardson (ed.), *Handbook of Theory and Research for the Sociology of Education* (New York: Greenwood Press.), pp. 241–58.

Heller, M. (1999), 'Alternative ideologies of "la francophonie"', *Journal of Sociolinguistics* 3(3): 336–59.

Ho, Patrick K. F. (21 February.2005), ' "Bahasa is boleh" shift welcome, but is it too little too late?' Retrieved 22 February 2005, *Today Online*.

Ismail, Rahil and Shaw, Brian J. (2006), 'Singapore's Malay Muslim minority: Social identification in a "9/11" world', *Asian Ethnicity* 7(1): 37–51.

Lee Kuan Yew (1959a), 'Precis to the Prime Minister's speech to the Chinese Union of Journalists on Tuesday September 1, 1959'. Retrieved 16 November 2004, www.sprinter.gov.sg

Lee Kuan Yew (1959b), 'Singapore Government Press Statement: Speech by the Prime Minister, Mr Lee Kuan Yew, on the Preservation of Security Amendment Bill at the Legislative Assembly on Wednesday October 14, 1959'. Retrieved 16 November 2004, www.sprinter.gov.sg

Lee Kuan Yew (1959c), 'Precis of the Prime Minster's Speech to the Chinese Union of Journalists on Tuesday September 1, 1959'. Retrieved 16 November 2004, www.sprinter.gov.sg

Lee Kuan Yew (1965), *Towards a Malaysian Malaysia*(Singapore: Government Printing Office), pp. 1–21.

Lee Kuan Yew (1998), *The Singapore Story: Memoirs of Lee Kuan Yew* (Singapore: Times).

Lee Kuan Yew (2005). Speech by Minister Mentor Lee Kuan Yew at the Tanjong Pagar Chinese New Year Dinner at Radin Mas Community Club, 17 February 2005. Retrieved 10 July 2006, www.sprinter. gov.sg.

Ministry of Foreign Affairs Retrieved 17 November 2004, www.mfa.gov.sg.Mutalib, Hussin (2005), 'Singapore Muslims: The quest for identity in a modern city-state', *Journal of Muslim Minority Affairs* 25(1): 53–72.

National Heritage Board (2000), *Singapore: Journey into Nationhood* (Singapore: Landmark Books and National Heritage Board).

Oh, John C. H. (1967), 'The Federation of Malaysia: An experiment in nation-building', *American Journal of Economics and Sociology* 26(4): 425–38.

Pakir, Anne (1991), 'The range and depth of English-knowing bilinguals in Singapore', *World Englishes* 10(2): 167–79.

Phillipson, Robert (1992), *Linguistic Imperialism* (Oxford: Oxford University Press)

Silver, Rita E. (2005), 'The discourse of linguistic capital: Language and economic policy planning in Singapore', *Language Policy* 4(1): 47–66.

Singapore Infomap Online, Retrieved 12 August 2004, www.sg

Singapore Statutes Online, Retrieved 28 February 2004, http://statutes.agc.gov.sg

Singapore Tourism Board Online, Retrieved 12 August 2004, www.visitsingapore.com

United States of America State Department Online, Retrieved 12 August 2004, www.state.gov .

Wee, Lionel. (2003), 'Linguistic instrumentalism in Singapore', *Journal of Multilingual and Multicultural Development* 24(3): 211–24.

Wikipedia. Online, Retrieved 12 August 2004, www.wikipedia.org

Beyond Linguistic Instrumentalism: The Place of Singlish in Singapore

4

Chng Huang Hoon

Singapore's participation in the global economy has motivated the Singaporean government to privilege languages that are deemed to have economic value over those that do not. More specifically, the government has called for the promotion of what has been locally designated as 'mother tongues' in addition to the constant exhortation that Singaporeans aspire towards internationally intelligible Standard (Singaporean) English. This overt promotion of specific economically and culturally valued languages has left Singlish out on a lurch. Amidst the forces of such overt commodification of specific languages, this chapter makes a case for the value of Singlish in the local linguistic marketplace as an essential marker of Singaporean identity.

Language policy and planning in Singapore

Singapore's language policy is very much tied to the history of national development. Two factors – the need for economic development and a racially diverse population – have influenced the thinking of the local leadership and guided many national initiatives. As Singaporeans, we are often reminded that Singapore is a small island, not blessed with rich natural resources. Internally, Singapore is a multiracial nation; externally, we are surrounded by predominantly Malay/Muslim states. In the 40-odd years of its independence, Singapore has maintained a population with a relatively steady spread along racial lines. In the most recent population census (2000), it was recorded that Singapore's 4.0 million people is made up of 76.8 per cent Chinese, 13.9 per cent Malay, 7.9 per cent Indian and 1.4 per cent Others (read: Eurasians, Europeans, etc.). These two factors, taken together, dictate the rationale for a bilingual education policy that has been in existence since the 1960s.[1]

Singapore's bilingual language policy privileges English as the first school language, and *de facto*, the most important of the four designated official languages in Singapore. The importance of English lies in its value as a world language that provides ready access to global trade and communication. In short, English has high instrumental value as the language used not just internally for inter-ethnic communication among the different ethnic groups but also employed externally for international communication. In order to manage the challenges of a multi-ethnic nation, the other prong of the national bilingual programme takes the form of requiring competence in a designated mother tongue: Mandarin (for the Chinese), Malay (for the Malays) and Tamil (for the Indians).[2] In this national plan, what Pakir (1992) has termed 'English-knowing bilingualism', there is little room for other languages – the many Chinese and Malay 'dialects', and the local tongue, Singlish.

Singapore's former Prime Minister Lee Kuan Yew was the man who spoke positively for the need of such a bilingual language policy (Lee 2000). In addition, Lee also said that

> When I speak of bilingualism, I do not mean just the facility of speaking two languages. It is more basic than that, first we understand ourselves . . . then the facility of the English language gives us access to the science and technology of the West. It also provides a convenient common ground on which . . . everybody competes in a neutral medium (*The Mirror* 20 November 1972, cited in Wee 2005: 55).

Back in the 1970s, when Singapore was still in her early stages of nation building, Lee argued strongly for the vision of a Singapore comprising Singaporeans who are plugged into the world through their command of English, and at the same time, remain true to their cultural heritage via the compulsory education in a second ethnic language like Mandarin, Malay or Tamil. However, in spite of years of compulsory bilingual education, the fact is, few Singaporeans are able to attain the standard of proficiency that qualifies them as competent bilinguals. In particular, many Chinese Singaporean students found the learning of Mandarin a challenge.[3] Recently, the official position seems to have shifted, if only slightly. In a 2004 speech, Lee said in relation to the learning of Mandarin and accessing the China market that '[b]ilingualism gets us through the front door, but it is only through biculturalism that we can reach deep inside China and work with them' (Lee 2004). There is now a call for a more focused approach to learning the various languages:

a. learning English – still important because of its status as a world language,
b. learning Mandarin – now instrumental with the ascent of China on the world stage,[4]
c. learning Malay – which remains an important language due in large part to Singapore's geographical proximity to Malaysia, Indonesia and Brunei,
d. learning Tamil or Hindi – possibly valuable in the near future with the re-emergence of India on the global scene.[5]

The above thinking on language planning and policy in Singapore has been termed by Wee as driven by a narrative of linguistic instrumentalism (see Wee 2003, also Chapter 2 this volume). This chapter attempts to examine the issue of the place and value of a local language, namely Singlish, by invoking an alternative narrative – the narrative of identity. My basic argument is that while it is true that Singlish has little instrumental value on the global stage, the fact remains that we live in a world that is diverse enough to accommodate the different roles played by different sectors of the population, each ably served by its own tongue. Similarly, the linguistic space in any society is sufficiently large to allow different varieties to co-exist and for each variety to serve identical, similar or slightly different functions. Simply put, my position is that Singlish is a variety that can co-exist with Standard (Singaporean) English, and that Singlish serves as a linguistic resource for many Singaporeans, and not only for the lower strata of Singaporean society. More importantly, it serves as an essential society-wide marker of Singaporean identity. In short, my perspective calls for a *less instrumentally driven* component in the local language planning and policy approach, a perspective that moves beyond linguistic instrumentalism.

The Speak Good English Movement (SGEM) in Singapore

As Tupas puts it, 'The problem of standards (. . .) is a problem of class: class-based issues that accrue to English in many societies in the world remain marginalized or ignored' (2006: 169). Similarly, in my view, the problem of a 'lesser', marginalized variety like Singlish is a problem of class, that it is associated with a less educated group of Singaporean speakers and nationally problematized as a less than comprehensible variety that does not fit well in a globalized first world economy like Singapore's.

The place of Singlish in the Singaporean linguistic landscape has been the subject of lively debate for a long time, and perhaps particularly in the last decade. As in any debate, there are proponents and opponents in the Singlish debate. Proponents of Singlish often appeal to the uniqueness of this distinct local variety of English and its place in the local culture. For example, the Singlish supporter below captures the positive alignment with Singlish among Singlish advocates:

> Singlish is a mark of how we have evolved as a nation and should surely have a place in our culture. Embracing Singlish as part of our heritage is not self-deception. It's about not being embarrassed by something that is unique and precious to how we express ourselves. (Lee M. 1998)

Very often, a sense of pride accompanies such expressed sentiments, as one informant of a recent study I conducted showed:

> It can help to make others feel more at ease/home, something that's unique to Singapore and we as Singaporeans should feel proud of [it]. (Informant 13, Chng, MS)

In contrast, opponents of Singlish tend to focus on the perceived or assumed lack of comprehensibility of this variety for non-Singaporeans, and the negative image Singlish is said to project. There is, for this camp, the tendency to privilege the importance of learning 'good' English and attribute to bad Singlish influence the oft-lamented decline of the standard of Singaporean English:

> It is indeed worrying that the standard of English used in Singapore has been dwindling steadily. . . . I certainly hope that Singaporeans will embrace the coming years with the common, fervent endeavour to speak and write proper English, as far as possible. (Chan 2000)

Indulging a hybrid [Singlish] is easy but what requires no effort is a cop-out and a luxury no struggling learner can afford. We must dissociate English from Singlish, its insidious enemy. (Lee A.M.Y. 1998)

Amidst fears of a decline in the command of internationally comprehensible Standard English, in March 2000, a national campaign to promote good English in Singapore was launched.[6] Known as the *Speak Good English Movement*, or SGEM,[7] this campaign aims to encourage 'the use of good English among Singaporeans'.[8] Many activities have been organized to propel the campaign along. These include short snippets of conversational dialogues published in the daily local newspapers illustrating 'good' (read: Standard usage) versus 'bad' (read: Singlish) English; skits and public performances at local libraries to convey the message that speaking 'good'/'proper' English is an asset; and production of booklets such as a five-book series called *Grammar Matters* by the SEAMEO Regional Language Centre in Singapore.[9]

May 2005 marked the fifth year of the launch of SGEM. The Guest-of-Honour at that year's launch was none other than the new Prime Minister Lee Hsien Loong, and the focal point of his speech centred on calling Singaporeans to 'drop the "lahs", use proper English'. Prime Minister Lee was reported as saying if we '[l]eave out the "lors" and "lahs" and use proper English, [then] it becomes second nature and will bring a host of advantages' (Ng 2005). Lee's message seems to be that

English is Singapore's bridge to the world as well as the common language that links the country's multiracial, multilingual communities. Because English is the lingua franca of commerce and globalisation, speaking it well – especially in the fast-growing service industry – would give Singapore a competitive edge. (Soh 2005)

The newly appointed chair of SGEM, Associate Professor Koh Tai Ann reinforced Lee's instrumental stance, saying that

If we are to be competitive, we ought to be able to use English well. The countries around us all are rapidly catching up. They, too, see that the acquisition of English is important. We would soon lose our edge in being English-speaking if we don't use it and speak it well. (Soh 2005)

In a recent small survey of 40 Singaporean informants aged between 18 and 23 on the subject of Singlish and SGEM, I asked informants if they had heard of SGEM (Chng, ms). In spite of the 5-year existence of SGEM, not all informants were able to correctly call to mind what SGEM was (9 informants drew a blank). Slightly more than half of the informants (21 out of 40) evaluated SGEM either as a movement with limited or little success. However, an overwhelming 36 informants felt that it was important to command and speak Standard Singaporean English (SSE). When I asked my informants whether SSE would replace Singlish one day, 32 informants said no, 4 said yes (possibly or maybe), 2 were unsure/don't know, 1 said 'depends' (but did not explain further), and 1 left the question unanswered. Small as this sample is, there was a clear majority who thought that it was unlikely that Singlish would be replaced totally by SSE, and by implication, that a movement like SGEM would not be successful in discouraging Singlish, which some had identified as the hidden agenda behind the movement. Chng (2003), among others, warned that if the success of the Speak Mandarin Campaign in Singapore was any indication of how a pragmatic attitude could override an emotional attachment (to the Chinese dialects), then it was not so unforeseeable that Singlish may one day be overtaken by Standard Singapore English. Randall and Teo (2005), for example concluded that

> The debate has centred on the importance of standard English for instrumental social reasons. It is not a tool for the individual but a tool for the society. In such a social/cultural climate, Singlish may not be as safe as it might seem.

This forewarning with regard to Singlish is reinforced by the fact that Young (2004) found a good 23 per cent of undergraduates she surveyed, that is, almost a quarter, agreeing to the proclamation that 'Singlish is a handicap we must not wish on Singaporeans' – a statement made by Singapore's then-Senior Minister Lee Kuan Yew. That 23 per cent agreed with the official sentiment says something about how seriously some educated Singaporeans have already taken heed of the official line in contrast to the 57 per cent who maintained that Singlish actually made them feel more Singaporean (Young 2004). This kind of results convinces me that the well-known pragmatic outlook attributed to Singaporeans plays a very key role in the Singaporean psyche as it has to a large extent guided some section of the population to actually put aside emotional attachment in the interest of attaining economic success in the world.

In no uncertain terms, Singapore's then Prime Minister Goh Chok Tong made the following pronouncement on Singlish:

> Singlish is not English. It is English corrupted by Singaporeans and has become a Singapore dialect. . . . Singlish is broken, ungrammatical English sprinkled with words and phrases from local dialects and Malay which English speakers outside Singapore have difficulties in understanding.. . . Let me emphasize that my

message that we must speak Standard English is targeted primarily at the younger generation . . . we should ensure that the next generation does not speak Singlish. (Goh 1999)

Goh's remark assumed wrongly that Singaporeans would use Singlish in the company of foreigners who did not know Singlish. It also assumed wrongly that Singaporeans did not have any understanding of how to exercise appropriate linguistic selection in specific situational interaction. Furthermore, it assumed that there was room only for monolingualism, more specifically competence in just one variety of English – the standard variety. In the above remark, the importance of Singlish goes unrecognized by a top official who is understandably just as concerned, if not more concerned about the need for a Singaporean identity. Instead, he constructs Singlish as a harm and an obstacle preventing the acquisition of Standard Singaporean English, and standing in the way of global access and communication.

Beyond linguistic instrumentalism: the place and value of Singlish

A number of linguists have argued for the importance of Singlish to Singaporeans. Chng (2003) for example has argued that Singlish is not a problem as there is room for more than one language in a nation's imagination and in Singapore's construction of its national and cultural identity. Rubdy has also spoken about the importance of Singlish as 'the quintessential mark of Singaporeanness' (2005: 11–12):

> Paradoxically, though, it is neither Mandarin Chinese nor Standard English that provides the cultural anchor that holds together the multi-ethnic, multicultural and multilingual populace of Singapore. Instead, Singlish, Singapore's local brand of colloquial English, has emerged as the symbol of intra-ethnic identity and cultural integration in Singapore, in total contravention with the ideologies of the language planners. Importantly, Singlish has come to be regarded as the quintessential mark of Singaporeanness by a large majority of young Singaporeans who now use it freely in informal domains of talk.

Furthermore, my own recent survey has indicated that many informants accept Singlish as a valuable cultural link among the different races in Singapore and believe Singlish is what defines us as Singaporean. Given these ready identification with Singlish as a truly Singaporean product, it is hard to fathom why at the official level, in spite of the recognized need for something that would bind all Singaporeans as one, and Singapore as one united nation, Singlish is still perceived as such a major threat. I agree wholeheartedly with Rubdy when she argues that

> In the race to stay ahead of the global competition economically, language cor-
> rectness has been indelibly linked to the 'collective' national good, the latter being
> defined in terms of concrete and tangible goals, both from the point of view of
> the government as well as its people. The pride Singaporeans might take in using
> and owning Singlish as a badge of cultural identity, social solidarity, personal
> linguistic affiliation and emotional identification associated with domains such as
> the home or the street – represents intangible (private) values and aspirations. It is
> these intangibles that are made short shrift of and become convenient casualty to
> 'the greater good' of the larger (public) 'collectivity' that is the national polity.
> (2003: 21–22)

Admittedly mine is a rather small sample. However, judging from the responses obtained, not just in this study, but in previous studies on this subject (e.g. Randall and Teo 2005; Young 2004), the *Speak Good English Movement* (SGEM) may be said to have not been as well received as officials have hoped for, at least among tertiary students in the two universities covered by these studies. In fact, SGEM is seen not so much as a movement to promote 'good' English in Singapore, but as an official effort to eradicate Singlish. It is perhaps a reflection of the coming of age of some Singaporeans and of Singapore that we do not always now find an unquestioning citizenry who would readily accept campaign messages, especially those that originate from the top.[10] In fact, even when the term 'campaign' is religiously avoided in the presenta-tion of SGEM, the Singaporean public is not fooled even in the absence of explicit rhetoric; and (a) does recognize that SGEM *is* a national campaign after all; and (b) that behind this campaign that overtly promotes 'the use of good English among Singaporeans' (see the SGEM website) lies the unspoken but ideological move to eradicate Singlish.

Indeed, in the marketization of Singapore on the world stage, Singlish is a poor choice by some determination. Singlish is after all a colloquial variety of English, and is widely seen as a poor cousin of even the mesolectal variety of Singaporean English, not to mention the acrolectal Standard Singaporean English. But 'unglamorous' as Singlish may be, it is still the language of choice when it comes to identifying with fellow Singaporeans, and with Singapore as home. As a homegrown local writer, Tan Hwee Hwee (2002) writes:

> Singlish is crude precisely because it's rooted in Singapore's unglamorous past.
> This is a nation built from the sweat of uncultured immigrants who arrived

100 years ago to bust their asses in the boisterous port. Our language grew out of the hardships of these ancestors. And Singlish is a key ingredient in the unique melting pot that is Singapore. This is a city where skyscraping banks towering over junk boats: a city where vendors hawk steaming pig intestines next to bistros that serve haute cuisine. The SGEM's brand of good English is as bland as boiled potatoes. If the government has its way, Singapore will become a dish devoid of flavor.

And it is precisely because 'SGEM's brand of good English is as bland as boiled potatoes' that we good ole Singaporeans steer clear of it whenever we can! Or as one informant put it, some of us 'dislike [SGEM] for trying to tell Singaporeans that the way we speak is problematic'. Doubtlessly, such a movement does not accord due recognition to the place and value of Singlish in Singapore, or to the reality of linguistic diversity, and more importantly perhaps, to key matters related to one's sense of cultural identity.

The case for the maintenance of Singlish in Singapore may be made via the following four non-instrumental motivations:

1. The current official position to weed out Singlish and promote only the standard variety of English assumes wrongly a state of linguistic homogeneity when in reality it is linguistic heterogeneity that rules the day. The fact is, in any society, and Singapore is no exception, there is social and linguistic stratification. Much as the government want to encourage every Singaporean to participate in the global economy, the truth is, individuals cannot and do not participate equally on the global stage. If we see this social stratification for what it is, we will then not unrealistically insist on a homogeneous level of participation that in Singapore, seems to also translate into the push for linguistic homogeneity – the promotion of a single variety of English.

2. Following from (1) above, we must recognize the need for Singlish at least in the local context. For speakers who have no access to the standard variety, Singlish is a valuable linguistic resource that enables this sector of the population to negotiate their ways within the local economy. The call for the maintenance of Singlish is therefore a call for the respect of the linguistic human rights of this group of speakers.

3. Furthermore, for Singaporeans who are fortunate enough to have access to the instrumentally valued standard variety of English, Singlish also plays a role, and that is the role of inter-class communication. In Singapore, there is a reluctance to admit that class differences exist in our society, perhaps because it goes against the ideals of meritocracy and equal opportunity. The push for Standard English and the corresponding call to rid ourselves of Singlish may be argued to be an attempt to mask existing class differences through a homogenization effort to have every Singaporean adopt 'good' English-speaking habits. In so far as class differences are not so easily erased, Singlish serves as a resource not just for inter-ethnic communication but also for inter-class communication, and this is particularly true in a society that is gradually seeing the disappearance of other local varieties such as the Chinese 'dialects'.

4. Finally, many Singaporeans do feel an emotional attachment to Singlish. It is not uncommon to hear Singaporeans characterize Singlish as a uniquely Singaporean trait that should be valued rather than feel ashamed about. There have been constant attempts to identify the elusive element(s) that constitute the Singaporean identity through for example, the design of a national dress, the debate over what the quintessential local cuisine is , and so on. The fact is, Singlish does fit that bill – Singlish is a uniquely Singaporean trait that immediately identifies a person as Singaporean. It seems ironical that a ready-made identity marker such as Singlish, a variety of language that is formed out of a local play of languages should be dismissed as a viable candidate, just because it does not have economic value. Granted that Singlish does not have the elevated status of a linguistic capital on the world stage, but Singlish has emotional capital for many Singaporeans and this is a reality that should not be denied.

Conclusion

To summarize, Singapore's effort to be a competitive economy in the global networks has for the greater part driven its language planning and policy approach. This economically driven agenda, while arguably necessary for national survival, seems to have ignored a very crucial part of a nation's well-being – its identity. As Chong (1999) puts it, '[w]ithout a healthy economy, Singapore would not survive; without culture, Singaporeans would be characterless and transient in nature'. I am in support of the original two-pronged approach to build a nation of Singaporeans who are plugged into the world economy and who are also in touch with our own cultural heritage. But I disagree that the former aim cannot tolerate a space for Singlish, and that the latter aim should only be achieved through education in the designated 'mother tongues'. Singlish has an important role to play in the nation's search for a uniquely Singaporean consciousness and the promotion of our own national heritage. What we have to do is to encourage not just an instrumentally driven outlook but to also accommodate the alternative reality – a less economically driven and more non-instrumental perspective that recognizes the value and place of Singlish in the Singaporean linguistic and cultural context.

Notes

1. Singapore's bilingual education policy was implemented for primary and secondary schools in 1966 and 1969 respectively.
2. The mother tongue designation for each ethnic group is not unproblematic of course. For example, many within the Chinese community are still struggling to identify with Mandarin as a 'mother

tongue' because for many, English has overtaken Mandarin while for others, one of the neglected Chinese dialects (like Hokkien or Cantonese) is still very much a home language.

3. A policy review of language education in the 1970s for example, revealed the problem of 'ineffective bilingualism' (Goh 1979, cited in Wu 2005).

4. In a speech in 2004, then Senior Minister Lee said, 'For deeper interaction, Singapore needs to nurture a few hundred students from each year's cohort to a higher level of Mandarin and a deeper appreciation of China's history and culture so that they can engage in China growth.

5. Similar to what Lee said about China and Mandarin, he also said that 'there is still a need to nurture a core of bicultural Singapore players to engage India' (Lee 2004).

6. Like others in the region, such as Hong Kong decision makers, the Singaporean leadership is perennially concerned about what they see as poor or falling standard of English. Like the local promotion of SGEM, in Hong Kong, there was a similar movement to improve English in the workplace. For the Hong Kong situation, see discussion in Bolton (2002) for example.

7. Wary of Singaporeans' fatigue over the endless series of national campaigns, this 'community-led initiative' resisted calling itself a campaign, and chose to name itself a 'movement'. Nevertheless, it is clear that many people still think of it as a campaign, as is evident from some of the responses obtained in a survey I conducted (Chng, MS).

8. SGEM website at http://www.goodenglish.org.sg/SGEM, accessed 22 June 2004.

9. Among the most recent efforts to instill 'good' English include mobile ads placed on public buses that ply Singaporean streets daily. What is featured on the exterior of these vehicles is a snippet in Singlish and its correspondent 'good' English equivalent.

10. As Edgar Schneider has pointed out, language engineering by governments is seldom successful (p.c.). For discussions on prescriptivism and degradation of vernacular languages, see Baugh and Cable (2002), Milroy (1991).

References

Baugh, Albert C. and Thomas Cable (2002), *A History of the English Language* (Fifth edition) (London: Routledge).

Bolton, Kingsley (2002), 'Hong Kong English: Autonomy and creativity' (introduction) in Kingsley Bolton (ed.), *Hong Kong English: Autonomy and Creativity* (Hong Kong: Hong Kong University Press), pp.1–25.

Chan, Kwang Ping (2000), 'Bad English in song for millennium', *The Straits Times*, 10 January 2000.

Chng, Huang Hoon (MS), '"I dislike it for trying to tell Singaporeans that the way we speak is problematic": An assessment of the Speak Good English Movement in Singapore'.

Chng, Huang Hoon (2003), '"You see me no up": Is Singlish a problem?', *Journal of Language Problems and Language Planning* 27(1):.45–62.

Chong, Ching Liang (1999), 'Inter-generational cultural transmission in Singapore: A brief discussion', 65th IFLA Council and General Conference, Retrieved 25 October 2006, http://www.ifla.org/IV/ifla65/65cc-e.htm

Goh, Chok Tong (1999), National Day Rally Speech, Retrieved 22 August 1999, http://www.sgem.org.sg/pm22.htm.

Goh, K.S. (1979), *Report on the Ministry of Education 1978* (Singapore: Ministry of Education).

Lee, Kuan Yew (2000), *From Third World to First: The Singapore Story, 1965-2000. The Memoirs of Lee Kuan Yew* (Singapore: Singapore Press Holdings, Times Education).

Lee, Kuan Yew (2004), Speech at the International Conference on National Boundaries and Cultural Configurations, 10th Anniversary Celebration of The Centre for Chinese Language and Culture, Nanyang Technological University, 23 June 2004.

Lee, Anthony M.Y. (1998), 'How long more can we go on speaking Singlish?', *The Straits Times*, 30 October 1998.

Lee, Michelle (1998), 'No shame in using Singlish', *The Straits Times*, 3 November 1998.

Milroy, James (1991), *Authority in Language: Investigating Language Prescription and Standardization*, (Second edition) (New York: Routledge).

Ng, Jane (2005), 'PM: Drop the "lahs", use proper English', *The Straits Times*, 14 May 2005, p.3.

Pakir, Anne (1992), 'English-knowing bilingualism in Singapore' in K.C. Ban, Anne Pakir and C.K. Tong (eds), *Imagining Singapore* (Singapore: Times Academic Press), pp. 234–62.

Randall, M and P. Teo (2005), 'Riding the tiger or leading a horse to water: The Speak Good English campaign in Singapore' in S. May, M. Franken and Barnard R. (eds), *Proceedings from International Conference on Language, Education and Diversity, 26–29 November 2003*, University of Waikato, New Zealand.

Rubdy, Rani (2004), 'Is Singlish an endangered variety?' in Leonard R.N. Ashley and Wayne H. Finke (eds), *Language in the Era of Globalization.* Selected papers from the International Conference of the American Society of Geolinguistics, October 2–4, 2003(New York: Cummings and Hathaway), pp. 131–44.

Rubdy, Rani (2005), 'Remaking Singapore for the new age: Official ideology and the realities of practice in language-in-education' in Angel M.Y. Lin and P.W. Martin (eds), *Decolonisation, Globalisation: Language-in-Education: Policy and Practice* (Clevedon: Multilingual Matters), pp. 55–73.

SEAMEO Regional Language Centre in collaboration with Curriculum Planning and Development Division, Ministry of Education, Singapore (2000) , *Grammar Matters*, Christopher S. Ward (Series Editor) (Singapore: Landmark Books Pte Ltd).

Speak Good English Movement website, http://www.goodenglish.org.sg/SGEM, Retrieved 22 June 2004.

Soh, Felix (2005), 'The Lunch Interview' with Associate Professor Koh Tai Ann, *The Sunday Times* (Singapore), 15 May 2005, p. 32.

Tan, Hwee Hwee (2002), 'A war of words over Singlish', *Time* (Asian Edition), 160(3), 29 July 2002.

Tupas, T. Ruanni F. (2006), 'Standard Englishes, pedagogical paradigms and their conditions of (im)possibility' in Rani Rubdy and Mario Saraceni (eds), *English in the World: Global Rules, Global Roles*, (London and New York: Continuum), pp.169–185.

Wee, Lionel (2003), 'Linguistic instrumentalism in Singapore', *Journal of Multilingual and Multicultural Development* 24(3).

Wee, Lionel (2005), 'Intra-language discrimination and linguistic human rights: The case of Singlish', *Applied Linguistics* 26(1): pp. 48–69.

Wee, Lionel (this volume), 'Linguistic instrumentalism in Singapore'.

Wu, Manfred Man-Fat (2005), 'A critical evaluation of Singapore's language policy and its implications for English teaching', Retrieved 25 October 2006, http://www3.telus.net/linguisticissues/singapore.html

Young, Caixia Lynda (2004), 'A Singaporean Sociolinguistic Review of the S[peak] G[ood] E[nglish] Movement]', unpublished honours thesis, National University of Singapore.

5 Linguistic Pragmatism, Globalization and the Impact on the Patterns of Input in Singaporean Chinese Homes

Ng Bee Chin

Chapter Outline

This chapter reports on a preliminary study which focused on the language use of bilingual Singaporean Chinese. It examines the background in which both bilingualism and biliteracy are acquired and used. The pattern and context of bilingualism was compared to models in other multilingual communities. The discussion centred on the linguistic repertoire of a select group of Singaporean parents and the type of input the children are receiving. In particular, the chapter focused on Singaporean families where the use of Singapore Colloquial English is the norm. Extrapolating from research on input in L1 and bilingual contexts, it was hypothesized that the input in some homes may not be enriching enough to help our school aged children develop bilingual competence that meets official expectations. The chapter concluded that there is a need to address our expectations of our school children's bilingual competence given the reality they live in. More importantly, the chapter stressed the need for parents to carefully reflect on the deployment of their linguistic resources and cautioned against a totally utilitarian and pragmatic approach to the use of languages.

Introduction

The main focus of research on bilingualism and multilingualism in countries where the dominant population speaks a variety of English is often on the issue of maintenance and education. In these contexts, the profile of the population has been altered by an influx of speakers of other languages through either migration or immigration. In such countries, for example, the USA, Canada, Britain and Australia, the pressing concern is one where the mother tongue or the home language of these immigrants is increasingly giving grounds to that country's dominant language of use. The situation is much the same for countries in Europe such as France, Italy and Germany which have a large immigrant population. In other situations, the research has focused on long-standing issues to do with negotiating access to power by various indigenous groups of different cultural and linguistic backgrounds (e.g. speakers of Basque in Spain). At a macro level, the debate is on how resources can be deployed equitably across different groups. To a certain extent, the competition for resources and the struggle to maintain cultural identity is the crux of the issue for most bilingual or multilingual communities. Another area which has generated heated discussion is the impact of the globalization and the spread of English – a theme in this current collection.

The situation in Singapore is different. Olshtain and Nissim-Amitai (2003) made a distinction between multilingualism in a natural environment and multilingualism due to transition. They argued that those born into a multilingual context usually see and accept multilingualism as a natural phenomenon. They are also more likely to be at ease with their language proficiency and less conflicted about their multilingual identity. On the other hand, speakers who were transferred into a multilingual context as a result of immigration have more difficult linguistic choices to make as they are more likely to be frustrated about their perceived lack of language competence. The authors explained that this discrepancy stems from a difference in the way language proficiency is perceived by both groups. In the first group, proficiency is a fluid concept which is pegged to the needs of the multilingual community. In other words, language proficiency is seen as a means to fulfil necessary communicative acts. In the second group, the individuals often use the monolingual benchmark to measure their own language proficiency. Bilinguals in this group fail to appreciate the complex interactive role that languages play in a multilingual setting.

The typology of Singapore fits the first group, that is, natural multilingualism. However, Singapore does not exhibit the fluidity of acceptance captured in Olshtain and Nissim-Amitai's study. The sociolinguistic situation in Singapore sets her apart from the 'norms' of bilingual situation that has been experienced in other bilingual communities.

On the surface, one can easily identify three major ethnic groups, those of Chinese origins, those whose fore parents come from India and the indigenous Malays. There is a remnant category loosely described as Eurasians. Kwan-Terry (2000) provides a succinct backdrop to the historical background of the sociolinguistic composition and the creation of separate ethnic identities within Singapore. The integral relationship between language use and nation building is comprehensively explored in Kuo and Jernudd (1993). For a discussion of how instrumental reasonings underpinned language choices and use, see Wee (2003), and Li and Milroy (2003). What is noteworthy about the Singaporean experience is that the central issue for the community here seems to be less on how culture resources can be retained than on how 'selective' linguistic resources can be maximized.

In some ways, Singapore is a model for other nations where the debate can still be held back by sections of the community who do not believe in bilingualism. Here, bilingualism is accepted. What the community at large is more concerned about are the economic and pragmatic returns that each language will give them. This is in part due to overriding market forces as well as a consequence of a series of orchestrated language planning policies.

The sociolinguistic history of Singapore is sharply demarcated by both political and economic interest. Since independence, there has been a strong homogenising force propelling the various ethnic groups to see English as the instrumental language to success. As argued by Wee (2003), the strand of this argument has taken a different shape at different times where the importance of the various 'mother tongues' waxed and waned. However, the prime significance of English has not been challenged over the last three decades. The 'Speak Mandarin Campaign' launched in 1978 was worrying to many non-ethnic Chinese as there was fear that the position of English may be played down. However, it is clear that Mandarin Chinese supplanted other Chinese languages but the position of English remains secure. The prominence of English is underscored by the fact that the main official language of school and work is English. Singapore, like many post-colonial nations has adopted English as the language of currency. Pakir (1999) documented the rise of English as a 'glocal' language which meets both global and local needs. The concern here is not one of how English is robbing us of our cultural heritage. In fact, 40 years after independence, Singapore has deftly navigated the divide between language and culture. In doing so, she has successfully moulded English to her needs. Singlish as a language may be disparaged by some, but there is no doubt that it remains an enduring marker of what it means to be Singaporean. The census data from 2000 indicated that 36 per cent of the children aged 5–14 years spoke English at home, a substantial hike from the figures in 1990. In the general population, 22.4 per cent of Singaporeans claimed English as their home language. Hence, English is not only a *lingua franca*; it has made its way into the homes and hearts of an increasing number of Singaporeans.

What is stark in this sociolinguistic landscape is the relentless strand of instrumental reasons for the promotion of languages. Some see this as a natural and optimistic response to 'the languages of the new world order' while others view this with scepticism. Whatever the reaction, there is no denying that instrumental motivations provide a strong and, indeed, a successful impetus for language learning. In most discussions of language learning in the Singapore context, the role of integrative motivation plays a minimal role. Then again, in the context of the study of English in Indonesia, Lamb (2004) presented a convincing argument that in a globalising world, the traditional construct of integrative motivation is losing its explanatory power. However, the conspicuous absence of integrative motivation, widely accepted as a trait for ultimate success in language learning has left an indelible mark on the cultural and linguistic experience of Singaporeans. This backdrop has given rise to a linguistic microcosm that is uniquely Singaporean. The purpose of this chapter is to examine this microcosm by studying the co-existence of English with other languages in the repertoire of three select groups of Chinese speakers in Singapore.

The sociolinguistic microcosm for Singaporean Chinese

As in other countries, the issue in Singapore is also one of language maintenance and language shift. However, these two concepts are interpreted in a way which is unique to Singapore. Language maintenance is typically used by linguists to describe a situation where 'members of a community try to keep the language(s) they have always used, that is, to retain the same patterns of language choice' (Hoffmann 1991:185). In the main, case studies of language maintenance or the success of language maintenance are often vicariously 'celebrated' in sociolinguistics research. An extreme of language shift is language death, but sometimes language shift can result in a stable form of bilingualism (Fasold 1986). Generally, language shift resulting in the loss of use of any indigenous language is a cause for concern. In Singapore, this phenomenon is often viewed with optimism and the shift to Mandarin Chinese–English bilingualism has often been cited as the key to Singapore's success (see Pakir 1994). This interpretation has prompted Gupta (1997) to reassess the negative connotations of 'language shift'. In the Singapore context, the fact that the shift to bilingualism has happened at the expense of other Chinese languages has always been officially celebrated.

In the local context, language maintenance often refers to the maintenance of 'mother tongues'. In the case of the Chinese community, it is Mandarin Chinese. Historically, neither Mandarin Chinese nor English were languages 'owned' by the local speakers. Chinese Singaporeans have been encouraged to part with their 'dialect' heritage and to embrace the homogenous world of Mandarin Chinese through a slew of campaign in the late 1970s and early 1980s (Riney 1995). Judging by the linguistic repertoire of post-1978 children, we can safely conclude that the campaign has been very successful.[1]

The impetus for this campaign is supplied through the schools, which play an unprecedented role in promoting this unique brand of language maintenance and shift. The curriculum of all schools is in English with Mandarin Chinese being taught as a language subject. Through the syllabi, the schools promote the use of standard English as well as Mandarin Chinese. Moral Education in the primary level is also taught in Mandarin Chinese. In select elite schools Mandarin may be taught at a more advanced level but by and large, Mandarin Chinese is not used for any content-based teaching (see James 1998 for a detailed argument of how the linguistic policies are socially constructed through the agency of the education system). Despite the minor role of Mandarin Chinese in the curriculum, it occupies a critical presence throughout the school years. The general expectation is for children to emerge bilingual and biliterate at a level which exhibits an internalization of the standard features in both languages. However, the reality is often far from the ideal.

From the point of view of literacy, a survey by Hsui (1996) found that literacy level in English far exceeded that of Mandarin Chinese. Hsui concluded that as a nation, Singaporeans are bilingual but not biliterate. Literacy is not the only issue. Kwan-Terry (1993) reported on the general dissatisfaction in the language competence achieved for both Mandarin Chinese and English despite the many years of schooling. This is evidenced in the Speak Good English

Movement launched in 2000 to promote the use of good English. The campaign is a series of sustained effort to weed out 'bad' English lest Singaporeans become unintelligible to the rest of the world. This is a source of grave concern even though for the general public, 'the rest of the world' is an abstract notion removed from their daily lives. As Chng (2003) pointed out, it is curious that there is such a mismatch between the official expectations for the language competence of our speakers and the reality for the people who use and speak the language. The disparity between reality and expectations has been a conundrum for educationists and speakers alike.

The underlying reason for the 'Speak Good English' campaign is a well-motivated one and one based on incontrovertible psycholinguistic truth. Basically, you will only acquire the variety of language you are exposed to. Simply put, it would be very unusual for someone born and raised in London to grow up speaking Singapore Colloquial English without sustained and intensive exposure to the language. By the same token, children growing up hearing Singapore Colloquial English are more likely to speak Singapore Colloquial English – hence, the need to stamp out the use of 'Singlish'. Whether stylistic choices can be legislated in this manner is another paper in itself. What is pertinent here is the assumption that quality of input can be manipulated by a campaign.

Input studies

The critical role that input plays in shaping the language use of young children has been robustly supported in the last decade. Though the relationship is not a simplistic one where language use directly mirrors language input, input has been shown to have a significant influence. In bilingual settings, the results echo those found in L1 situations. A host of studies focusing on different linguistics features in bilingual populations found an effect for input. Fore example, input frequency was found to have pronounced effect on the use of compounds in English–Chinese bilinguals (Nicholadis and Yin 2002). In a study on Tzotzil–Spanish bilinguals, input has also been found to modulate lexical and syntactic development. Other studies have found that discourse strategy adopted by parents, code choice, pragmatics etc. have an impact on the level of bilingualism attained by the children (Juan-Garau and Pérez-Vidal 2001; Comeau, Genesee and Lapaquette 2003; Morita 2003). More importantly, the role of input is even more critical in the sensitive period of language acquisition (cf. Long 1993 and Perry and Harris 2002 for a review of studies in this area). Though the precise nature of which aspect of the language is susceptible and the extent of the impact has been controversial, there is incontrovertible evidence to support the case that most people who learn a language at a young age surpass those who learn it as an adult. However, critical in this argument is the role that input plays. Research shows that though children are better than adults in acquiring language without having to figure out the rules and structures explicitly, they require 'massive' amounts of input (DeKeyser 2000). This view is also shared by Hamers (2004) who argued that efficient learning cannot take place in the absence of an adequate input model. Though the point was not made explicit, by input, the authors were referring to 'native-like input'.

What type of input do Singaporean children have access to? Assuming that Singaporean children receive standard input in both languages in the school system (though this is clearly not the case as reported by Rubdy (2007) for the case of English), we need to examine the home environment the children grow up in.

In order to gain a better understanding of the linguistic environment of Singaporean Chinese homes, an exploratory study was taken to identify the context and use of the various languages at the disposal of a select group of Singaporeans who speak Singapore Colloquial English as a norm.

The research questions are:

1. What are the participants' language choices with various interlocutors?
2. What is the participants' evaluation of their own language and literacy skills?
3. What expectations do the participants have in terms of language maintenance?
4. What is the relationship between language proficiency and pattern of language use?

Method

Participants

The participants were drawn from three main samples, laboratory technicians, second-year university students and first-year university students in remedial English classes. They were all Chinese Singaporeans.

The first sample (Group A) consisted of 21 laboratory technicians with children (10 females and 11 male). Their age range was 28–43. The highest education level attained by the technicians was GCE 'A' levels. All had gone through at least 10 years of primary and secondary education. The laboratory technicians were generally bilingual, switching fluently from Singapore Colloquial English to Mandarin Chinese. Though they were capable of making minor stylistic adjustment when the situation required, their ability to code-switch to a standard variety was limited. Generally, their speech was characterized by the use of 'Singlish' features in terms of lexicon, syntax and intonation.

The second group (Group B) were 40 second-year undergraduates (28 females 12 males) drawn from an engineering faculty in Nanyang Technological University. This group had better English proficiency and though there were individual differences in their abilities to switch to Standard Singapore English, they were generally linguistically more competent than Group A and Group C. Their ages ranged between 22 and 24 years.

The third group (Group C) consisted of 20 first-year students in an English proficiency class. These were students who failed the University's qualifying English test. Their English proficiency was comparable to that of the technicians. Their age range was between 21 and 23 years.

The target sample for this study was the laboratory technicians. The student groups were added to see if language competency had an influence on language use. The two samples were there for comparison purposes.

Procedure

A questionnaire with 15 questions investigating frequency and patterns of language use in the home domain was administered to all participants in May 2004. Participants were asked to specify the language they use with their parents, siblings, partner, children and friends. For each item, they were also asked to indicate the frequency level of use. To gain a better picture of the input received by the children, the participants were also asked to comment on the type and frequency of languages used by their partner with the children. A self-evaluation task was also incorporated to investigate the perception of their own competency in the languages they use. Finally, the participants also answered questions examining the functional literacy of each language used. Participation was anonymous and voluntary.

Results

General pattern of language use

Parents – Of the 21 participants from Group A (laboratory technicians) 17 (81 per cent) used local vernaculars[2] with their parents. Only four indicated Mandarin Chinese as a choice. In comparison, students from the general population and the remedial English class used a range including a mixture of all three options; Mandarin Chinese, local vernaculars and English,[3] Mandarin Chinese only, mixture of Mandarin Chinese and English and local vernaculars only. However, the general trend is one which moved away from local vernaculars (less than 5 per cent chose this option) to the use of Mandarin Chinese, a mixture of Mandarin Chinese and English and English only situations. For the students from the general population, the choice was evenly divided between English only, Mandarin Chinese only,- and a mixture of English and Mandarin Chinese. Very few students from the remedial English class (10 per cent) indicated English as a choice.

Overall, when comparing the three groups, there is evidence to indicate that there was a shift from the use of Chinese vernaculars to Mandarin Chinese and English. This is consistent with the 2000 census data and Gupta and Yeok's (1995) study on Cantonese–English bilingual Singaporeans which also indicated a strong intergenerational shift away from the use of local vernaculars. The shift to English was more pronounced for the students from the general population. What is interesting is that only 12 per cent indicated a consistent language choice strategy where they consistently used one language with one parent.

Siblings – Of the laboratory technicians 28 per cent used a mixture of Mandarin Chinese and English with their siblings. Only one person indicated a consistent use of English. The choices were spread out evenly for all other options (Mandarin Chinese only, Mandarin Chinese and local vernaculars, local vernaculars only and a mixture of all three languages). In the general student population, 30 per cent indicated that they only used English with their siblings and 45 per cent indicated that they used a mixture of both English and Mandarin Chinese. Only 5 per cent spoke Mandarin Chinese solely to the siblings. For the remedial English group, 40 per cent indicated that they used both English and Mandarin Chinese and 30 per cent indicated that they used Mandarin Chinese only and 5 per cent spoke only English to their siblings.

These responses clearly showed that the two languages were used extensively in the same environment. This percentage rose from 28 per cent for the technicians to 40–45 per cent for the student population.

Close friends – For the laboratory technicians, the main choice here was again a mixture of Mandarin Chinese and English (34 per cent), followed by Mandarin Chinese only (25 per cent) and English only (14 per cent). While no one chose local vernacular as the sole language used with friends, 9 per cent still used both local vernaculars and Mandarin Chinese when conversing with friends. In contrast, 70 per cent of the students from the general population used both English and Mandarin Chinese, followed by English only

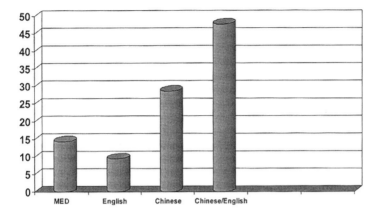

Figure 5.1 Parents' choice of language with children.

(15 per cent) and Mandarin Chinese only (5 per cent). No one reported using local vernacular as the sole language of communication with friends.

Children – The laboratory technicians were asked what languages they used with their children while the university students were asked what languages they were likely to use with their children.

As can be seen in Figure 5.1, the dominant strategy was for parents to use both English and Mandarin Chinese. Close to 50 per cent of the participants used both Mandarin Chinese and English when interacting with their children. Other options included using Mandarin Chinese only (28 per cent). About 10 per cent chose English only as their option. It is noteworthy that a small percentage (13 per cent) used all three languages (Mandarin Chinese, English and local vernaculars) with their children.

The dominant choice of using both languages is most striking when compared with their evaluation of their own language competence. As shown in Figure 5.2, 65 per cent of the laboratory technicians indicated Mandarin Chinese as their most proficient language as well as the one they were most comfortable in. In contrast, only 10 per cent indicated proficiency in both and only 25 per cent indicated that they were comfortable speaking in both languages. However, English emerged as the language participants were most comfortable with for writing.

Figure 5.3 shows what the students from the general population were likely to use with their children. The results were neatly split between English only and the use of both Mandarin Chinese and English. Though close to

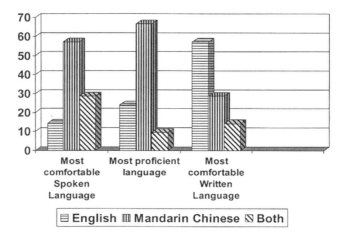

Figure 5.2 Parents' evaluation of their own language competence.

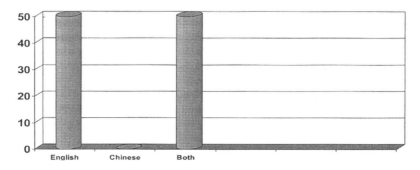

Figure 5.3 Language most likely to use with children by students from the general population.

40 per cent of the students indicated Mandarin Chinese as their most proficient language and 60 per cent claimed to be comfortable in both languages (see Figure 5.4), it is intriguing that none chose Mandarin Chinese as the language they would use with their children.

As seen in Figure 5.5, the scenario for the students from the remedial English class was slightly different. Here, 70 per cent indicated that they were likely to use both Mandarin Chinese and English while 20 per cent said they would use English and only 10 per cent said they would use Mandarin Chinese. This was despite the fact that 60 per cent chose Chinese as the most comfortable spoken language and 50 per cent indicated that they were most proficient in Mandarin Chinese (see Figure 5.6).

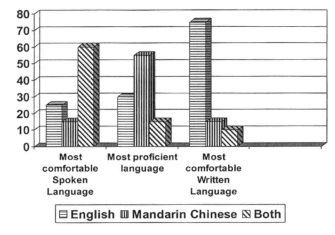

Figure 5.4 Student from the general population's evaluation of their own proficiency.

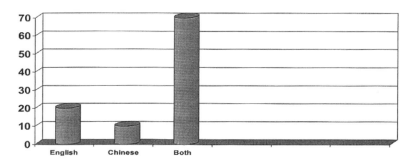

Figure 5.5 Language most likely to use with children by students from the remedial English group.

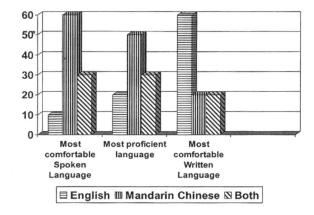

Figure 5.6 Students from the remedial English class evaluation of their own language proficiency.

When comparing the choice vis-à-vis language use with children for the three samples, there is a rising trend towards the choice for using two languages regardless of the language proficiency of the speakers. While the participants were more likely to choose Mandarin Chinese as the spoken language they were comfortable with, they also overwhelmingly chose English as the language they prefer to write in. This matches the profile of Singaporean bilinguals drawn by Hsui (1996).

Discussion

Overall, the bilingual population in this sample is one which generally incorporated both English and Mandarin Chinese fluidly in their spoken repertoire. The use of local Chinese vernaculars still played a role in the lives of the laboratory technicians who were older than the student population with parents and siblings in the domain. However, apart from this specific context, the use of local vernaculars has shrunk across all three groups.

The fact that both English and Mandarin Chinese occupied fairly central roles in the close-knit circles of the participants meant that the children are exposed to both varieties at home. In the follow-up interview, the parents indicated that they did not consciously make a deliberate language choice when speaking with their children. Most claimed that they feel that they had to use both Mandarin Chinese and English as these were the options which best prepared the children for school. The extreme apprehension and concern the parents had about failing to prepare the children adequately for school should they fail to use the right language is a point emphasized repeatedly. As responsible parents, they were convinced that they were doing the best thing for their children.

In the research on bilingual language acquisition, the one-parent-one-language system is one that has been widely reported to promote successful bilingualism. It is widely believed that it is conducive to separate the contexts in which each language is presented. The context can be a place or a person. For example, Language A could be spoken at home and Language B can be designated to be used outside of home. Alternatively, the context could be signalled by the interlocutors. Language A could be used consistently by one parent and Language B by the other parent. This latter strategy has come to be known as the one-parent-one-language system. And it is this system which has been reported to provide the most facilitative bilingual environment. This is particularly the case in the early years as the association of speaker and code encourages the child to develop contextually driven heuristic strategies (Juan-Garau and

Pérez-Vidal 2001). Though less supported, there is also evidence to suggest that bilingual children brought up in the one-parent-one-language system are less likely to 'mix' the two languages (Dopke 1992). However, there is also evidence to suggest that in a situation where the minority language is under threat, the use of the minority language by both parents works better than the one-parent-one-language system to promote successful bilingualism.

Within the one-parent-one-language approach, parents were advised to choose the language they were most proficient in. In fact, parents were strongly encouraged to only use the language they had near-native competence in. In general, the advice was for parents to capitalize on linguistic resources and to use the language they were confident in. Though the literature is replete with studies that map out the influences of input on the language of bilinguals, there are very few studies with a focus on the consequence of language acquisition in an input-poor environment. However, scarce as it may be, the existing evidence indicates that the 'quality' of input is significantly related to the bilingual development of a child.

In a single case study of a trilingual, Quay (2001) drew correlations between input quality and the level of competence achieved in a trilingual child. More indirect evidence came from studies of deaf children's acquisition of sign language in a non-native setting. In this study Ross (2001) showed that inconsistent (non-native) input is correlated to non-native-like usage especially in instances where the structures were more complex.

In this preliminary study, we note that parents still chose to use a language which they were not fully comfortable in with their children. This study clearly shows that there is an increasing trend to use both English and Mandarin Chinese in the home domain regardless of the competence of the speakers. Assuming that a substantial proportion of our school-age children are exposed to Singapore Colloquial English both at home and in the wider environment, where do they get standard input from? Some have argued that the school system serves to provide standard input but we know from anecdotal evidence that this is not consistently the case. More recently, Rubdy (2007) found strong evidence of the use of Singapore Colloquial English in the classroom. The teachers in Rubdy's study use 'Singlish' for various pragmatic reasons: to explain difficult concepts to students of lower English proficiency, they use it as a tool to build rapport with the students, to get a point across and most interestingly, they also use 'Singlish' as a resource to teach standard English. Given this scenario, is it realistic to expect Singaporeans to be able to adjust their English in response to a campaign? More pertinently, is it realistic to take a normative approach to assess the speakers?

In the rare elite households where parents have near-native competence in both languages, this is not an issue. However, the norm is the reverse. To varying degrees, it can be argued that the laboratory technicians in this study are typical of most middle- to lower-middle-income households in Singapore. In this case, the failure to use Mandarin Chinese when it was chosen as the language the participants were most comfortable in translates into missed opportunities to harness the resources of the speakers. On the contrary, the use of English in cases when the participants felt less than competent in the language poses a bigger problem when one considers the fact that quality of input is critical in the child's language development.[4]

At this juncture, it is important to acknowledge that children grow up in a complex environment and the parents are not the only people in their lives. It is also true that, often, the prime caregivers are people other than their parents. There is also the considerable amount of time which they spend socialising in schools. Generally, it is often not possible to attribute the course or direction of language development to a singular factor. However, the strong modulating influence of parents cannot be understated. As reported by De Houwer (2003), four-fifths of the variation in her study of trilingual input and language use could be attributed to parental input. If we were to take a bold step and argue that parents and the home environment play a significant role in moulding the children's language development, we cannot ignore the impact of input in the child's environment.

There are arguments that non-standard Singapore English is developmental and that children who speak such variety soon grow out of it. There are also arguments claiming that for the majority of speakers, this is a question of context and given the right context, speakers are able to code-switch to an acceptable variety. This is indeed true for a segment of the population. Chew (1995) referred to this ability as 'lectal power'. In her study, Chew identified speakers who were still unable to code-switch to Standard English after completing secondary education. It is undeniable that despite years of English education, there are a substantial number of speakers who speak a variety which will not be considered standard in any English-speaking community. Given that such speakers exist in our community, we need to question the validity of insisting on expecting that children produce standard English when the input they are exposed to is not consistent with the model expected.

A practical approach may be to encourage parents to speak in the language they are most comfortable in. While it is true that 'comfortable' may not mean proficient, it will be a start in the long road in this area that is fraught with more questions than answers.[5] The linguistic challenges faced by our young children are too many to list and no one can claim that the conundrum of language learning can be reduced to the simple equation of input and outcome. Other factors such as integrative orientation towards the target language and instrumental gains from acquiring target such as proficiency are all factors which are relevant in the discussion of this issue. Nonetheless, given the background that most Singaporean speakers are immersed in, educators may have to adjust or moderate their expectations from our school-going children by considering the contexts in which the languages are acquired. On the home front, parents should be advised to carefully weigh up their language options and as far as possible, they should be encouraged to have the courage to choose a language they are proficient in as a home language rather than choose languages that they believe best facilitate the children's survival in school.

Another approach may be to change the way we view the issue. Olshtain and Nissim-Amitai (2003) put across a cogent argument distinguishing perceptions of the proficiency of bilinguals from a monolingual and a multilingual standpoint. They based their study on the perception of proficiency in communities which are multilingual due to transition (migration; immigration) and communities which became multilingual in a natural setting. Using monolingual standpoints and norms, the language competence of bilinguals will always appear to be wanting. In communities which have a multilingual perception of proficiency, the speakers operate in a more open and liberal system and mastery of languages is viewed in the context of compatibility with social and cultural needs of the individuals. This view is expansive in that it encourages language learning and language choice with the key emphasis on the communicative function of language. As illustrated in Rubdy's (2007) study, Singapore Colloquial English can be used as a perfect bridge to Standard English and should be seen as a resource rather than an encumbrance. In this framework, speakers regulate their own degree of proficiency. Obviously, there are inherent pitfalls in this proposal. The danger in this framework is that it assumes equal access to opportunities. In such a system, there will be a need to create conditions where the language proficiency required for success in the community can be readily negotiated and attained.

Notes

1. This is supported by the 2000 census data (Lee 2003) which indicated a 20 per cent decrease in the use of local vernaculars between 1900 and 2000.

2. Participants were classified as using a particular language solely (e.g. only local vernaculars) if they indicated that they used that particular language 'all the time' with the interlocutor.

3. Participants were classified as using two or more languages if they responded 'some of the time' or 'most of the time' to two or more languages with the same interlocutor.

4. The recent move to modify the Chinese syllabus is based on streaming the students by the language used in the family. The assumption is that those children who come from an English-speaking background will have poorer command of Mandarin Chinese in comparison to those with Mandarin Chinese input at home. As can be seen from this sample, most families have dual-language input. It would be interesting to see how this group of children is categorized in comparison to the children who only receive Mandarin Chinese input.

5. Naturally, this may not agree with official policy as the language the parents are most comfortable in may well be a Chinese local vernaculars. However, given the profile of our Chinese speakers, this scenario is becoming less likely.

References

Chew, P. G. L. (1995), 'Lectal power in Singapore English', *World Englishes* 14(2): 163–80.

Chng, H. H. (2003), '"You see me no up": Is Singlish a problem?', *Language Problems and Language Planning* 27(1): 45–62.

Comeau, L., Genesee, F. and Lapaquette, L. (2003), 'The modeling hypothesis and child bilingual codemixing', *International Journal of Bilingualism* 7(2):113–26.

De Houwer A. (2003), 'Trilingual input and children's use in trilingual families in Flanders' in C. Hoffmann and J. Ytsma (eds), *Trilingualism in Family, School and Community* (Clevedon: Multilingual Matters), pp. 118–38.

DeKeyser, R. M. (2000), 'The robustness of critical period effects in second language acquisition', *Studies in Second Language Acquisition* 22(4): 499–533.

Dopke, S. (1992), *One parent, one language: An Interactional Approach* (Amsterdam: John Benjamins).

Fasold, R. (1986), *The Sociolinguistics of Society* (New York: Blackwell).

Gupta, A. F. (1997), 'Language rights', *English Today* 13(2(50)): 24–26.

Gupta, A. F. and Yeok, S. P. (1995), 'Language shift in a Singapore family', *Journal of Multilingual and Multicultural Development* 16(4): 301–14.

Gupta, A. F. (1994), *The step-tongue: Children's English in Singapore* (Clevedon: Multilingual Matters).

Hamers, J. F. (2004), 'A sociocognitive model of bilingual development', *Journal of Language and Social Psychology* 23(1): 70–98.

Hoffmann, C. (1991), *An Introduction to Bilingualism* (London: Longman).

Hsui, V. Y. (1996), 'Bilingual but not biliterate: Case of a multilingual Asian society', *Journal of Adolescent & Adult Literacy* 39(5): 410–14.

James, J. (1998), 'Linguistic realities and pedagogical practices in Singapore' in S. Gopinathan, A. Pakir, V. Saravanan and W. K. Ho (eds), *Language, Society and Education in Singapore: Issues and trends* (Singapore: Times Academic Press), pp. 99–116.

Juan-Garau, M. and Pérez-, C. (2001), 'Mixing and pragmatic parental strategies in early bilingual acquisition', *Journal of Child Language* 28(1): 59–86.

Kuo, E. C. Y. and Jernudd, B. H. (1993), 'Balancing macro- and micro-sociolinguistic perspectives in language management: The case of Singapore', *Language Problems and Language Planning* 17(1):1–21.

Kwan-Terry, A. (1993), 'Cross-currents in teaching English in Singapore', *World Englishes* 12(1): 75–84.

Kwan-Terry, A. (2000), 'Language shift, mother tongue, and identity in Singapore', *International Journal of the Sociology of Language* 143: 85–106.

Lamb, M. (2004), 'Integrative motivation in a globalizing world', *System* 32(1): 3–19.

Lee, E. E. F (2003), 'Profile of the Singapore Chinese Dialect Groups', *Statistics Singapore Newsletter*, Retrieved 17 July 2004, http://www.singstat.gov.sg/ssn/feat/2Q2001/pg2–6.pdf

Li Wei and Milroy, L. (2003), 'Markets, hierarchies and networks in language maintenance and language shift' in J. Dewaele Housen and Li Wei (eds), *Bilingualism: Beyond Basic Principles. Festschrift in Honour of Hugo Baetens Beardsmore* (Clevedon: Multilingual Matters), pp. 128–40.

Long, M. H. (1993), 'Second language acquisition as a function of age: Research findings and methodological issues' in K. Hyltenstam and A. Viberg (eds), *Progression and Regression in Language: Sociocultural, Neuropsychological, and Linguistic Perspectives* (Cambridge: Cambridge University Press), pp. 196–221.

Morita, E. (2003), 'Children's use of address and reference terms: Language socialization in a Japanese–English bilingual environment', *Multilingua* 22(4): 367–95.

Nicoladis, E. and Yin, H. (2002), 'The role of frequency in acquisition of English and Chinese compounds by bilingual children', *Proceedings of the Annual Boston University Conference on Language Development* 26(2): 441–52.

Olshtain, E. and Nissim-Amitai F. (2003), 'Being trilingual or multilingual: Is there a price to pay?' in C. Hoffmann and J. Ytsma (eds), *Trilingualism in Family, School and Community* (Clevedon: Multilingual Matters), pp. 30–52.

Pakir, A. (1994), 'Educational linguistics: Looking to the east', *Georgetown University Round Table on Languages and Linguistics* , pp. 370–83.

Pakir, A. (1999), 'Bilingual education with English as an official language: Sociocultural implications', *Georgetown University Round Table on Languages and Linguistics,* pp. 341–49.

Perry, G. M. J. and Harris, C. L. (2002), 'Linguistically distinct sensitive periods for second language acquisition', *Proceedings of the Annual Boston University Conference on Language Development* 26(2): 557–66.

Quay, S. (2001), 'Managing linguistic boundaries in early trilingual development' in J. Cenoz and F. Genesee (eds), *Trends in Bilingual Acquisition* (Amsterdam: John Benjamins), pp. 149–99.

Riney, T. (1995), 'Language in Singapore: A taxonomy of shift', *ICU Language Research Bulletin* 10: 103–20.

Ross, Danielle S. (2001), *Disentangling the Nature-Nurture Interaction in the Language Acquisition Process: Evidence from Deaf Children of Hearing Parents Exposed to Non-native Input*, Unpublished PhD dissertation, University of Rochester.

Rubdy, R. (2007), 'Singlish in the School: An impediment or a resource?', *Journal of Multilingual and Multicultural Development* 28(4): 308–17.

Singapore Census of Population, 2000 Advance Data Release No. 3 Literacy and Language, Retrieved 17 July 2004, http://www.singstat.gov.sg/papers/c2000/adr-literacy.pdf

Wee, L. (2003), 'Linguistic instrumentalism in Singapore', *Journal of Multilingual and Multicultural Development* 24(3): 211–24.

Anatomies of Linguistic Commodification: The Case of English in the Philippines vis-à-vis Other Languages in the Multilingual Marketplace

6

T. Ruanni F. Tupas

Chapter Outline

In this chapter, I would like to map out a specific configuration of linguistic commodification in the Philippines. Although recent research around the world has shown how certain languages, which used to be seen simply as cultural conduits of identity, have now also been commodified in the midst of various demands from globalizing forces, the case of the Philippines would show that what is actually happening is the further commodification of English. I would like to argue therefore that linguistic commodification follows various ideological tracks because it is influenced by different processes and conditions of globalization as well. In the end, the study of linguistic commodification can bring to light the various roles people, corporations and states play in the fierce, but unequal, competition for the world's resources.

Introduction

The notion of the commodification of language is not new. Since the dismantling of formal colonial structures in many countries in the world in the mid-1900s, the role of the English language in newly independent nations has often been couched in economic, pragmatic or, in a more general sense, instrumentalist discourse. Not only was English language use capable of writing against the Empire, but it could also help nations achieve (capitalist) development. Implicated in the complex processes of decolonization, English and, for that matter, other colonial languages like French, Spanish and Portuguese, were delinked from their ideological moorings through the creation of a convenient, albeit simplistic, dichotomy: colonial languages for economic/pragmatic/instrumentalist purposes and local languages for symbolic/identity/nationalist aspirations.

In recent years, however, owing mainly to the shifting structural movements of globalization, several scholars have started to probe into a different anatomy of linguistic commodification. Heller (2003, 1999), in the case of French in Canada; Pomerantz (2002), in the case of Spanish in the USA; and Wee (Chapter 2 this volume), in the case of Mandarin in Singapore, have strongly shown the changing fortunes of such languages, from being repositories of culture and ethnic identity, to being valuable capital and commodity needed for 'participation in a multilingual marketplace' (Pomerantz 2002: 276). Heller and Pomerantz note the growth of regional markets requiring multilingual skills, and Wee similarly points to China's open-door economic policy, as some of the major forces generating such shift in perspectives on language and identity.

In other words, linguistic commodification refers mainly to how certain local languages have become valued commodities in communities which previously used them solely as markers of identity, for example to ground their speakers in a history of great culture and civilization (as in the case of Mandarin in Singapore) or to espouse an ethnolinguistic nationalism with separatist aspirations against a dominant state (as in the case of French in Canada). Broadly speaking, it may be argued that all languages are commodified in one way or another, but the kind of commodification referred to here is specific to particular economic and sociopolitical global movements in recent years which have engendered some people's shifting views of the languages they speak and learn. This shift, of course, is not straightforward; in fact, linguistic commodification embodies the yet unresolved ideological tension between the treatment of such languages as identity markers and as economic resources (Wee, Chapter 2 this volume).

While carefully emphasizing important differences among the three countries' experiences with the emergence of local languages as economic resources, Wee nevertheless provides some 'discernible' similarities among the three situations. Some general features of what he prefers to call 'linguistic instrumentalism' are

1. Linguistic instrumentalism is a later addition to a previously existing view that treats the language as a marker of cultural identity and authenticity, resulting in a tension that is not yet reconciled.
2. One consequence, though, is the tendency to devalue or marginalize local vernaculars.
3. Linguistic instrumentalism assumes the continued importance of multi-/bilingualism, so that the language whose economic value is being championed is acquired in addition to English, never in place of it (Wee, Chapter 2 this volume).

Against the backdrop of this framework, I discuss the anatomy of linguistic commodification in the Philippines, arguing that it actually has very different features from what has earlier been said about languages as economic resources in Canada, the USA, and Singapore. Indeed, linguistic commodification or instrumentalism is very much alive in the Philippines – it has always been, especially for the last three decades now – but such a phenomenon, which can be traced back to American colonialism in the country, almost exclusively remains with a foreign language, English, while Filipino, the national language, continues to be seen as the symbol of national identity. The country's bilingual education policy (implemented in the early 1970s) and debates about it are grounded in this dichotomy (Tollefson 1991, 1986), which leaves all other local or mother languages effectively marginalized in education and other formal communication contexts like government and business (Nical, Smolicz and Secombe 2004).

What I hope to do in this chapter, therefore, is not to invalidate other accounts of linguistic commodification, but enrich it by providing a different outline of it such that what we have are possibly different anatomies of linguistic commodification brought about to some extent by the different roles countries play in globalization processes. In this sense, to be able to adequately understand linguistic commodification in the Philippines, we need to situate this phenomenon in the broadest framework possible. The question of English in the country is tied up with past, present and future political, ideological and socioeconomic issues besetting the Filipino people today (Tollefson 1991, 1986; Bernardo 2004; Tupas 2003a,b).

What I do first, therefore, is to discuss some general political questions about the welfare and affairs of Filipinos today; they help position in a general way similar questions about language politics in the country as well. I then move on to trace the general contours of linguistic commodification in the country by contextualizing it within the political economy of development in the Philippines. That is, I show how the commodification of English can be clearly understood in the light of the commodification of labour in the Philippines, a cornerstone economic policy of all administrations since Marcos.

Third, I zero in on some specific ways the English language has been developed as a commodified language. To do this, I discuss its roles in the educational system, the chief ideological battleground for the inculcation of particular ideologies on development and training centre for the generation of skills for local and global consumption. What emerges is not a commodified homogeneous English but a hierarchy of proficiencies in the language serving the various needs of a stratifying market. Fourth, I then bring the discussion back to my argument that linguistic commodification follows various ideological tracks because it is influenced by different processes and conditions of globalization as well. In the end, the study of linguistic commodification can bring to light the various roles people, corporations and states play in the fierce, but unequal, competition for the world's resources.

Contextualizing the issues

Philippine labour migration and foreign policy

The Philippines was, in 2004, in the international limelight as a result of the hostage crisis in Iraq involving a Filipino driver named Angelo de la Cruz. The Philippines drew flak from many countries, especially Australia and the USA, after the President Gloria Arroyo decided to withdraw the country's small military contingent from Iraq in exchange for the life of de la Cruz. From the perspective of critics, the pullout meant the Philippines' capitulation to terrorism. The crisis was simply a matter of two sides: either sacrifice the life of one person 'in the name of a unified front against terrorism' or save it through a pullout and surrender to terrorism.

I do not wish to be drawn into the dynamics of yet another *either/or* discourse emanating from the ideological underpinnings of the US-led military campaign in Iraq and elsewhere in the world, but one thing seems clear: if viewed within Philippine political and socioeconomic realities, the hostage crisis was complex and exposes the vulnerabilities and renewed strengths of the Philippine state and its people. The case of Angelo de la Cruz, according to University of the Philippines Law Professor, Merlin Magallona, former under-secretary for Migrant Workers of the Department of Foreign Affairs and now director of the Institute for International Legal Studies (IILS):

> illustrates in a more dramatic manner the involvement now of ordinary Filipino citizens in foreign relations . . . . The global presence of Filipinos is likely to connect itself to the conduct of foreign policy or in [sic] making of foreign policy in the first place.

The average Filipino family consists of five members; since there are currently around 8 million Overseas Filipino Workers or OFWs deployed all over the world, with close to 1 million in the Middle East alone, around 40 million Filipinos (or half of the country's population) are directly or indirectly affected by political and socioeconomic global movements involving migrant Filipinos.

What we can infer from Magallona's statement, in other words, is the argument that the country's foreign policy has not been cognizant of Filipino migrant issues and problems, even if the exportation of human labour has been the cornerstone of economic policies of practically all administrations since Marcos. In particular, with a huge concentration of OFWs in the Middle East, and with a worldwide upsurge of Islamic radicalism, Philippine policy security issues in international relations must take account of the security of its own migrant people. Such lack of connection between foreign policy and migration realities was starkly demonstrated by the recent hostage crisis.

> When it erupted, the government had no contacts with the right intermediaries. Special envoy Roy Cimatu said they had to work from 'zero'. None of the high-level officials who went to Iraq speaks Arabic. When Undersecretary for Special Concerns Rafael Seguis spoke in English on Al Jazeera television, some of his phrases were not accurately translated into Arabic.

The question that we need to ask, therefore, is that if the plight of ordinary Filipinos around the world generally has not fed back into the crafting and (this is more important perhaps) implementation of relevant policies, including a wide-ranging and calculated Middle East policy, what socioeconomic and political conditions and principles guided such policies instead?

I would like to locate my discussion of linguistic commodification within such a complex question. I do so for some related reasons. First, a policy of labour migration which incorporates language policy as well, also 'constitutes one form of foreign policy' (Tyner 2000: 133). Second, thus, issues of language in the Philippines – and I believe also in other contexts – are deeply implicated in wider social issues as well. Answers to the question above will bring to light a more nuanced understanding of the dynamics of language use in the country. No amount of talk about the commodification of language in the Philippines, therefore, can adequately capture its sociopolitical embeddedness without tying it up with the issue of the commodification of labour in the Philippines, which in turn is one of the chief implications of the Philippine state's cooptation with neoliberal globalization.

Contextualizing linguistic commodification

Liberalization, export-driven economic development and Filipino labour

Towards the end of the 1960s and especially during the whole of 1970s, under pressure from the World Bank and the International Monetary Fund (IMF), the government under Marcos developed an export-oriented economic liberalization programme which 'deliberately hitched economic development in the Philippines to the locomotive of expanding demand in the advanced capitalist markets of Japan and the West' (Bello et al. 1982: 67–78).

Internally, Marcos then had few choices since the economy was very weak and, consequently, his political fate was dependent largely on how he could curtail growing popular resentment against his administration. Though evaluations of economic conditions prevalent immediately before, during and after Marcos's 20-year rule (1965–1986) would vary depending on who is doing the analysis (Boyce 1993), the following sketches of the political economy of the country during those times are deemed plausible:

> Between 1961 and 1971, the rich became richer, while the poor became a bit poorer. Between 1971 and 1985, both rich and poor experienced real income declines, but in percentage terms the incomes of the poor fell more than the incomes of the rich. Hence inequality continued to widen. (Boyce 1993: 43)

> As the upper classes divided in internecine strife over political office and over the response to US economic domination, thousands of youths, workers, and peasants burst out of the straitjacket of patronage politics and rocked the country with massive demonstrations, strikes, and marches for anti-elite and anti-American causes. (Bello et al. 1982: 20)

> . . . repressive labour conditions in the Philippines served the Philippine govern-
> ment well in its promotion of an overseas employment programme. Within this
> context, therefore, overseas employment was constructed as a viable strategy for
> thousands of Filipinos. (Tyner 2000: 136)

Therefore, the infusion of much needed cash in the form of aids and loans as well as the prospect of increased foreign investments could help Marcos rescue himself from acute pressures of the left, the oligarchy (which he marginalized in favour of his few trusted allies or 'cronies'), the middle class, and the huge working class, who all complained about decaying social and economic institutions in the country.

Externally, the same economic institutions like the World Bank and the IMF and other bearers of neoliberal ideologies like the MNCs (multinational corporations) and powerful Western nations like the USA, were swiftly consolidating their resources towards the creation of a singular capitalist world economy, through the elimination of protectionist policies of independent states in order to bring down economic and political barriers between nations and allow for faster and more efficient flow of goods and services across national borders. Through an economic programme which would accept the same ideological principles imposed by the World Bank and the IMF, the Philippines could then 'plug' itself even deeper into the global capitalist economy (Bello *et al.* 1982: 41).

One of the immediate implications of the country's export-oriented liberalization policy was access to the labour markets of rich capitalist countries which were then coping hard with an undersupply of labour to run their industries and to support their social infrastructures as a result of the changing demographics of their own workforce. Such need for capitalist labour, in turn, conspired with existing Philippine socioeconomic realities: the exportation of cheap labour was not such a bad idea after all since it could help solve quickly the severe unemployment problem of the country and, thus, help contain political dissent. So while modern-day Philippine migrant history could trace itself back to the early years of the 20th century (Catholic Institute for International Relations 1987), it was then during the tumultuous years of the Marcos dictatorship – with the backing of the USA, the World Bank and the IMF, because it purportedly established and supported democratic institutions – that the exportation of cheap labour was institutionalized as the centrepiece component of the economic liberalization programme of the Philippines (Bello *et al.* 1982; Cariño 1998). Consequently, the practice of exporting labour has become a fundamental defining feature of the ideologically consistent economic policies of all post-Marcos administrations (Aquino, Ramos, Estrada and Arroyo). What used to be a 'temporary strategy' (Abrera-Mangahas 1998: 45) to a temporary severe unemployment problem became ironically a permanent diatribe against enduring unemployment and other socioeconomic problems in the country, consequently making the country 'the world's largest exporter of government-sponsored labour' (Tyner 2000: 132).

Another, but related, result of the neoliberal policy was access to foreign capital mainly through the MNCs which established factories and other related industrial outposts in the country, such as the Export Processing Zones which were established officially immediately after the imposition of Martial Law in the early 1970s. In this case, cheap domestic labour was utilized as yet another quick way out of poverty although, on hindsight, it never accomplished this objective. These MNCs capitalized on cheap Filipino labour which thus closely tied up the local economy in a disadvantageous way with the escalating capitalist development of some industrialized countries where such MNCs originated. Therefore, whether Filipino labour remained or left the country, certain facts emerged from the economic restructuring of the 1970s: the production of cheap labour was the cornerstone policy of the country's economic development; the local economy was made dependent even more on external economic and political pressures, thus allowing the 'celebrated fable of the invisible hand' (Boyce 1993: 349) of the global market to exert extreme pressure on the shape and direction of Philippine economic development, even if the Philippine state actively pursued such shape and direction (Tyner 2000); the policy did not solve the unemployment problem of the country, nor did it address the restiveness of a great number of Filipinos. The communist insurgency grew fast during these times and, as has been well known now, Marcos was thrown out of office through people power in 1986.

Contextualizing English

The commodification of English language proficiencies

However, the successful implementation of economic restructuring (never mind its results) did not depend solely on the state's economic institutions. In fact, it also depended much on non-economic infrastructures, the most critical of which was the Philippine educational system which became both the ideological battleground for the inculcation of neoliberal ideas among the youth and the training centre of docile bodies out of which skills needed locally and abroad were generated (Tupas 2001). In the *Philippine Development Report, 1978*, of the National Economic Development Authority, the 'development of the country's manpower' was carried through a 'comprehensive educational process' (1979:110), such that the 'realignment of education and training' was implemented in the service of 'national development thrusts' (1979: 115). Among out-of-school youths, the same developmental agenda was carried out by the National Manpower and Youth Council (NMYC). In simple terms, this meant the crucial utilization of educational resources (both formal and non-formal) for export-driven economic development.

The National College Entrance Examination (NCEE) was the chief educational, thus social, stratifier (PNCRC 1983). With standards set by the central government, the NCEE determined who among the high school graduates could go on to college, earn their degrees and most possibly become white-collar workers. Those who did not pass could either enrol in technical education certificate courses or start working in low-paying jobs because by then they would have been taught vocational skills in high school through institutionalized technical programmes. I was myself a product of such an educational structure even if I went to secondary school in the late 1980s. I majored in Industrial Electricity, but also studied Machine Shop Practice, Automotive Mechanics, and Furniture and Cabinet Making. I passed the NCEE (which tested abilities in English, Math, Science and Verbal Reasoning) and was thus able to enter college.

It is in the intersection of these economic, social and ideological practices where the role of the English language in the Philippines then and now could be clearly understood. The economic restructuring did underscore the need for an English-proficient labour force, but the nuances of its use in the country could be more clarified if we locate it within particular institutionalized practices meant to perpetuate neoliberalism and the developmentalist agenda of the government. In other words, not only was English the language for labour, but – silently, though no less insidiously – it was also an instrument for educational segregation. The language of the NCEE was English and those who passed it apparently were more proficient in the language than those who failed the test. What emerged, therefore, was a labour force of varying English language proficiencies which would cater to the various demands of the international labour market (Tollefson 1991; see also Sibayan and Gonzalez 1996). Such linguistic hierarchization, in turn, has helped perpetuate the socioeconomic status quo, as pointed out below by Bernardo who concludes out of research made on the impact of English as medium of instruction in the Philippine schools.

> The small proportion of the population who have easily acquired English language proficiencies in their enriched milieu will have the best chances of learning in the various domains taught in English. They will have an ever-widening array of options available for education, even in foreign countries. But the overwhelming majority of the population, who will forever struggle with English as a foreign language, will likely find their limited proficiencies in English a major stumbling block to learning in the various domains of knowledge. . . . They are the ones most likely to fail in examinations and writing requirements in English, to perceive much of formal education as irrelevant, and to drop out of school altogether. (2004: 27)

To speak of the commodification of English in the Philippines, therefore, we need to stop thinking of English as a monolithic language since, more importantly, it is the different English language proficiencies that are commodified in terms of the varying monetary, instrumental and symbolic values attached to them by the market. This explains why the economic restructuring in the 1970s resulted in the acute problem of brain drain because the majority of those who responded to the allure of capital locally and abroad were Filipino professional, technical and related workers like doctors, nurses and artists (53.5 per cent), as opposed to service workers like maids and other housekeeping service workers (22 per cent), and production workers, labourers and drivers (20.8 per cent) (Go 1998). And this likewise explains why the problem of brain drain continues to be a problem today, where teachers are in demand in the US, and where doctors study nursing to work as nurses in countries like the UK and the US. Similarly, the recent incursion into the call centre market of our 'low cost country' with a 'very open economy' (*Philippines* 2003) in order 'to become the new star in the global outsourcing business' (*RP gets serious* 2003), revealed an undersupply of highly proficient English language speakers because those who can speak 'good' (American) English mainly come from a small group of schools, especially expensive exclusive schools concentrated in urban centres like Metro Manila. In other words, there are 'good jobs' in the Philippines – but only for 'good English speakers' (*Good jobs* 2004: 1 and 5).

Meanwhile, those with low-level English language proficiencies – and they constitute the majority of the country's labour force (Go 1998: 15) mainly because much of the educational system is mediocre (Sibayan and Gonzalez 1996) – consequently become marginalized economically, socially and politically. Those who leave the country to work abroad – and again, they constitute the great majority of exported labour – become, among many possibilities, domestic helpers in Singapore and Hong Kong, entertainers in Japan, and construction workers in Taiwan and in several countries in the Middle East. Thus, just like in the past, education today fulfils the same function as noted by Ordoñez (1999) in the following statement:

> The role of Philippine education (through Education 2000) seems to be that of supplying the world market economy with a docile and cheap labor force who are trained in English and the vocational and technical skills required by that economy (2).

Therefore, the practice of using 'education' for 'manpower development' remains true even today, albeit couched in a slightly different discourse to respond to recent concerns of the market, but which is nevertheless ideologically anchored in the same economic project of export-driven liberalization. It may be noted that the Philippines in recent years has become a so-called 'model' human exporting country in terms of an elaborate system of laws and regulations which help protect the rights of its migrant workers and protect them from all kinds of abuse. For example, *The Migrant Workers and Overseas Filipinos Act of 1995* (RA 8042 or the Magna Carta for Overseas Workers) (itself largely a response to public furore over celebrated abuses of Filipino workers by foreign employers), has articulated the need for the government to no longer promote overseas employment as a key national development strategy and, instead, make sure that the welfare of its people who desire to work abroad are highly protected. In short, while the earlier state policy explicitly promoted the 'exportation' of Filipino labour as a major source of economic stability, the government's role now is that of migration 'management'. As will be shown below, however, despite recent attempts to 'manage' migration flows (apparently making individual Filipinos responsible for their decisions to seek employment abroad), such semantic callisthenics in the Magna Carta cannot hide the fact that labour exportation remains a government strategy for economic development because of its apparent economic benefits, and that, in the first place, 'it does not touch the structure which continues to create displacement and unemployment' (Batistella 1998: 107).

The Ramos administration's *1993–98 Medium-Term Development Plan*, which expressed the government's desire to achieve the status of a newly industrialized country (NIC) by the year 2000, continued to over-emphasize an export-driven approach to economic development. The new slogan was education for 'global competitiveness', thus the emergence of a new capitalist rhetoric – 'English for global competitiveness' (Lorente and Tupas 2002).

Ordoñez, though, finds this problematic in the following ideological unpacking of the discourse:

> *English for global competitiveness* fits into the types of education that would conform to the requirements of an export-oriented economy pushed by the IMF–World Bank for the Philippines, an economy controlled by multinational companies – extracting raw materials from our natural resources, involved in light industries like the assembly of knockdown cars and electronic equipment, textile, manufacturing, food processing, the making of crafts, and service industries. (1999: 19–20, emphasis as original)

To complete the process, the *Export Development Act of 1994 and Technical Education and Skills Development Act of 1994* were put into law during the Ramos administration. The first act was meant to 'evolve export development into a national effort' because exporting was 'the key to national survival' (Sec. 2) while the latter act, as its first objective, was meant to 'Promote and strengthen the quality of technical education and skills development programs to attain international competitiveness' (Sec. 3). In a sense, the former made sure that the Philippines compete for increased share of its exports in the international market, while the latter would complement such efforts with technical know-how, this time for the exportation of human labour. The latter created TESDA – or Technical Education and Skills Development Authority – which was tasked to develop 'the quality of human resource' (Sec. 8) in the country. TESDA replaced and absorbed all existing programmes, bureaus and personnel engaged in various aspects of human skills development but which could be found in different spaces in the bureaucracy. The major ones were the NMYC, which was mentioned above, the Bureau of Technical and Vocational Education (BTVE), and all other technical-vocational education-related work at the Department of Education, Culture and Sports (DECS) and the Bureau of Local Employment of the Department of Labour and Employment. What this latter act envisaged, therefore, was to create an Authority which would consolidate all of the country's efforts and resources to develop various skills for 'international competitiveness'. The result is aptly articulated by Parreñas: our OFW's have become 'manufactured products of the Philippines, placed in the same category as electronic goods' (2001: 54).

While indeed, much of human labour contributes to the Philippine economy through billions of dollars of remittances (although their long-term effect on the economy continues to be a contested issue, see for example, Battistella and Paganoni 1992), a study of Philippine labour will demonstrate how the hierarchy of skills (including English language skills) that governs the deployment of labour actually perpetuates, rather than reconfigures, both the Philippine social structure (which, in turn, also reproduces such hierarchy), as well as the globalized unequal structure of relations between the Philippines as a labour-producing country and labour-using countries and corporations (Tupas 2001; Lorente and Tupas 2002). All of this is supposed to occur under the clutches of neoliberal globalization which has promised all countries and people material prosperity (e.g. see Fukuyama 1992). Apparently, countries and people respond variedly to the pressures of globalization, with some through sheer economic and political power able to design and impose policies for their own benefit, while others with minimal power largely unable to set the pace and direction of globalization. The dichotomy between the haves and have-nots of globalization is not absolute, but the deepening disparity of wealth and other forms of power between them certainly cannot be denied.

The anatomy of linguistic commodification in the Philippines, thus, is such that it is inextricably bound with the commodification of labour in the Philippines which, in turn, is a by-product of the Philippine state's export-driven developmental strategies within the broad framework of capitalist liberalization vigorously promoted by advanced countries and their MNCs, and channelled through the political and ideological influence of the World Bank and the IMF. Therefore, English – or rather, English language proficiencies – fits perfectly well in such a framework of political economy of linguistic commodification, as it is the language that helps allow the deployment of labour all over the world.

Conclusion

Linguistic commodification in a developing multilingual country

The consequent, but last, important question that we address in this chapter, therefore, is to what is the impact of this particular nature of linguistic commodification (where English is the only language commodified) on the local languages of the Philippines? We remember that in other accounts of linguistic commodification presented at the start of this chapter, local languages such as French, Spanish and Mandarin in contexts where they used to take on the main role as repositories of culture, identity and tradition, are now increasingly seen as economic resources chiefly as a response to changes in the new economy. We remember, too, as in Wee's general rendering of these accounts, that these languages are learned not in lieu of, but in addition to, English. In the Philippines, aside from the fact that local languages have not been viewed as economic resources, the dominance of English in both Philippine economic practice and discourse has effectively marginalized the local languages in the crafting of policies in education and economic development. On the one hand, the local languages are considered unfit as languages of instruction; at best, they are deemed (officially) as auxiliary media of instruction or as transitionary languages in Grades 1 and 2. On the other hand, their use is anathema to economic progress and technological advancement; it may be counterproductive to promote them as they may come in the way of learning English (Tupas 2008).

Filipino, the national language, is perhaps the strongest candidate among the local languages to mount a strong challenge to English as the only viable economic resource for the country's development as well as the people's upward mobility and individual economic upliftment. But while Filipino has, in fact, challenged the dominant position of English in Philippine society for much of the 1900s, it has done so on nationalist, symbolic grounds, and not on the same terms that English has consistently embodied (see Gonzalez 1980; Fullante 1983). Some scholars argue that, indeed, for Filipino to be truly dominant in both symbolic and instrumentalist ways, the domains of its use must be expanded to include academic, professional, economic and government domains (Sibayan 1988, 1999). People, in other words, must find reasons to use it pragmatically, for example to extricate them from poverty, ensure their success in school, or use it for academic reasons. Unfortunately, as shown in the experiences of French in Canada, Spanish in the USA and Mandarin in Singapore, the expansion of domains for the local languages cannot be accomplished simply through decrees and policies alone. The local languages, and I suppose all other languages in the world as well, are located in the intersections of sociopolitical and economic phenomena, at once both localized and globalized, such that what they are and what roles they can play in society and in the world may also depend on the amount of power of the people who speak them.

In the end, therefore, the varying anatomies of linguistic commodification demonstrate the non-uniform development of globalization processes. Countries, people and communities respond to the challenges of globalization in different ways; they play different roles in the globalized or globalizing world economy (e.g. Nayyar 1997). And just like the fact that among countries there are losers and winners in globalization, in the global multilingual market, only a few languages become dominant (or are becoming so). New economic regional blocs and the opening of more national economies to global capital may alter the futures of some languages (e.g. French, Spanish, Mandarin), but people who mainly serve the market, not dictate it (and they are the large majority in the world), can perhaps continue to carve out spaces of resistance against the excesses and delusions of capital, using the dominant language, English (e.g. see Danaher and Burbach 2000), or their own local languages (Canieso-Doronila 1998), for the development of their own local literacies and cultural knowledges in order to survive and safeguard their welfare as human beings. Making commodities out of languages, after all, is not necessarily a good thing.

References

Abrera-Mangahas, M. A. (1998), 'Violence against women migrant workers: The Philippine experience' in Benjamin V. Cariño (ed.), *Filipino Workers on the Move: Trends, Dilemmas and Policy Options* (Philippines: Philippine Migration Research Network), pp. 45–80.

Battistella, Graziano (1998), 'The Migrant Workers and Overseas Filipinos Act of 1995 and Migration Management' in Benjamin V. Cariño (ed.), *Filipino Workers on the Move: Trends, Dilemmas and Policy Options* (Philippines: Philippine Migration Research Network), pp. 81–113.

Battistella, Graziano and Anthony Paganoni (eds) (1992), *Philippine Labor Migration* (Quezon City, Philippines: Scalabrini Migration Center).

Bello, Walden, Kinley, David and Elinson, Elaine (1982), *Development Debacle: The World Bank in the Philippines* (USA: Institute for Food and Development Policy).

Bernardo, Allan B. I. (2004), 'McKinley's questionable bequest: Over 100 years of English in Philippine education', *World Englishes* 23: 17–31.

Boyce, James K. (1993), *The Philippines: The Political Economy of Growth and Impoverishment in the Marcos Era* (Honolulu: University of Hawaii Press in association with the OECD Development Centre).

Canieso-Doronila, Maria Luisa (1998), 'The emergence of schools of the people and the transformation of the Philippine educational system', *UP-CIDS Chronicle* 3: 63–97.

Cariño, Benjamin V. (ed.), *Filipino Workers on the Move: Trends, Dilemmas and Policy Options* (Philippines: Philippine Migration Research Network).

Catholic Institute for International Relations (1987), *The Labour Trade – Filipino Migrant Workers Around the World* (England: CIIR).

Danaher K. and Burbach, R. (eds) (2000), *Globalize This! The Battle against the World Trade Organization and Corporate Rule* (Monroe, Maine: Common Courage Press).

Fukuyama, Francis (1992), *The End of History and the Last Man* (New York: Free Press; Toronto: Maxwell Macmillan Canada; New York: Maxwell Macmillan International).

Fullante, Luis Cruz (1983), The national language question in the Philippines, 1936–the present, unpublished PhD dissertation, University of California, Los Angeles.

Go, Stella P. (1998), 'Towards the 21st century: Whither Philippine Labor Migration?' in Benjamin V. Cariño (ed.), *Filipino Workers on the Move: Trends, Dilemmas and Policy Options* (Philippines: Philippine Migration Research Network), pp. 9–44.

Gonzalez, Andrew B. (1980), *Language and Nationalism: The Philippine Experience thus Ffar* (Quezon City, Metro Manila: Ateneo de Manila University Press).

'Good jobs for good English speakers' (August 2004), *Philippine Daily Inquirer*, pp. 1and 5.

Heller, Monica (2003), 'Globalization, the New Economy, and the Commodification of Language and Identity', *Journal of Sociolinguistics* 7: 473–92.

Heller, Monica (1999), 'Alternative ideologies of *la francophonie*', *Journal of Sociolinguistics* 3: 336–59.

National Economic Development Authority (1979), *Philippine Development Report, 1978* (Manila: National Economic Development Authority).

Nayyar, D. (1997), 'Globalization – the game, the players and the rules' in S. D. Gupta (ed.), *The Political Economy of Globalization* (USA: Kluwer Academic Publishers), pp. 15–40.

Nical, Iluminado, Smolicz, Jerzy J. and Secombe, Margaret J. (2004), 'Rural students and the Philippine Bilingual Education Program on the island of Leyte' in James W. Tollefson, James W. and Amy B. M. Tsui (eds), *Medium of Instruction Policies – Which Agenda? Whose Agenda?* (Mahwah, New Jersey and London: Lawrence Erlbaum Associates), pp. 153–76.

Ordoñez, Elmer A. (1999), 'English and decolonization', *Journal of Asian English Studies* 2 (1–2): 17–21

Philippine Normal College Research Centre (1983), 'The coming revolt against the educational system', *Diliman Review* January–February: 24–27.

Philippines views for back-office operations, 'The International Herald Tribune', Retrieved 23 May 2003, www.iht.com

Pomerantz, Anne (2002), 'Language ideologies and the production of identities: Spanish as a resource for participation in a multilingual marketplace', *Multilingua* 21: 275–302.

RP gets serious on outsourcing biz. Retrieved 23 October 2003, www.mctimes.net

Saving Angelo = Saving Gloria, *Newsbreak* (Isagani de Castro Jr.). Retrieved 18 August 2004, http://www.inq7.net/nwsbrk/2004/aug/16/nbk_4-1.htm

Sibayan, Bonifacio P. (ed.) (1999), *The Intellectualization of Filipino and Other Essays on Education and Eociolinguistics* (Manila: Linguistic Society of the Philippines).

Sibayan, Bonifacio P. (1988), 'Transcript of the discussion' in Andrew B. Gonzalez (ed.), *The Role of English and Its Maintenance in the Philippines – The Transcript, Consensus and Papers of the Solidarity Seminar on Language and Development* (Manila, Philippines: Solidaridad Publishing House), pp. 19–69.

Sibayan, Bonifacio P. and Gonzalez, Andrew (1996), 'Post-imperial English in the Philippines' in Fishman, Joshua A., Conrad, Andrew W. and Rubal-Lopez, Alma (eds), *Post-imperial English – Status Changes in Former British and American Colonies, 1940–1990* (Berlin and New York: Mouton de Gruyter), pp. 139–72.

Tollefson, James W. (1991), *Planning Language, Planning Inequality – Language Policy in the Ccommunity* (London and New York: Longman).

Tollefson, James W. (1986), 'Language policy and the radical left in the Philippines: The New People's army and its antecedents', *Language Problems & Language Planning* 10: 177–89.

Tupas, T. Ruanni F. (2008). 2008. *Kalayagan, tawid-buhay* and other uses of language in a marginal Philippine community: the place of language in literacy and social development, *International Journal o Bilingual Education and Bililgualism* 2: 226–245.

Tupas, T. Ruanni F. (2003a), 'Back to class: the medium of instruction debate in the Philippines', invited paper presented at the *Workshop on Language, Nation and Development in Southeast Asia*, Institute of Southeast Asian Studies, NUS, Singapore. 26–27 November 2003.

Tupas, T. Ruanni F. (2003b), 'History, language planners, and strategies of forgetting: The problem of consciousness in the Philippines', *Language Problems & Language Planning* 27: 1–25.

Tupas, T. Ruanni F. (2001), 'Linguistic imperialism in the Philippines: reflections of an English language teacher of Filipino Overseas Workers', *The Asia-Pacific Education Researcher* 10: 1–40.

Tupas, T. Ruanni F. (2008), Kalayagan, tawid-buhay and other uses of language in a marginal Philippine community: The place of language in literacy and social development, *International Journal of Bilingual Education & Bilingualism* 2: 226–45.

Tyner, James A. (2000), 'Migrant labour and the politics of scale: gendering the Philippine state', *Asia Pacific Viewpoint* 41: 131–54.

7

The English Language as a Commodity in Malaysia: The View through the Medium-of-Instruction Debate

Peter K. W. Tan

This chapter discusses the commodification of the English language by focusing on the debate and comments that arose from a suggestion made by the former Malaysian Prime Minister Mahathir Mohamad in 2002 that English-medium education in state schools, phased out in Malaysia in the 1970s, could be reintroduced. January 2003 saw the start of the school term with an English–Malay mixed medium of instruction. I examine the extent to which the rhetoric of English as an economic resource is surfaced or assumed and whether alternative reasons are pushed aside or attenuated. I make reference to articles from the Malaysian English (then) broadsheet New Straits Times *in the period April to July 2002.*

Introduction

One of the features of 'high modernity' (Giddens 1990), as opposed to *mere* modernity, is that the essentializing,[1] apparently self-evident, notions of language, race, nationhood and identity break down. Furthermore, the relationship between language between community, ethnicity and nationality are seen as complex (rather than straightforward), having the propensity to be over-simplified (rather than inherent), or simply as outmoded. Among the things that put paid to all those old certainties are porous borders, easy communication and travel, and especially easy buying and selling. All of these things can be seen as evidence of globalization. The pressures of globalization have led to an increased commodification of language with respect to its usefulness in the global as well as the local market place.

Increasingly therefore languages are evaluated in economic terms. The term used by Fairclough to refer to this is *marketisation*, which he defines as 'the extension of market modes of operation to new areas of social life' (2000: 163). Areas previously not considered subject to market forces are co-opted into this new way of doing things.

Not surprisingly, English, as a 'global language' (Crystal 2003), is therefore often seen as valuable from this point of view; other major languages such as Mandarin Chinese are also being seen as valuable. Witness the cover story of *Time* magazine of 26 June 2006, 'Go ahead, learn Mandarin' (Ramzy 2006). Tellingly, the subtitle is 'China's *economic* rise means the world has a new second language – and it isn't English' (my emphasis). Ramzy quotes a Chinese-language professor at the College of the Holy Cross in Worcester in the USA who says that the enrolment in first-year Chinese doubled because '[t]here are dollar signs attached to it' (Ramzy 2006: 18).

The notion of commodification is of course not new and was developed by Engels and Marx in their *Communist Manifesto* (1848): one consequence of according a dominant position to capital is that all elements have to be accorded a value, and thereby turned into a commodity – that is, be commodified or commoditized – and this underlies all capitalist systems. This of course prepares the ground for Bourdieu's notion of linguistic capital, so that there is a linguistic market because linguistic exchange

is also an economic exchange which is established within a particular symbolic relation of power between a producer, endowed with a certain linguistic capital,

and a consumer (or market), and which is capable of procuring a certain material
or symbolic profit. (1991: 66)

Giddens sees all of this within the bigger sweep of modernity, where individuals are freed from the constraints of time and space and the local, and
because of this, modernity is 'inherently globalising' (1990: 63).

In this phase of globalization, Castells (1993) suggests that we have moved
on from capitalism to new capitalism as characterized by five features: (1) there
is increased reliance on science and technology for the production of goods;
(2) the production is shifting from that of material to information; (3) the
organization of production has changed in that we are moving away from
mass production to adaptability, and from a hierarchical organization structure to a flatter one where individual employees take on more responsibilities;
(4) economies now involve other parts of the world in 'real time' in terms of
market competition; and (5) production is highly influenced by the information technology revolution.

Lankshear (1997) suggests that there is a six-fold consequence to Castell's
new capitalism on language. (1) There is an emphasis on new literacies that
can cope with personal, impersonal and virtual communities with the assumed
importance of Standard English and key foreign languages. (2) Literacy
becomes instrumentalized and languages become economized – that is, languages or varieties are promoted for reasons of economic advantage. (3) Literacies become overtly commodified in that certification (indicating proficiency
levels) becomes available and becomes standardly included in an individual's
CV. (4) The fact that the means–end equation is so tightly defined means that
critical practice receives little emphasis. (5) The new work order can result in
using language in opaque ways for outsiders. (6) Literacy becomes technolo-
gized in the emphasis on learning with the help of computers and the internet.
These are echoed by other commentators (e.g. Block and Cameron 2002).

Drawing together all the above and relating them specifically to English, we
might therefore expect to see its commodification evidenced or manifested in
these ways:

1. An increased focus on the importance of English-language skills for dealing with
   foreigners.
2. An increased reference to English as 'the international language of business'.[2]
3. An increased reference to English as the language of the information technology.
4. A consideration of how officially certified proficiency levels on English might play an
   important role.
5. Nay sayers in relation to an increased emphasis in English might be branded in negative
   ways.

However, the discourse of modernity and globalization is not the only one found in discussions about the direction in which language education policy or language change should move. We also find the discourse of identity prominent in some areas of linguistics including language policy. We can also make reference to the discourse associated with the New Englishes. (Elsewhere, I have used the term *Non-Anglo Englishes* to underline the different cultural underpinnings of these Englishes, but here I keep to the more familiar term to refer to Englishes used in former British or American colonies such as Malaysia and Nigeria.) Schneider (2007), for instance, suggests that various New Englishes or Postcolonial English varieties are emerging as a result of communities appropriating English for themselves and identifying with these New Englishes. The notion of pluricentrism (Clyne 1992) – that languages can have differing norms – has also been fairly well established: this can be discussed in relation to English (Leitner 1992) as well as other languages.

The context

This chapter discusses the points made in relation to a specific context in Malaysia. On 6 May 2002, the then prime minister of Malaysia, Mahathir Mohamad, announced that the government would be willing to re-introduce English-medium education 'if the people [wanted] it'. This of course generated much discussion and on 11 May 2002 the then Education Minister, Musa Mohamad, stated that he would set up a bilingual system where English would be the medium of instruction for science- and mathematics-based subjects in schools and universities; this would mean, for example, that history would be taught in Malay[3] and biology in English. On 21 July 2002, Musa Mohamad provided details about how this would be implemented in national schools (this term will be explained below): the bilingual system would be introduced in phases beginning on the new school term in January 2003 at Year 1 of primary school, and Forms 1, 4 and Lower 6 of secondary school (equivalent to Years 7, 10 and 12 of a 13-year education system).

Malaysia has had a fairly long history in relation to English-medium education. We can see the development of bilingual education in Malaysia in four phrases (for details, see Watson 1983; Gaudart 1987; Solomon 1988; David and Govindasamy 2003; Hashim 2003; Pandian 2003).

Phase 1. Prior to 1970, primary school education was available in four mediums in Malaya.[4] Immediately before independence from Britain in 1957, schools were either 'standard schools' or 'standard-type schools', distinguished by medium of instruction. Standard schools employed Malay, and standard-type schools employed English, Mandarin Chinese or Tamil for teaching. Malay-, Tamil- and Mandarin–Chinese-medium schools were closely linked to ethnicity and almost all pupils in these schools would be from one ethnic group. English-medium schools, the majority set up by church missions, were mainly found in towns[5] and attracted many Chinese pupils; Indian, Eurasian and Malay pupils were also represented. Tertiary education was only available through English. The situation immediately after independence remained largely the same, though 'standard schools' were renamed 'national schools' (*sekolah kebangsaan*), and 'standard-type schools' became 'national-type schools' (*sekolah jenis kebangsaan*).

Phase 2. This phase, covering the 1970s and 1980s, marked the aggressive promotion of Malay as the national language, as the title of Asmah's (1979) book suggests, for 'unity and efficiency' or, as David and Govindasamy (2003) put it, because of 'nationalistic fervour'. English was co-official with Malay as national language at independence but the status of English as official language was removed in 1967. Severe race riots in Kuala Lumpur in May 1969 prompted the then Minister of Education, Dato Haji Abdul Rahman Ya'akub to declare in July that English-medium schools would be converted to national (Malay medium) schools: Year 1 pupils in primary school in January 1970 would be taught in Malay. The sudden change caused consternation among many teachers. A significant group was the transitional group of pupils who were already in English-medium schools. Because some subjects such as history and geography were only introduced in Year 4, they had these subjects taught in Malay whilst other subjects introduced in Year 1 (such as science and maths) taught in English. This might have been the model for the system in Phase 4.

Phase 3. This phase marked the loosening of the medium-of-instruction requirements at the periphery when in the 1990s, colleges set up in Malaysia could offer English-medium programmes to prepare students for degree courses overseas or even the initial years of a foreign degree course. With these, Asmah asserts that 'local English-medium education has made a comeback, and with great vigour' (1996: 519).

Phase 4. This takes us to the events of 2002 mentioned above which led to the development of a mixed-medium education from January 2003. Among the impetuses that might have given rise to this about-turn include concerns about low proficiency of English among school-leavers, lack of competitiveness, unemployment attributable to low English proficiency and the ethnic segregation in schools.

The data

The data are articles from the *New Straits Times* that focus on the issue of the medium of instruction in schools, published between April and July (inclusive) of 2002. This yielded 40 articles of varying lengths. Of these, 7 (or 17.5 per cent) were leaders (editorials) or comment articles, 4 (or 10.0 per cent) were on various courses offered. The rest reported on views of various personages of some authority although a few reported on informal surveys conducted by the newspaper itself. The vast majority therefore reported views or positions on the issue: the newspaper, authorities and readers of the *New Straits Times*. It should be noted that the *New Straits Times* is a pro-government newspaper and is controlled by UMNO (United Malay National Organisation, the main component in the ruling party, the Barisan Nasional or National Front). This would in fact be in line with the intention of this chapter which is to examine the official justifications given for giving English a more prominent position in the Malaysian education system. Of particular interest would be the exemplars of linguistic commodification mentioned above and the emphasis given to the instrumentalist reasons for reinstating English.

Justifications for English

A large proportion of the comments were focused on implementation issues rather than why English was required, or on explaining the reasons for the patchy acquisition of English in different sections of Malaysian society. I focus on comments that pertain to the reasons for strengthening the position of English in schools made by various personages, the editors or members of the public, and by doing so build up a picture of the kinds of views put forward publicly as good reasons for increasing the amount of teaching through the English medium in Malaysian schools.

Initial comments

I look in a little more detail at the points raised in the early leading articles in the *Straits Times* and by the then prime minister and Education Minister initially before summarizing the main issues raised subsequently.

Here is the view expressed in relation to the employment of English as a medium of instruction in the leading article of 8 April.

> Plainly, the Education Ministry is no longer gripped by the politics of linguistic chauvinism. The retraining of some 30,000 teachers nationwide to teach English

> in primary and secondary schools will no doubt enrich their encounters, as well as
> that of their pupils, with the language and its learning process.
>
> . . . we are suffering the price of benign neglect of the subject. Nursing this
> neglect should not be narrowly linked to nationalistic concerns.
>
> . . . English is the language of global interaction. It is the technical language of the
> sciences. Current developments in the field of knowledge are nearly always articu-
> lated in English. Depriving our children of proficiency in this language has already
> set us back and will handicap tomorrow's Malaysians even more.

First of all, English is seen as a language that is not associated with chauvinism
and all that is associated with this, that is, irrationality, high emotional content
or unreasonableness. There is reference to 'nationalistic concerns', so that it
looks as if the *chauvinism* mentioned earlier can be equated to excessive
nationalistic concerns.

The view that is being negated is picked up by Ibrahim Ahmad Bajunid,
Dean of the Faculty of Humanities and Social Sciences, Universiti Tun Abdul
Razak: 'English has been viewed [by some Malay groups] as the language
of Christians and then as the language of colonialists' (17 July), and it is presumably this sort of association that is seen as chauvinistic, irrational and
unreasonable.

Of interest is the employment of two kinds of metaphors. One pertains to
disease: lack of English is likened to a *handicap* and not having the full use of
one's limbs. *Benign* could be a medical term (contrasted to *malignant*) but in
this case *benign neglect* is a set phrase. *Nursing* is what one does to one afflicted
with disease, though the expression 'Nursing this neglect' is ambiguous in
meaning. Does it mean *act in such a way so as to 'cure' the neglect* (in the way
one would say 'nurse a cold') or does it mean *allow to fester and worsen* (in the
way one would say 'nurse a grudge')? On balance, I assume the intended meaning is the curative one and this reinforces the disease metaphor.

The other metaphor relates to constriction and widening. Teachers trained
in English and their pupils will have *enriched* (widened) encounters; being
overly concerned about nationalism leads to *narrowing* (constriction); English
allows for interaction beyond the national level to the global level (widening)

Therefore, not having English leads to ill health and English opens the
world to its users.

We turn to comments made by the then prime minister and the Education
Minister, reported on 7 May.

> With less emphasis given to English in recent years, Dr Mahathir said, the Government found that those lacking a good command of the language were handicapped in integrating and facing the challenges of the new economy.
>
> 'So we have to overcome our weakness in this area. How we overcome this, it depends on us.'
>
> . . . In Sungai Petani, Education Minister Tan Sri Musa Mohamad said his Ministry would gather public opinion before making a decision [on reviving English-medium teaching].
>
> 'We are living in the era of globalisation where we need to communicate with the international community which predominantly uses English. We need to study this from all aspects and the Ministry wants as much public input before making a decision on the matter,' he said after launching a national-level 'Safe School' concept convention today.

The first paragraph presents Mahathir's words in indirect speech before moving into direct speech. The report appears to closely represent Mahathir, and the non-standard grammatical structure in the final sentence (which might have been silently amended in other newspapers) is left intact; this also suggests that the first paragraph follows the structure of Mahathir's speech closely. Once again, lack of English is represented as a disease or disability (*handicapped*). The ground of the metaphor is specified, but only through a gerundial construction that omits information. Those with poor English have problems in integrating: this presumably means integrating *themselves*, but with whom or into what? The reference could be to integrating these people with the workforce or integrating with people with different backgrounds or people of different races. The new economy is said to make *challenges* to those with poor English; this is another metaphor, but with the ground left unstated and we are not told what kind of challenges are made.

The leading article of 8 May quotes Mahathir and attempts to flesh out his comments. It reiterates his comments, 'it has been proven beyond doubt that those less proficient in the language are handicapped when it comes to integrating and facing the challenges of the new economy.' Mahathir's key terms, *handicapped*, *integrating* and *challenges*, reappear; the editor states that his points have been *proven* but does not offer any proof himself. The subsequent paragraphs expand on the challenges and comment on the importance of competitiveness in the face of globalization, and that English is the *lingua franca* of knowledge.

Key words

The Education Minister appears much more direct and matter-of-fact, when he declares that English is useful as an international language and it is the language of wider communication. He uses two key terms *globalization* and *international* which will recur in many of the discussions to follow. The other key terms are *competitiveness* (because the global market implies competition between producers) and *lingua franca* (because the enlarged global market requires a common means of communication). These key terms could obviously appear in their various cognate forms (*global, competition*, etc.). All of these obviously relate to the notion of English as a commodity in the manner raised earlier. Indeed, the metaphorical allusiveness of the earlier comments are replaced by more down-to-earth comments. (In all the quotations below I have italicized these key terms; the italicization is not in the original.)

We find this in the comments made by various personages in industry. The president of the Malaysian Trades Union Congress (MTUC), who is quoted as saying that competence in English 'would be able to improve [Malaysia's *competitive* edge, especially in the context of the Asean Free Trade Area (8 May).

The president of the Free Industrial Zone Penang Companies' Association (Frepenca) is quoted as saying that, with English, 'Malaysia would be at an advantage in *competing* with countries that offered the same [free trade incentive' and that 'English was widely used at Frepenca member factories and among professionals around the globe' (11 May).

The president of the Institute of Engineers Malaysia announces that '[a] English is the *lingua franca* in technical and research documents *internationally*, it is vital for our future engineers and other scientists to know the language to understand the material' (12 May).

Social activist Lee Lam Thye is also quoted as saying that '[t]he decreasing standard should be of concern to Malaysians especially at a time when we are preparing ourselves for the challenges of *globalisation* and an industrialise nation in 2020' (10 May). Lee Lam Thye was a long-time Member of Parliament for a constituency in Kuala Lumpur in the opposition Democratic Action Party until he retired from politics.

The key terms feature dominantly when Mahathir, as president of Umno (United Malays National Organisation) gives a press conference after the meeting of the Umno supreme council, reported on 11 May:

> Dr Mahathir said the council acknowledged English as the *lingua franca* and stressed the importance of Malaysians mastering the language. 'English is widely

used in trade and *international* dealings. Agreements are often in English and if we do not have a good command of the language, we might agree to clauses which are actually against our interests.'

Deputy Prime Minister Abdullah Badawi echoes this view and he is quoted as saying that 'Malaysians must accept the reality that it was crucial to master at least one main foreign language in order to be relevant in the era of *globalisation*' (17 May).

The Education Minister Musa Mohamad is also quoted as saying, 'We want [Malaysians] to build networks with people from *other nations* … we cannot help but acknowledge the instrumental role of the English language in this regard' (13 July).

Knowledge and information

A strand in the argument that was certainly picked up in the early discussion in May but that received emphasis from official circles is the point that English is the language of knowledge. Towards the end of the debate in July, it is this point that interestingly receives attention to the exclusion of others. This, presumably, does not negate the earlier emphasis on globalization, competitiveness and international communication and could in fact be seen as the basis for the former.

Here are some comments from various personages in the earlier stages. The MTUC (Malaysian Trades Union Congress) president is quoted on 12 May: 'He said knowing English meant enrichment in *knowledge* as most books were in the language'.

The President of the Institute of Engineers Malaysia is quoted as saying that having science and maths taught in English 'would go a long way towards strengthening the base for the country of further progress in science' (12 May).

The government is attributed the view that 'it is integral that Malaysians have a good command of English for it is the language of *information* and *knowledge*' (16 May).

Not surprisingly, there is also reference to the internet as source of all information *par excellence*:

[Then Deputy Prime Minister] Abdullah said it was imperative to start teaching the subjects in English as English was the language of the Internet and information technology. 'Teaching them English early will enable them to grasp the language at a young age. What the Education Ministry is doing is to make early preparations for the students. (15 July)

The clue to putting down the importance of English as being related to its status as the language of knowledge is contained in the Education Minister's statement:

> There is no need to view the English language as a threat to Malay, as it is just a tool to gain access to international sources of *information*, Education Minister Tan Sri Musa Mohamad [said] today. (13 July)

Negatives are always of interest because they presuppose a view that needs to be negated. Musa Mohamad's response here also suggests that the increased emphasis in English has no implications on identity construction; English is denied this function. The instrumental function of English is foregrounded the following week, when what he said was reported in indirect speech:

> He added that the move [to teach science and maths in English] was *purely* to enhance the *knowledge* of students in the two subjects, and not really a platform for them to learn English. (21 July, my italics)

We note the use of *purely*, in Hallidayan terms, a mood adjunct of intensity with a limiting function (Halliday 2004: 129). Any other presumed reason for emphasizing English, not stated explicitly here, is again denied. I suggested above that these might be the reasons that pertain to English having a role in identity construction.

Finally, Mahathir also lends his voice in underlining that the fact it was merely incidental that English, rather than some other language, received attention – this time a more explicit denial of English having any identity construction function:

> The Government realises the obvious need for Malaysians to master the two subjects [science and maths] because the bulk of available resources for the subjects is in English . . . The issue is not so much about improving the standard of English but more about equipping Malaysians with knowledge. (20 July)

Employability

Finally, the other pragmatic reason for renewed emphasis on English that is cited is the relationship of English to the job market.

> At least 2,000 entry-level executive jobs remain unfilled in the professional services sector because of a shortage of English speaking graduates, a public relations expert has declared.

'Advertising agencies, public relations firms and a whole host of other disciplines in marketing look at proficiency in English as a must-have skill because our clients deal simultaneously in Bahasa Malaysia and English. So being proficient in just one language is simply not good enough,' said Razak Abu Bakar, a senior consultant at Alpha Platform public relations. (28 May)

Indeed, the employability issue can become extended to become an economic sovereignty issue.

'If we do not act with speed, I am afraid that we will soon be engulfed by other nations, perhaps not politically, but definitely our economic sovereignty will suffer,' he [Abdul Rafie Mahat, director general of the Ministry of Education] said. (30 May)

The term is grandiose-sounding and not transparent. Perhaps the point made is that without English, Malaysia will have to rely on foreign or expatriate employees who would then jeopardize the 'sovereignty' of Malaysia. Or perhaps it just means that other nations will overtake Malaysia in economic growth.

Discussion

What then are we to make of the kinds of justifications given for an increased emphasis on English in the Malaysian educational context? The initial comments appear to be more open ended with its use of metaphors. Subsequently, there is a surfeit of the rhetoric of commodification and globalization. Many of the key points and issues given as the justification for English reflect the five manifestations of commodification given above (page 108). English is for getting jobs, English is for dealing with foreigners, English allows Malaysia to be competitive, English allows access to the internet and knowledge in general. Judging from the justifications given, it would appear that there is an indisputable commodified view of English in the Malaysian debate.

Indeed, the later comments by Musa Mohamed and Mahathir seem to up the ante of the commodified view of English by denying other justifications for wanting English apart from its ability to provide knowledge and information.

It might look puzzling to many that these later comments were so restrictive in contrast to the opening comments when it was suggested that English leads to enrichment, good health and wholeness (*integration*). Admittedly, the earlier comments analysed included points made by the editor of the *New Straits*

Times in a leading article; however, Mahathir's comments have been captured in the earlier and later comments and the contrast is telling:

> . . . Dr Mahathir said, the Government found that those lacking a good command of the language were handicapped in integrating and facing the challenges of the new economy. (7 May)

> The issue is not so much about improving the standard of English but more about equipping Malaysians with knowledge. (28 May)

Obviously we could imagine that the more open-ended comments in contrast to the highly commodified view at the end could be the result of the greater awareness of the various sensibilities in the country.

The Singaporean *Straits Times* singles out the function of English as a link language, and suggests that this is the reason for the renewed emphasis. For instance, Leslie Lau (2002) has an article entitled 'Mahathir sees English healing inter-racial rift'. Another article in December 2002 emphasizes this view.

> The aim is simple: If children from all races attend the same school, sit side by side in the canteen and tough it out on the playing fields, everyone will get on better. Racial integration will be better and chauvinism and intolerance will be at more acceptable levels in Malaysian society. The task of getting everyone to attend national schools is not going to be a walk in the park, though. At present, about 95 per cent of Chinese students attend Chinese-language schools, about 700,000 Malay students are in religious schools and about 90 per cent of Indian students are in Tamil schools. (Pereira 2002)

What is of interest is that this function of English does not receive any space in the Malaysian *New Straits Times* at all – none, except for the perhaps coded reference in Mahathir's comments about those without good English being 'handicapped in integrating'. Malaysians will know that national integration is an issue. National integration was certainly the ostensible reason for Mahathir introducing 'vision schools' (in Malay, *sekolah wawasan*) just before this in 2000. These 'vision schools' house different sub-schools which employ different mediums of instruction, but have common facilities such as the canteen; in this way, it is argued, there would be a multi-racial mix of pupils at recess or lunch time. If the *Straits Times* view is correct, English has a significant non-commodified, identity-construction function in the Malaysian context which has to be suppressed in public forums. This link function is also arguably instrumental in nature, but it would have nothing to do with the notion of a commodified language associated with the new capitalism mentioned earlier.

I mentioned earlier as well that there was a great deal written about the significance of the New Englishes in asserting national identity. English in Malaysia has been seen as being advantageous because it transcends ethno-linguistic loyalty. In Nair-Venugopal's study of the use of English in the Malaysian workplace, she notes the use of Malaysian(ized) English and goes on to comment that

> localization frustrates the cultural hegemony of [ideologies that claim that exonor-
> mative standards are the most suitable for the seemingly globalised workplace] . . .
> so that the cultural identity of the local workplace is maintained. (Nair-Venugopal
> 2000: 212)

This suggests that Malaysian English could have a role in maintaining local cultural identity. In the discussion, English is associated with the global, employed for communication with foreigners, and not quite seen as a Malaysian language. That it could be useful for communicating with other Malaysians is only implied when we are told that many job positions in Malaysia are unfilled because job applicants lacked proficiency in English. And of course we should not forget that the debate in the *New Straits Times* is in English. Here again, we have another lacuna and the whole discourse of the New Englishes is ignored.

Conclusion

The debate in Malaysia is certainly indicative of the prevalence of the discourse of economic commodification and globalization to the exclusion of other kinds of discourse. Does this tell us something about today's world view or Weltanschauung? Have economic concerns outweighed all other concerns and have these become the only credible justifications in any kind of debate? If so, this would feed into Fairclough's marketization thesis: that credibility in today's world rests on arguments based on the assumption of a market place.

I have also noted that the whole discourse of New Englishes is ignored in the discussion. Is it the case that the Malaysian debate simply shows how work within academic circles is just ignored in the public domain? Is it the fault of linguists that their work is not appreciated by non-specialists? There are no easy answers to the question.

Perhaps the Malaysian debate cannot be generalized, and the kind of narrowing observed is something peculiar to the Malaysian context. After all, there are many lobby groups with their own specific agenda, all of which have forced the hand of Mahathir and the Ministry of Education, and they end up saying less than what they mean.

It would seem that there can be no doubt that English is seen in commodified terms in today's world. Arguments and justifications that allude to this are overwhelming. We should however not mistake the rhetoric for the real thing. Other kinds of arguments and justifications, such as those based on identity, exist, but it would appear that the discourse associated with them do not have the power and appeal of the discourse associated with economic commodification.

Notes

1. An essentialist position is one that considers particular characteristics relating to particular groups as fundamental and immutable, rather than open to change or differentiation.

2. On 23 March 2006, French President Jacques Chirac stormed out of a European Union summit when Frenchman Ernest-Antoine Seillière, head of an employers' federation, addressed the audience in English. When challenged about his linguistic choice, he replied, 'I'm going to speak in English because that is the language of business'.

3. As noted by Alsagoff (Chapter 3 this volume), Malay is known as either *Bahasa Melayu* (i.e. the Malay language) or *Bahasa Malaysia* (i.e. the Malaysian language). The former label links the language to ethnicity and the latter to the nation and would parallel the name of the Malay language in Indonesia – *Bahasa Indonesia* (i.e. the Indonesian language).

4. When the federation of Malaysia was formed in 1963, Malaya came to be referred to as 'Peninsular Malaysia' or 'West Malaysia'.

5. Kuala Lumpur became a city only in 1972.

References

Asmah Haji Omar (1979), *Language Planning for Unity and Efficiency* (Kuala Lumpur: Penerbit Universiti Malaya).

Asmah Haji Omar (1996), 'Post-imperial English in Malaysia' in Joshua A. Fishman, Andrew W. Conrad and Alma Rubal-Lopez (eds), *Post-imperial English: Status Change in Former British and American colonies, 1940–1990* (Berlin: Mouton de Vruyter), pp. 513–33.

Block, David and Deborah Cameron (2002), 'Introduction' in David Block and Deborah Cameron (eds), *Globalization and Language Teaching* (London: Routledge), pp. 1–10.

Bourdieu, Pierre (1991), *Language and Symbolic Power* (Cambridge: Polity & Basil Blackwell).

Castells, Manuel (1993), 'The informational economy and the new international division of labor', in Martin Carnoy, Manuel Castells, Stephen S. Cohen and Fernando Henrique Cardoso (eds), *The New Global Economy in the Information Age: Reflections on Our Changing World* (University Park, PA: Pennsylvania State University Press).pp. 15–43.

Clyne, Michael G. (ed.) (1992), *Pluricentric Languages: Differing Norms in Different Nations* (Berlin: Mouton de Gruyter).

Crystal, David (2003), *English as a Global Language* (Second edition) (Cambridge: Cambridge University Press).

David, Maya Khemlani and Subra Govindasamy (2005), 'Negotiating a language policy for Malaysia: local demand for affirmative action versus challenges from globalization' in A. Suresh Canagarajah (ed.), *Reclaiming the Local in Language Policy and Practice* (Mahwah, NJ: Lawrence Erlbaum), pp. 123–45.

Engels, Friedrich and Karl Marx (1848), *Das Manifest der Kommunistischen Partei* (London). Translated into English, *The Communist Manifesto*, by Samuel Moore in 1888.

Fairclough, Norman (2000), 'Multiliteracies and language: orders of discourse and intertextuality' in Bill Cope and Mary Kalatzis (eds), *Multiliteracies: Literacy, Learning and the Design of Social Futures* (London: Routledge), pp. 162–81.

Gaudart, Hyacinth (1987), 'English language teaching in Malaysia: a historical account', *The English Teacher* XVI. Retrieved 17 July 2006, http://www.melta.org.my/ET/1987/main2.html

Giddens, Anthony (1990), *The Consequences of Modernity* (Cambridge: Polity Press).

Halliday, M. A. K. (2004), *An Introduction to Functional Grammar* (Third edition) (London: Arnold).

Hashim, Azirah (2003), 'Language policies and language education issues in Malaysia', in Jennifer Lindsay and Tan Ying Ying (eds), *Babel or Behemoth: Language Trends in Asia* (Singapore: Asia Research Institute), pp. 93–102.

Lankshear, Colin (1997), 'Language and the new capitalism', *International Journal of Inclusive Education* 1(4): 309–321.

Lau, Leslie (14 August 2002), 'Mahathir sees English healing inter-racial rift', *The Straits Times* (Singapore). Retrieved 14 August 2002,: http://straitstimes.asia1.com.sg

Leitner, Gerhard (1992), 'English as a pluricentric language' in Michael G. Clyne (ed.), (1992), *Pluricentric Languages: Differing Norms in Different Nations* (Berlin: Mouton de Gruyter), pp.179–238.

Nair-Venugopal, Shanta (2000), 'English, identity and the Malaysian workplace', *World Englishes* 19(2): 205–13.

Pandian, Ambigapathy (2003), 'English language teaching in Malaysia today', in Ho Wah Kam and Ruth Y L Wong (eds), *English Language Teaching in East Asia Today: Changing Policies and Practices* (Singapore: Eastern Universities Press), pp. 269–292.

Pereira, Brendan (3 December 2002), 'Malaysia mines the past for future harmony', *The Straits Times* (Singapore). Retrieved 3 December 2002, http://straitstimes.asia1.com.sg

Ramzy, Austin (2006), 'Go ahead, learn Mandarin', *Time* 167(25) (26 June 2006), pp. 16–22.

Schneider, Edgar W. (2007), *Postcolonial English: Varieties Around the World* (Cambridge: Cambridge University Press).

Solomon, J. S. (1988), *The Development of Bilingual Education in Malaysia* (Petaling Jaya: Pelanduk).

Watson, J. K. P. (1983), 'Cultural pluralism, nation-building and educational policies in Peninsular Malaysia', in Chris Kennedy (ed.), *Language Planning and Language Education* (London: George Allen & Unwin), pp. 133–150.

English in India: The Privilege and Privileging of Social Class

Rani Rubdy

Chapter Outline

This chapter examines the ways in which the politics of English and English language-in-education in India plays an invidious role in re-producing economic and social inequalities by reinforcing the hegemony of the privileged class and perpetuating certain social structures and practices that legitimize their privilege (Gramsci 1988). It traces the historical development that led to the unique position English occupies in India and attempts to eke out some of the complex issues relating to its role as symbolic capital by analysing its potential for the privileging of certain groups in India while shutting doors on others. Bringing the discussion forward to a rapidly globalizing and modernizing India that is undergoing enormous social and economic transformation, it suggests that a more nuanced analysis that integrates alternative conceptual and interdisciplinary frameworks may be called for in deconstructing the often paradoxically complex factors that contexts such as India present than the commodification framework that is currently favoured affords.

Introduction

The most perfect political community is one in which the middle class is in control,
and outnumbers both of the other classes.

Aristotle

Gurcharan Das, author of *India Unbound*, begins his chapter on the rise of
the middle class in India with this quotation, which aptly sums up the main
thesis of his book, namely, 'how a rich country became poor and will be rich
again' (2002: 348). He presents an insightful analysis of the tortuous economic
path India has trodden since it cast off the shackles of colonial rule, and paints
a highly optimistic picture of the transformation being wrought by India's
current economic and sociopolitical developments, following a 40-year long
period of staggering failure in its post-independence economic performance.
He attributes this transformation to the rise of a confident new middle class
that is 'full of energy and drive and [is] making things happen' (Das 2002:
280). According to Das, a true measure of India's failure in the past is not its
abysmal record of poverty but its lack of a true middle class. When India
became independent, the middle class was tiny – around 5 per cent of its
population. Since its economic growth in the 1980s and its acceleration after
the reforms in the 1990s, the middle class has tripled, although it is still less
than 20 per cent of the population. Speaking from an economist's perspective,
Das believes that with a dynamic and rapidly growing middle class pushing
the country's politicians to liberalize and globalize in its path of a liberal
market-based democracy, India, now unleashed like an imprisoned tiger, so to
speak, stands on the brink of the biggest economic transformation in its
history.

As the chapter aims to show, the emergence of a burgeoning Indian middle
class does not come unencumbered, however. In a country where two-thirds
of the people live in poverty and half are illiterate, and are ridden with an
infrastructure of the poorest quality – a situation made worse by a bureaucracy characterized by a tortuously slow pace of decision making – Indian
society is rife with many deep divides and chasms of inequality. If caste and
gender divisions characterize the oldest and most marked among these
inequalities in pre-colonial times, they are steadily being superseded by a new
set of inequities created by a rising new middle class, modernization, urbaniza-
tion, and more recently, the digital divide. And English, with a high premium

in linguistic and symbolic capital in an increasingly globalizing India, plays a significant role in creating and sustaining these divides.

Within the traditional Indian social system, the higher castes have always had more access to means of production, including better schooling, better jobs and more material and social goods, usually denied to the lower castes. The construct of caste in India thus exemplifies hegemonic practices that are historically associated with keeping the labouring or Shudra caste (officially called the Dalits and the Other Backward Classes or OBCs) in a disadvantaged position. Despite a strong affirmative action policy whereby slots are reserved for Dalits and OBCs in almost all walks of life – including education and employment – discrimination against them still exists (Ramanathan 1999: 215).

In the 19th century a new professional middle class emerged under the British rule with the introduction of the English language and Western education. This class produced not only clerks for the East India Company but also lawyers, teachers, engineers, doctors, bureaucrats – all the new professions that were required to run the country. Once they learned English and acquired an education, rewards and prestige were showered upon them. They became the new elite and closed ranks. But while the rise of a new English-educated, Westernized urban elite was matched by the decline of the powerful landed gentry, the position of the upper-caste Brahmins, however, remained secure since many of them took to English education, passed exams and became part of the new middle class.

Yet another divide is that between the urban and the rural population, created by the concentration of a large percentage of the English-speaking upper and middle classes in the urban centres. This has ensured that there are at least two cultures in India: the first, primarily rural and dominated by strong traditional Hindu beliefs; the second, an urban élite culture, comprising professionals, more modern, secular and cosmopolitan in outlook. Socially, culturally and economically distanced, the two communities inhabit separate worlds, with differing life styles and world views.

When we speak of English in India, it is worth noting that it is primarily this small but powerful percentage of upper- and middle-class Indians that English serves today as both economic and symbolic capital. As Lin and Martin (2005: 3) put it, English very often 'comes as a package with all these desirable "goodies", or it is the indispensable medium for bringing in and acquiring these goodies'. Owing to the emphasis laid on the instrumental value of English right from its introduction into colonial India, English has always been associated with social aspiration for some sections of Indian society. However, English symbolic capital remains unevenly distributed across different social groups. Today English continues to rule supreme as the language of power and privilege associated with the newly emergent and increasingly influential middle class, engendering connotations of cultural superiority and imperialism which, while working to their advantage, disadvantages the vast majority who have limited access to English.

The market value of the English-conversant middle class is high indeed. Its association with educational, economic and social success, and the identification of this successful socioeconomic group with the fast rising middle classes has motivated the millions of have-nots in India to seek to emulate the life styles, the mind sets, and the world views of the Indian middle class. And since one of the key characteristics that distinguishes this class is their English-medium education background and/or the fluency of their English-speaking skills, there is at present a kind of 'craze' to learn English at any cost. This trend clearly disadvantages those who get their education mainly through the vernacular medium (VM), both minimizing their life chances and chances of social success. English thus stands at the core of class-based inequalities (intricately intertwined with caste and gender dimensions in India) which often manifest themselves in the English–Vernacular divide.

Historical context of English language education in India

There are many reasons why English has such a dominant role in Indian society. Historically, India was the 'jewel' of the British Empire, following extensive trading with England in the era of the East India Company and then about 150 years of British rule. But it is not due merely to the British presence in India and the use of English in modern India. There were conscious decisions on the part of the British imperial administration that ensured the widespread use of English in government, law and education.

English was first introduced to Indians when the colonial masters found they needed a class of bilingual linguistic middlemen to mediate between the English-speaking ruling class and the indigenous language-speaking subjects. In creating a cadre of people to assist the colonial government by working in subordinate positions and act as the buffer between the rulers and the masses, the rulers had to make sure that the subjects would acquire the necessary knowledge and skills, scientific and social, as well as the moral values and world view that would ensure allegiance to the colonial government. There were also political considerations: to make the local population 'more English than Hindus' (as stated in the now infamous Minutes of Macaulay). As is well known, 'the content and goal of education were dictated by the need to produce consenting subjects to serve the interests of the colonial government. They also aimed at moulding their minds by negating their native values and knowledge and substituting them with European values that were accepted as superior' (Annamalai 2005: 22). Given these objectives, English, in which the European knowledge and values of enlightenment were encoded and in which the administrative skills needed for governance were available, was the obvious choice as the language to be taught and the medium of teaching.

Under what came to be known as the Anglicist position, English-medium education was made available selectively to the upper segment of the Indian population (to keep government expenditure on English-medium education low and contain any feelings of political disquiet that might arise from the failure of English-educated subjects in obtaining employment), who in turn, as teachers and opinion-makers, would impart European knowledge and values to the masses through the medium of the vernaculars. This strategy, which was meant to create a new elite that was loyal to the colonial government, clearly had an assimilatory goal. Analysing the basis for adopting this strategy of elitist education, Annamalai comments: '(T)he medium and content of education became an instrument for the control of minds and the assimilation of behaviour. Thus the question of medium of instruction became an integral part of the principle and purpose of governing' (Annamalai 2004: 180–81).

The recruitment of Indians for the civil service in the colonial government in order to offset the rising administrative cost of governing India, clerical employment in the government and the new industries, and positions in professions such as law, medicine, accounting and teaching, all obtained through English-medium education, created a new urban elite among Indians. The new elite became part of the ruling class, and the nexus between the foreign rulers and the general population. They also gained access to power, wealth and status.

Commenting on the way the introduction of English transformed Indian public life, Khilani states: 'It obviously divided the British rulers from their Indian subjects; it also divided Indians themselves, between those who could speak English, who knew their Dicey from their Dickens, and those who did not' (Khilani 1998: 44).

Das is scathingly critical in his description of the pretentiousness that characterized the intellectual and cultural snobbery of the English-educated bourgeoisie of this period, leading them to devalue their Indian roots and identity:

> We are Macaulay's children, not Manu's. Our ambivalence goes back to that day when Macaulay persuaded the British government to teach English to Indians. . . . Our inner lives are a parody. We have one foot in India, the other in the West, and we belong to neither. We speak a hodgepodge of English and our regional language, the combination varying with the status of the listener. When speaking to a servant or a shopkeeper, our verbal brew leans towards the local language; with a peer we are capable of invoking the purest English. We are alienated from the mass of our people. We mouth platitudes about Indian culture without having read the classics in Sanskrit. Instead we read *Time* magazine to 'keep up'. We are touchy about India and look to the West for inspiration and recognition. (Das 2002: 283)

It should be noted, however, that although assimilation in the sense of co-opting the native elite into the government and to the ideology of European Enlightenment was successful, the economic and political outcomes were contrary to the goal of assimilation of the ideology of acceptance of the legitimacy of the colonial government by the local population. English education, besides opening avenues of employment, also opened entry to university education to Indians from 1857, when the first three universities were established. Western education provided the stimulus for the most dramatic change in the minds of Indians in a thousand years as Indians embraced Western knowledge with vigour, with English functioning as their 'window on the world'. Das is quick to point to the rich irony whereby while English introduced to Indian minds the liberal ideas and ideals of the French Revolution, the British empire was practising the opposite through colonial rule, thus stirring nationalist ideas of emancipation generated through English. 'Schools and colleges taught liberty and equality while the rulers practiced subjugation and inequality. After college the same students joined the nationalist movement. By introducing English in India, the British dug their own graves' (Das 2002: 11).

The requirement of proficiency in English as a condition for admission into universities increased the demand for English-medium education in schools, ensuring the downward spread of English-medium education, which in turn was accelerated by the missionary schools. These schools whose primary goal was bringing about 'moral improvement' of the masses started out by using the vernaculars as the media of instruction in order to take the gospels directly to the people but soon turned to providing English-medium education so as to be able to attract upper-caste students.

Significantly, the political objective of imparting knowledge and skills to the population that serve the interests of the ruling elite has not changed in post-colonial India. At the time of independence in 1947, the consensus was that English would be replaced as the medium of education by Indian languages throughout the secondary level. This was in line with the pro-vernacular sentiments that prevailed at the time, inspired partly by Gandhi's views of providing all children the right to an education in their mother tongue, as reflected partly in the formal stance adopted by the National Policy on Education (Ministry of Education 1968). However, since the Constitution did not specify any time frame for the change, despite the recommendations of the various education committees and commissions constituted by the government of India both immediately before and after independence, the lack of a definitive time frame allowed the government to drag its feet in implementing this decision, reflecting its general ambivalence and casual attitude towards the medium-of-education policy.

Several other factors came together to divert attention from the serious implementation of the change over to Indian vernacular languages on the part of the government, besides this lack of commitment. These include the flexibility that individual states typically exercise in relation to the use of Indian languages as the medium of education across levels of education and across states and conflicting political interests which often force the government to make compromises with regard to vernacular language medium education. As a result, the VM policy is often compromised when alternative sources of schooling are allowed to operate, such as those established by the Central Board of Education and the private Matriculation schools in the state of Tamilnadu, which adopt English as the medium of instruction for different reasons, including parental and political pressures (Annamalai 2004).

Today, of the 200-odd languages that actively contribute to making India a functionally multilingual country and not just demographically so, 41 languages are available for study in the school curriculum (NCERT 1999, cited in Annamalai 2004: 177) to be learned as first, second and third language under what is known as the 'three language formula'. The first language in most cases is the mother tongue or regional language (generally the official language of the state or a minority language different from that of the state). The second language is English and the third language is Hindi (where it is not the regional language). English is the only language taught in all states as first, second and third language and it is taught in the largest number of schools. From one point of view, making English compulsory in Indian schools has rendered hundreds and thousands of children handicapped. According to some scholars (Chatterjee 1992: 302), apart from being educationally unsound to use a foreign language, it is a negation of democracy because it divides the Indian people into two nations: the few who govern and the many who are governed.

Such is the legacy of British colonialism that strong parental demand for English-medium schools persists in the belief that learning through an Indian language will disadvantage students because they will not be able to access modern knowledge, which is mostly encoded in English. Furthermore, it is feared that this disadvantage will hinder their efforts to seek educational and economic opportunities in developed English-speaking countries (Annamalai 2004: 188). Thus its currency as the language of educational and socioeconomical advancement and a vehicle of modernity makes English the dominant resource in the symbolic market (Bourdieu 1991) in India. Students are keenly aware of the importance and value of English for future studies and jobs. Business corporations prefer employees with a good command of English to employees with a good command of either Hindi or any of the regional languages. Most importantly, English remains the sole medium of instruction in most universities, in prestigious science colleges and professional training programmes. The pull of English in post-independent India is thus remarkably strong, desired alike by urban poor and rural parent, whether in the slums of Bombay (now Mumbai) where the English-medium school is a prestige symbol (Phillipson 1992: 27) or the most socially backward parts of West Bengal where parents have a keen understanding of the competitive nature of life chances.

English language-in-education policy (EM) validates the role of English while devaluing VM education and simultaneously sending implicit messages about the low regard the vernacular holds, as described by Ramanathan:

> All 'prestigious', science-based disciplines at the tertiary level such as computer science, engineering, the hard sciences, pharmacy and medicine seem to be available only in English. This means that if the English proficiency of students educated in the vernacular is deemed insufficient at the end of the 12th grade, which by and large is the case, they are denied access to these 'prestigious' disciplines. Furthermore, in instances where VM students are admitted to EM colleges they face the uphill task of not only taking classes with their EM counterparts,

> but of having to take the same set of state-mandated examinations in English.
> In many cases, this proves to be insurmountable for many low-income VM students
> and many of them drop out of the educational system during and after college.
> (Ramanathan 2005: 6)

The continuance of EM in education at school level and near exclusively at college and university levels thus marginalises VM students and defeats the policy goal of nation-building with equal educational opportunities for all. Nor is the divisiveness it creates conducive to building a cohesive nation (Annamalai 2005: 27).

Some scholars maintain that English in India no longer coexists with other languages in a complementary relationship but seems to have acquired such a privileged status that literacy in local indigenous languages is threatened (Dua 1996). The Indian government has tried to balance English language teaching with the teaching of other languages by promoting the teaching of regional languages, including the students' L1 and Hindi as an official language. However, due partly to the government's ambivalent attitude and the lack of a strong infrastructure that supports the study of the regional languages, such as adequate reading materials and administrative autonomy, VM education has acquired inferior connotations and is seen as a less attractive option. One study that compares students' reactions towards English and regional languages as media of instruction concludes that a 'fear of being treated as an inferior category among the educated unless the courses are taken in the English medium' is an important factor in 'their aversion to the regional language medium' (Jayaram 1992: 103, cited in Ramanathan 1999: 227).

In sum, under British colonialism, English was not meant to be a social equalizer. After independence, English remained as the language of government, law and commerce, modern rational knowledge and progress, and this helped to consolidate its power and prestige. At the individual level, its supremacy has been reinforced by its privileged association with employment opportunity, career advancement, material achievement and a premier place in the educational system, especially in higher education. Thus, as Annamalai observes, 'contrary to the claim that schooling is a means of leveling social differences, a two-language system of education in schools, one with English language medium for the select few and another with Indian language medium for the masses, perpetuates social inequality and creates social tension' (Annamalai 2004: 190). Paradoxically, the socioeconomic inequality is taken by many in a way that substantiates the belief in the necessity of English for one's economic and social survival and success, hence reinforcing the power and dominance of English.

English in India **131**

The currency of English as symbolic capital in postcolonial India

The notion of cultural capital (Bourdieu and Passeron 1977; Bourdieu 1991) has been used by educationists (e.g. Delpit 1988; Lin 1996; Luke 1996) 'to describe the disadvantaged position of ethnic and linguistic minorities and to problematize the notion that state education in modern societies is built on meritocracy and equal opportunity' (Lin 1996: 394). Defining cultural capital to include language use, skills and orientations, attitudes, dispositions and schemes of perception that a child is endowed with by virtue of socialization in her/his family and community, Bourdieu argued that familial socialization bestows on children of the socioeconomic elite the right kind of cultural capital (also called habitus) for school success. Children from disadvantaged groups, with a habitus incompatible with that presupposed in school, are not competing with equal starting points with children of the socioeconomic elite. They are placed in an unfair game where the rules are already laid down by the privileged class who are way ahead of them in the race. Hence, the reproduction of social stratification.

The key to understanding the socially divisive role that English plays in India lies in understanding the two major features associated with situations of symbolic domination (Bourdieu 1991): first, the formation of a language-in-education policy that legitimized and consolidated the place English occupies today in the symbolic market, as discussed in the previous section. Second, the perpetuation of the uneven distribution of symbolic capital across different social groups, with the dominated group having the most limited access to symbolic resources, an aspect I turn to in this section.

In the socioeducational landscape of India, English and the privileges associated with it remain inaccessible to those who are disadvantaged because of their economic situation, their caste, or both. As a result, English is increasingly implicated in the production of socioeconomic disadvantage and new subaltern identities, opening up life opportunities and possibilities for some, while closing doors and erecting barriers for others. The divisive nature of English is thus at the core of class-based inequalities, its differential value being most strongly located in the English–Vernacular divide. In India, students are generally educated either in EM or VM schools. While theoretically all students can 'choose' which types of school they want to attend, such 'choice' is socially conditioned because of a number of intersecting factors, including socioeconomic and familial reasons. EM schools are generally well funded and provide English immersion to students, who already have access to English symbolic capital in the home and out of class. These students have the good fortune (literally in terms of wealth and also metaphorically) to receive instruction from well-trained teachers familiar with up-to-date methodologies and classroom techniques, whereas those who study English as a subject in the VM schools are often taught by teachers with inadequate training or qualifications who resort to outdated methods of teaching, and who in turn, receive little support by way of enhancing their professional skills.

Referring to the immense power/knowledge differential that exists between those who have access to English and those who do not, Ramanathan (1999), in her study on the English–Vernacular divide in Gujarat, likens the privileges associated with EM education to the unequal power relations that reside between the inner and outer circles of countries (Kachru 1985) that result from the privileged standard-setting position of inner circle countries (Phillipson 1992; Pennycook 1994). She observes how even within an outer circle country such as India, an English-related inner–outer power dichotomy appears to exist, where the Indian middle class assumes a position of relative power through access to English in Circle 1, with Dalit or lower-caste students and students from so-called Other Backward Classes (OBCs) placed in Circle 2 (Figure 8.1).

The Dalits and the OBC students, who are also typically the most economically and educationally handicapped, are unable to acquire proficiency in English because they lack the requisite cultural orientation, or habitus, to use Bourdieu's term. When these students enter tertiary education on the fringes of Circle 2 with poor English language skills, they seem to struggle more

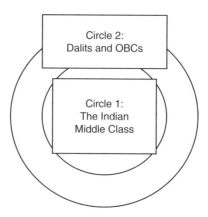

Figure 8.1 Inner and Outer Circles of Power in India (from Ramanathan 1999).

than others. The importance of developing English language skills for future studies and jobs is well understood among students even though the government is careful not to overtly stress the importance of English above the indigenous languages for political reasons. They, however, often find English difficult to learn, uninteresting and irrelevant to their daily life. Deep in the rural interiors of India, similarly, students find themselves forced to learn English and have mixed feelings towards it. They live in a lifeworld where few have adequate linguistic resources to use English and even if they had, they would find it unnatural and pompous using it. They are thus placed in a frustrating dilemma, universally recognizing the importance of English for their future but at the same time having little access to the symbolic capital necessary for successfully acquiring it. Ramanathan notes the irony of their predicament as follows:

> These are the students most in need of English yet English seems farthest from them. Their economically disadvantaged status does not permit them to enroll in language classes in the city, nor does it afford them access to other realia available to learners in Circle 1: the Internet, newspapers, TV shows in English, and English movies. They realize more and more that they need to be computer literate for the simplest of jobs, but to gain access to knowledge about computers they have to first become fluent in English – that is, they have to develop the language that allows them to enter and become part of Circle 1. For most, however, their worst fears become reality: they never really gain fluency in English or entry into that circle and thus never become qualified for the jobs they desire. (Ramanathan 1999: 228–29)

Similarly, describing the advantage of EM in higher education and employment as a mirage for a majority of students who receive poor education and whose command of English is poor in the end, Annamalai, cautions that the often cited success stories of Indian students who get into professional, managerial and academic positions, nationally and internationally because of their mastery of both English and subject knowledge can be misleading:

> These highly successful students are most likely to have studied through English medium in well-funded schools. They are also likely to have come from families that have used English as a second language for at least one preceding generation and to have had exposure to reading materials and conversations at home. These students already have a solid cultural and linguistic foundation in English; their education merely supplements this advantage . . . A much larger population is made up of first-generation learners from poor families, who do not have access to the same kind of support at home as their middle class counterparts. Thus, a

social advantage for the minority of students has been misleadingly projected as
the advantage of English-medium education. (Annamalai 2004: 189)

Ramanathan demonstrates how the two types of schools – EM and VM –
generate two broad sets of class-based and class-indexed ideologies and practices which 'slot students into invisible grooves' (Ramanathan 2005: 38), and
which create and sustain well-entrenched 'gulfs' and 'chasms' in Indian society.
She attrributes the privileged access that the Indian middle-class student has
to English literacy to what she calls a shared *assumptions nexus* – 'a collective
syndrome of values, assumptions, perspectives, motivations, behaviours and
world view that the middle class has by sheer virtue of just being so, a nexus
that seems to remain out of reach for low-income vernacular medium students'
(Ramanathan 2005: 6) – much like Bourdieu's notion of habitus. She goes on
to describe how macro-structures such as institutional and larger state- and
nationwide policies as well as curricular and pedagogical materials align 'in
specific ways so as simultaneously to engage in combined relations of power to
empower the upper and middle classes in particular social ways that directly
yield certain social goods' (Ramanathan 2005: 6). The *assumption nexus* is thus
a construct that helps to explore the ways in which the values and aspirations
of the Indian middle class dovetail with this complex socioeducational system
and to explain how the overall apparatus works to maintain the status quo.

This hegemony of the middle class is further strengthened by particular
socioeducational structures and practices that have become firmly entrenched.
Some of the institutional practices which keep English out of reach of the lower
income and lower caste groups and push them into the outer circle include
practices such as (a) tracking students into college-level streams that bar some
students from EM instruction; (b) teaching English literature rather than the
English language throughout India, which limits English to the elite and middle class; and (c) using grammar translation methods, all of which inhibit the
communicative competence of these students and help to keep them in their
disadvantaged positions and out of Circle 1.

For instance, that the teaching of English literature has deeply entrenched
roots in the Indian soil from colonial times is common knowledge. But those
familiar with Viswanathan's (1994) analysis of the beginnings of English literary studies in India would also know how the development of what counted as
'education' and 'literature' in Indian schools was intimately tied up with colonial power relations and the creation of docile colonial subjects. Ramanathan's
(2005) study shows how current practices in literature teaching in the Indian
context become not only entirely counter-productive but assume a neocolonial

impact, when they become associated with gatekeeping functions in streaming students, when they force teachers to resort to translation methods instead of a meaningful interpretation of texts and spawn the widespread use of study guides and rote memorization, and when they create cultural dissonance and alienation between students and the overly Western themes found in the course material. Her depiction of the complexity and conflict surrounding literature teaching, which places the EM and VM students in 'unequal grooves', and devalues the vernacular, ties in with Viswanathan's historical account of the development of a construction of an English literature 'canon' in India as a form of social, cultural and political control.

Thus, although motivation to learn English is very strong, the cumulative effect of practices such as those described by Ramanathan combined with the poor infrastructure and quality of instruction available to them keep the poorest and most disadvantaged students from learning it. A compounding factor is the lack of autonomy on the part of both institutions and teachers. This partially explains why much of the teaching is exams oriented, why teachers opt for particular methods, why the students resort to memorizing and using study guides to get through the exams as well as why English-speaking skills are not emphasized (Ramanathan 1999: 228). Learning English in this way is not only high in social and intellectual cost. It is also highly counter-productive.

The domination of the symbolic market by English and the perpetuation of the uneven distribution of English linguistic capital has continued to construct 'social failures' out of the majority of the children in India. There is a widening gap between the rich and the poor and educational researchers cannot ignore the role played by educational institutions, policies and practices in the reproduction of social stratification based on the possession or the lack of a mastery of English.

The dynamics of global structures and local markets

If English has been a key tool of ideological subjugation and social oppression in colonial times, creating as it did Westernized colonial subjects whose tastes and sensibilities betrayed their indigenous make-up, in today's era of globalization its potential for domination is almost limitless. Globalization has made the borders of the nation state more porous and reinstated the importance of the English language for all communities, through multinationals, market forces, pop culture, cyber space and digital technology. Riding on the wave of globalization and the forces of global capital, and abetted by resources of the media, the internet and satellite communication, the 'soft power' of English neocolonialism is positioned to control minds even more completely, as Annamalai notes, 'not by coercion but by seduction' (2005: 33). The cultural violence that the pursuit of imperialistic and capitalist goals can wreak has been attested by scholars such as Giddens (1991), Phillipson (1992), Pennycook (1994), Fairclough (1999) and Canagarajah (1999).

In India's case though, the fear of cultural homogenization is perhaps of less immediate concern, given India's cultural vibrancy and its capacity to accommodate creatively to non-indigenous influences without losing its own identity and distinctiveness. Indians are not easily persuaded to give up their cultural roots even after migrating to powerful, developed countries of the West, but tend to foster indigenous linguistic and cultural mores and take much pride in passing them on to their offspring. The additive nature of English-bilingualism in India is a case in point, wherein Indians have appropriated the English language and made it one of their own, nativizing and hybridizing it in inventive ways in a seamless blending that Bruthiaux (Chapter 1 this volume) refers to as a potential benefit to be welcomed, provided of course that cultural continuity is safeguarded. As Annamalai observes, the attitudinal integration with English culture associated with English language-in-education during the colonial period is therefore politically irrelevant to postcolonial India. Nor has the motivation for learning English been purely, or mainly, economic, as in the case of Singapore, for instance (Wee, Chapter 2 this volume). A combination of various forces – economic, political, intellectual and social – has propelled the craze for English, successfully marketed as the language of development, modernity, and scientific and technological advancement.

For most Indians the primary motivation for learning English has been instrumental rather than an integrative one (Gardner and Lambert 1972; Agnihotri and Khanna 1997). English has long held sway as a 'library language', or the language of knowledge acquisition (Tickoo 1996). Consequently, English is the language in which most of the academic material is published and the number of Indian publishing firms makes the country one of the leading publishers of English language books in the world. Indeed, as Kurzon comments '[T]o be educated tends to be synonymous with the ability to speak fluent English. Any chance meeting with an academically educated Indian will naturally be conducted in English. Internal migration among different states of the Union further strengthens the status of English not only as a library language or a link language, but as an all-Indian language, more so than any other language spoken in India apart from Hindi' (Kurzon 2004: 18–19).

There is, however, as Annamalai notes, a new kind of cultural integration in which English plays a pivotal role, that of class culture, with its distinctive group behaviour, ideas about life and view of the world, and it is disseminated to the members of the class by English. 'English is the cross-linguistic symbol of the identity and solidarity of this class, which is economically the middle and upper class of the country' (Annamalai 2005: 32). He goes on to state:

> English has also assumed a role in another kind of cultural integration, which puts a premium on what is called global culture, but which is heavily drawn from Western cultural values . . . . English is the key to this overpowering culture that offers material rewards to its adherents. This cultural role of English marks down the value of nation-building, in the cultural sphere through identification with Indian languages. The ideological and behavioural integration with Europe planned through the language in education policy in the colonial period re-enters in the guise of global integration,

with English playing the same instrumental role (Annamalai 2005: 32).

This inter-connectedness of English with a global culture that supersedes the national and ethnic cultures, not only works to heighten its seductive power. With all the social selection mechanisms unchanged which use the mastery of English as the chief screening and gatekeeping measure for access to higher education and the recruitment of professionals in job settings, it ensures that the parents', students', teachers' and principals' as also the employers' and the company executive's choices are necessarily constrained under the hegemonic effect of the dominance of English in a way that the mechanisms of social mobility are newly re-legitimized in the postcolonial era by the discourses of globalization.

Such trends justify the view held by critical theorists that '[G]lobalization has given more opportunities for the extremely wealthy to make money more quickly . . . In fact, globalization is a paradox: while it is very beneficial to a few, it leaves out or marginalizes two-thirds of the world's population' (Kavanagh, cited in Lin and Martin 2005: 7). And that it is elusive to the most disadvantaged members of a society because they are positioned to reap the least benefits from it:

> While the cosmopolitan multilingual elite well-versed in global English and new knowledge technologies (often mediated through global English) can find jobs anywhere across the globe (i.e. gaining transnational mobility), those monolingual

locals who never catch on to the new skills and new languages (often due to lack of class-based capital and habitus) are ever more locked up in non-mobility both geographically and socioeconomically. (Lin and Martin 2005: 8)

From this perspective, it seems clear that like the discourse of opportunity, a discourse of equality is being used to justify English as a soft option and the emergence of a new middle class.

Not everyone shares this perception of globalization or of the hegemonial potential of English in perpetuating it, however, and I return here to Gurcharan Das's prediction, referred to at the beginning of this chapter, namely, that India's prosperity will increase in proportion to the extent of increase of its middle class. Dismissing the gloom-and-doom vision of globalization as a spectre that university-based post-modernist thinkers in particular like to raise, Das's primary concern is with the economic potential of globalization for India's development agenda, perceiving its function as a lever to revitalize the economy and generate tangible social change by effecting a break from past inefficiencies and incapacities that stifled and suppressed the nation's economic growth.

Thus, analysing the situation from an economist' point of view, Das sees globalization as a fresh new opportunity that can work to India's advantage precisely on account of the number of people available in India today who are English-speaking bilinguals. Das rues the fact that in the post-independence era of development and re-structuring, India was miserably left behind by the East Asian 'tiger economies' when it skipped the industrial revolution, owing partly to stubbornly persisting with an inward-looking socialist model of development, which protected local industries and the slow-paced implementation of its reforms. Noting the curious historical inversion wherein unlike many democratic countries in the West, India embraced democracy first and capitalism much later, he observes that the making of money was never a priority for Indians. But there are reasons to rejoice – one of them being what he terms 'the commercialization of Indian society'. This time round it is the educated young in India's largest cities who are leading the change. And this commercial spirit, in his view, is not just limited to the cities; the smallest village has found it. He visualizes a 'trickle down effect', particularly when, given that the discourse of knowledge can only be effective to the extent that it is congruent with the discourse of power, these developments are accompanied by decentralization, with the local self-government (*panchayat raj*) emancipating the Indian village politically. The lively informal economic activity gathering force in these villages marks a healthy proactive spirit that is capable of leading the people from endemic poverty to empowerment and better living conditions. As the rewards of economic growth penetrate downward he is optimistic that more people will share in the prosperity.

In Das's view, the present change from an industrial to a global information economy speaks to India's advantage. For one thing, the new economy is largely a service economy and creates more jobs, unlike the cost-cutting, downsizing and mechanizing economy of the past. Besides, because in today's global economy a country's status is determined by the share of brains that it uses, he contends that India with its vast intellectual capital is in an excellent position to provide knowledge workers to the global economy and benefit from the knowledge revolution. The communications revolution is creating masses of job opportunities in India. For instance, helped by cheap telecommunication networks and English language-speaking skills, the call centre industry, which employs about half a million people between 20 and 26 years, is already girded to sell itself as the face of globalized India. India's advantage over other countries is that English is pervasive and call centre operators have found that it takes only 6 weeks to get Indians talking with an American accent. Increasingly, powered by the knowledge sectors of economy, India's emerging success in information technology is yet further evidence of its competitive edge. India's software companies have the best computer engineers in the world and Indian entrepreneurs in Silicon Valley are at the heart of the internet revolution. The internet has levelled the playing field, promising to make up for past inefficiencies (Friedman 2006). Aggressive recruiting by global companies have pushed the programming wages in the homegrown software industry in India and the fact that the number of workers for these companies have doubled in the course of 12 months (March 2004–2005) with a 7 per cent increase in average revenue productivity makes for impressive statistics, reflecting a whole new reality. The software and outsourcing boom has also resulted in an environment that has drawn to India research centres from across the world. Das therefore argues that the spread of information technology is an opportunity to overcome historical disabilities and compress the time needed to reach important developmental goals. And what makes all this possible is India's universities, which produce 2.5 million fresh graduates every year who have varying levels of proficiency in English, while India's business schools provide around 89,000 MBAs per year. With India's competitive advantage in the new knowledge economy, it may in the end have been all right to skip the industrial revolution.

Similar views have been put forward by Thomas Friedman (2006), author of the international bestseller, *The World is Flat*, who argues that globalization has gone to a whole new level in the 21st century. Dividing the era of globalization roughly into three broad periods, he identifies brawn as the key driving force in Globalization 1.0 (from 1492, when Columbus set sail, opening trade between the Old World and the New World – until 1800) – that is, 'how much muscle, how much horsepower, wind power or, later, steam power your country had and how creatively you could deploy it'. In the second era (roughly from 1800 to 2000), Globalization 2.0, the dynamic force driving global integration was multinational companies spearheaded by the Industrial Revolution and breakthroughs in hardware – that is, from steamships and railways in the beginning to telephones and mainframe computers towards the end. But, he argues, while in Globalization 1.0 it was countries globalizing and in Globalization 2.0 it was companies globalizing, the dynamic force in Globalization 3.0 that gives it its unique character is the newfound power for *individuals* to collaborate and compete globally. And the phenomenon that is enabling, empowering, and enjoining individuals and small groups to compete in this way is what he calls the *flat-world platform*, because of its powerful potential to level the playing field. What is more, Globalization 3.0 differs from the previous eras not only in how it is shrinking and flattening the world and how it is empowering individuals. But, he maintains, while in the previous eras 'it was Western countries, companies and explorers who were doing most of the globalizing and shaping of the system, . . . Globalization 3.0 is going to be driven not only by individuals but also by a much more diverse – non-Western, non-white – group of individuals . . . and you are going to see every color of the human rainbow take part' (Friedman 2006: 9–11).

Friedman's predictions find empirical endorsement in Nayar's (2006) recent monograph *India's Globalization: Evaluating the Economic Impact*, excerpted by Yale Global Online (1 February 2007). Compared to the derisively termed 'Hindu' rate of growth of 3.4 per cent over the period 1956 to 1975, in the dozen years from 1995 to 2007 the growth rate has been over 6.5 per cent; and during the last four years, an unprecedented average growth rate of over 8 per cent. Nayar concludes: '[C]ontrary to the position of the critics, globalization has served as the agent of deliverance for India from economic stagnation and perpetual economic crises even as it has reduced poverty. However, India continues to be dogged by deep-seated societal problems that persisted throughout the autarkic period. But it is precisely the accelerated growth generated by globalization that has provided the additional resources to alleviate, if not yet to remove, them.'

This analysis seems to run counter to the approach I have adopted so far which associates the politics of English language education in India with socially and culturally undesirable consequences as viewed within the commodification of language framework. Yet the perspective put forward by economists such as Das is worthy of serious consideration not just because it is extremely interesting and persuasive but in that it presents an alternative conception. Das's analysis of current developments in the Indian economy, and the high regard with which he views English's role in them, provides a good example, noted by Bruthiaux (2002), of the disparity between the views held by mainstream economists and many critical theorists and applied linguists. Commenting on the tendency of these two parties to operate independently of each other, Bruthiaux points out that while many applied linguists see the phenomenon of globalization as nothing but having negative linguistic consequences, they show a general reluctance to engage more deeply with the views held by mainstream economists, or to examine the factual basis of the debate. He argues for the need to adopt a greater plurality of positions and suggests that if we take a more nuanced view of the spread of English and its effect on local cultures and languages, it is possible to see globalization as a process of social and cultural transformation, liberation even. Listening to what mainstream economists are saying will also help invigorate the debate.

Das, for instance argues that, rather than condemn developments such as the global information revolution and economic liberalization as the 'pathology of modernization', one might be persuaded to accept that modernization offers the only opportunity for the majority of Indian people to raise themselves to a decent standard of living: 'To eschew modernization is to condemn the masses to degrading poverty and the injustices of caste in our traditional society'. Hence, paradoxical though it may seem to critical theorists and applied linguists, the conclusion he comes to is that the only way for India to prevent economic stagnation and achieve prosperity is by increasing its middle class:

> When half the population in society is middle class, its politics will change, its world view will be different, its poor will be fewer, and society will have greater means to look after them. Thus, to focus on the middle class is to focus on prosperity, unlike in the past, when our focus has been on redistributing poverty. This does not mean that one is callous. On the contrary, the whole purpose of the enterprise is to lift the poor – and lift them into the middle class. (Das 2002: 252)

Understandably, many are sceptical about India's ability to succeed in th knowledge economy or its ability to spread the rewards of its success t the masses. There are contending views about India's entry into global compe tition and trade even among Indian thinkers. The critical questions bein asked are: 'Is international trade a public good for all participants? Or is it mor accurately seen as a zero-sum game, where certain nations and groups prospe at the expense of others?' (Khilani 1998: 206). Even if one discounts the fac that Indian software programmers are earning one-fifth the wages paid in th West, and that the youngsters employed at the call centres risk losing their cul tural moorings while being urged to learn more about Western lifestyles an imitate Western accents in order to gain the approval of their clients, how wil a few thousand 'knowledge workers' transform the destinies of a billion people particularly when 40 per cent are illiterate and the infrastructure crying out t be overhauled? For a majority of working-class Indians, English remains some thing beyond their reach. Unlike their middle-class counterparts, they typicall live in a lifeworld where few will, or can, use English for any authentic commu nicative or sociocultural purposes. Besides, as Bruthiaux rightly asserts, for large majority of the poor L1 literacy is the essential factor because they neec the basic skills to participate in their local economies, not the English that i needed for participating in the global economy (Bruthiaux 2002).

To be fair, Das is throughout passionate in his zeal for alleviating India' poverty. He is of the firm view that if indeed there is one thing that coulc secure India's future, it is the vigorous attention to building human capabili ties – and that the most effective means of doing this is to unleash the powei of human capital through education (Das 2005: 226). He contends that attain ing success in the knowledge economy will necessitate both the expansion o primary education and improving the quality of higher education – whereas the Indian state's failure in these areas has been glaring. In the post-indepen dence years, led by the notion that modernization meant greater attention t advanced research and development, the country's scarce educational resource: were devoted entirely to furthering tertiary education while the more urgen needs of primary education, particularly for women, were put on hold. Despitc this disproportionate channelling of funds to higher education, tertiary edu cation at present is in the doldrums while primary education has only recently begun to be given serious thought. Accordingly, in his recommendations foi reforms towards a more liberalized economy, Das rightly argues that the mos powerful and immediate reform for the poor is more and better primary schools – a need long neglected by the government in its concern to prioritize higher education. Not being an applied linguist, Das does not go into the details of what this education must constitute, except to recognize simply that English's position as the tool of choice for worldwide communication is unassailable at a time when the shift towards a global information economy is intensifying (Warschauer 2000). In the end, neither English for all, nor for a select few, may be the solution. Recognizing the importance of English, while actively cultivating and encouraging the development of the indigenous vernaculars, and providing a better quality of education in both is the goal to strive for. As Annamalai puts it: 'The greatest challenge for education in post-colonial India and the choice of language for delivering new education is in combining inculcation of self-pride with self-criticism, of cultural rootedness with cosmopolitanism, and of modernization with tradition' (Annamalai 2005: 37).

Conclusion

The chapter aimed to eke out some of the complex issues relating to the hegemony of English in its role as symbolic capital by examining its potential for the privileging of certain groups in India while shutting doors on others. I have not attempted to offer solutions, or touch on those being worked out by the participants themselves in negotiating or resisting the hegemonical effects of English dominance. This is not to say that the politics of English is without resistance and struggle. The marginalized and oppressed peoples are not entirely powerless, and happily, English's divisive role has not gone uncontested. The counter-discourses to the politics of English are evident from the rhetoric of the anti-colonial struggle; and the English–Vernacular divide, which is only one aspect of its unequal practice in the social cog, 'continues to be resisted, mitigated and bridged' as has been described in Ramanathan's recent noteworthy study (2005). Such responses to oppression show that institutions and individuals are capable of negotiating their destinies with and within the system, in both creative and constructive ways. Das (2002) too provides examples of how the socially oppressed have shown remarkable skills of endurance, resilience and entrepreneurship in overcoming overwhelming odds to achieve economic independence where the state had miserably failed them.

While there is little doubt that the linguistic consequences of globalization at its worst can be 'profoundly unjust because it serves the interests of one side at the expense of the other, and that it must therefore be resisted', it is possible to envisage globalization as a process of social and cultural revitalization and liberation, that has the effect of 'raising individuals and groups out of limiting or even damaging mindsets and reorienting them in novel and potentially beneficial directions' (Bruthiaux, Chapter 1 this volume). Though this view may appear controversial, resonating as it does with the 'corporate-friendly stance of mainstream economists', travelling between different disciplinary perspectives in examining the interplay of English and the new global and local markets should help develop interilluminating lenses (Lin 2005: 52) for the study of language-in-education policies in particular settings.

References

Agnihotri, R. K. and A. L. Khanna (1997), *Problematizing English in India* (New Delhi: Sage).

Annamalai, E. (2004), 'Medium of power: The question of English in education in India' in, James W. Tollefson and Amy Tsui (eds), *Medium of Instruction Policies: Which Agenda? Whose Agenda?* (Mahwah: Laurence Erlbaum), pp. 117–94.

Annamalai, E. (2005), 'Nation-building in a globalised world: Language choice and education in India' in Angel M. Y. Lin and Peter Martin (eds), *Decolonisation, Globalisation: Language-in-education Policy and Practice* (Clevedon: Multilingual Matters), pp. 20–37.

Bourdieu, P. (1991), *Language and Symbolic Power* (Cambridge, MA: Harvard University Press).

Bourdieu, P. and J. C. Passeron (1977), *Reproduction in Education, Society and Culture* (London: Sage).

Bruthiaux, P. (2002), 'Hold your courses: Language education, language choice, and economic development', *Teachers of English to Speakers of Other Languages Quarterly* 36(3): 275–96.

Canagarajah, A. Suresh (1999), *Resisting Linguistic Imperialism* (Oxford: Oxford University Press).

Chatterjee, L. (1992), 'Landmarks in official educational policy: Some facts and figures' in R. S. Rajan (ed.), *The Lie of the Land* (New Delhi: Oxford), pp. 300–08.

Das, G. (2002), *India Unbound* (New Delhi: Penguin Books).

Delpit, L. D. (1988), 'The silenced dialogue: Power and pedagogy in educating other people's children', *Harvard Educational Review* 58 (3): 280–98.

Dua, H. R. (1996), 'The spread of English in India: Politics of language conflict and language power' in J. A. Fishaman, A. W. Conrad and A. Rubal-Lopez (eds), *Post-Imperial English: Status Change in Former British and American Colonies* (New York: Mouton de Gruyter), pp. 557–88.

Fairclough, N. (1999), 'Global capitalism and critical awareness of language', *Language Awareness* 8: 71–83.

Friedman, T. L. (2006), *The World is Flat: The Globalized World in the Twenty-first Century* (London: Penguin Books).

Gardner, R. C. and W. Lambert. (1972), *Attitude and Motivation in Second Language Learning* (Rowley MA: Newbury House).

Giddens, A. (1991), *Modernity and Self-identity, Self and Society in the Late Modern Age* (Cambridge Polity Press in association with Blackwell).

Gramsci, A. (1988), *A Gramsci Reader: Selected Writings* (D. Forgacs, ed.) (London: Lawrence and Wishart).

Jayaram, N. (1993), 'The language question in higher education: Trends and Issues' in S. Chitnis and P. Altbach (eds), *Higher Education Reform in India.*(New Delhi: Sage), pp. 84–119.

Kachru, B. B. (1985), *Standards, Codifications and Sociolinguistic Realism: The English Language in the Outer Circle* (Cambridge: Cambridge University Press).

Khilani, S. (1998), *The Idea of India* (New Delhi: Penguin).

Kurzon, D. (2004), *Where East looks West: Success in English in Goa and on the Konkan Coast* (Clevedon: Multilingual Matters).

Lin, A. M. Y. (1996), 'Doing-English-lessons in the reproduction or transformation of social worlds?', *Teachers of English to Speakers of Other Languages Quarterly* 33 (3): 393–412.

Lin, A. M. Y. (2005), 'Critical, transdisciplinary perspectives on Language-in-education policy and practice in post colonial contexts: The case of Hong Kong', in Angel M. Y. Lin and Peter Martin (eds), *Decolonisation, Globalisation and Language-in- education Policy and Practice* (Clevedon: Multilingual Matters), pp. 38–54.

Lin, A. M. Y. and P. Martin. (2005), 'From a critical deconstruction paradigm to a critical construction paradigm: An introduction to decolonisation, globalisation and language-in-education policy and practice' in Angel M. Y. Lin and Peter Martin (eds), *Decolonisation, Globalisation and Language-in-education Policy and Practice* (Clevedon: Multilingual Matters), pp. 1–19.

Luke, A. (1996), 'Genres of power? Literacy education and the production of capital' in Ruqaiya Hasan and Goeffrey Williams (eds), *Literacy in Society* (London: Longman), pp. 308–38.

Nayar, B. R. (2006), *India's Globalization: Evaluating the Economic Consequences. Policy Studies 22.* East–West Centre, Washington. Online at: www.eastwestcenterwashington.org/publications

Pennycook, A. (1994), *The Cultural Politics of English as an International Language* (London: Longman).

Phillipson, R. (1992), *Linguistic Imperialism* (Oxford: Oxford University Press).

Ramanathan, V. (1999), 'English is here to stay: A Critical look at Institutional and Educational practices in India', *Teachers of English to Speakers of Other Languages Quarterly* 33(2): 211–31.

Ramanathan, V. (2005), *The English–Vernacular Divide: Postcolonial Language Practice and Politics* (Clevedon: Multilingual Matters).

Tickoo, M. L. (1996), 'English in Asian bilingual education: From hatred to harmony', *Journal of Multilingual and Multicultural Development.* 17(2–4): 225–40.

Viswanathan, G. (1994), 'The beginnings of English literary studies in British India' in Janet Maybin (ed.), *Language and Literacy in Social Practice* (Clevedon: Multilingual Matters), pp. 215–32.

Warschauer, M. (2000), 'The changing global economy and the future of English Teaching', *Teachers of English to Speakers of Other Languages Quarterly* 34(3): 511–35.

9 Negotiating Language Value in Multilingual China[1]

Agnes S. L. Lam and Wenfeng Wang

Chapter Outline

Policy makers in bilingual or multilingual societies often have to negotiate between competing concerns such as the need to promote an international language for the purpose of modernization, the need to maintain or develop national cohesion through a common language as well as the need to retain other indigenous languages for cultural integrity. In a country like China, with its many languages and dialects, such considerations are inevitably at the crux of its language policy. The majority population, the Han Chinese, is expected to acquire competence in Standard Chinese (Putonghua) and English, while the minorities are encouraged to be bilingual in their own minority language and Chinese. The day-to-day circumstances for both the Han Chinese and the ethnic minorities, however, are more complex with most learners having to negotiate among at least three linguistic systems: Standard Chinese, English and a local or regional Chinese dialect (especially for the Han Chinese) or a minority language (for the minorities). This chapter draws upon the findings from the Language Education in China project to illustrate this state of affairs. After a brief outline of the policy perspective of the state, the discussion focuses on the analysis of interview excerpts from six learners: three from the majority Han Chinese group and three from the minorities. It will be shown that learners, like the state, do covertly or overtly ascribe value to each of the languages in their repertoire. It is also argued that the apparent discrepancy between the official bilingual policy and the day-to-day trilingual or multilingual realities in learner experience is not an impracticable mode of trading language value and is, in fact, inherent in the process dynamics of the Multi-agent Model of Language Choice involving agents such as language planners, educators, family members, learners and other competent language users.

Introduction

In the making of language education policy, governments around the world need to take account of the various functions of languages used in their countries and assign values to them as appropriate in their policy models. For example, languages can be valued for instrumental (Gardner and Lambert 1972) or cultural considerations (Kramsch 2001). Instrumental reasons may include using a language as a tool to gain knowledge, whereas cultural reasons may include using a language as a means of cultural expression or identity formation or integration. Such considerations also operate at the level of individual learners, who may, of course, also enjoy learning a language just because they are intrinsically interested in the language, that is, to acquire linguistic competence for its own sake, and not primarily because they wish to use it for any practical or cultural purpose, though they may eventually do so as well. In reality, motivation in language learning often involves a host of motives within and surrounding the learner (Dornyei and Skehan 2003: 616–17). The interactions between national assignment of language value and individual learner apportionment of such are also complex, and not easily delineated, perhaps because there is a certain degree of fluidity inherent in such negotiation. This chapter is an attempt to address such concerns at both the national and individual levels in the context of the People's Republic of China (PRC), with reference to some of the findings from the Language Education in China (LEDChina) project (Lam 2005).

Multilingual and multidialectal China is an interesting case in the study of the trading of language value. The majority ethnic group, the Han Chinese, speaks a number of Chinese dialects, falling into two main categories: the northern dialects and the southern dialects. The northern dialects can be subdivided into seven sub-groups and the southern dialects into six sub-groups (Huang 1987: 33–45). Chinese dialects (especially the southern ones) often differ in pronunciation, vocabulary and some aspects of syntax but share one writing script of about 3,500 years old. The national language, Chinese, is also known as Hanyu (Han Language). The standard dialect for oral interaction is Putonghua (Common Language) or Mandarin, a northern dialect corresponding well to Baihua, the written variety of Modern Standard Chinese propagated from around 1920. Among the ethnic minorities (106,430,000 people constituting about 8.4 per cent of the total population in China) (National Bureau of Statistics of the People's Republic of China 2001), 55 groups are officially recognized and over 80–120 languages are spoken (State Language Commission 1995: 159; Zhou 2003: 23).

In the context of such linguistic complexity and with an enormous population, China has to make language choices that are both politically peaceable and practically implementable. The official language policy appears to promote bilingualism and the reasons given have been both instrumental and cultural. The Han Chinese, the majority population, are expected to be bilingual in Chinese (Putonghua being the standard dialect) and English while the minorities are encouraged to be bilingual in Chinese (Putonghua) and a minority language. It is generally acknowledged that the value of English in China's national agenda is to accelerate her economic progress and enhance her diplomatic profile in the global arena. The rhetoric surrounding the propagation of Putonghua has emphasized instead national integration, while the teaching of minority languages cites the maintenance of cultural identity. While the official discourse stresses bilingualism and almost discrete roles for the languages in interplay, this chapter argues that, in reality, most learners in China often negotiate among at least three languages: Putonghua (the national standard Chinese dialect), English (the favoured foreign language) and a local Chinese dialect (for the Han Chinese) or, for the minorities, a minority language or at least a minority culture. In other words, the explicit bilingual policy is underpinned by an implicit trilingual model in practice.

It is also proposed that the value attached to each of the languages used in China is not discretely instrumental or cultural but is often a mixture of more than one type of motivation, a perspective quite consistent with current research on motivation (Dornyei and Skehan 2003: 614–21), or specifically on motivation in Chinese learners (Gao *et al.* 2004). In fact, whenever two or more languages, and hence cultures, are being negotiated within a learner or a group of learners, there is some degree of volatility in the incorporation of elements from different languages, which has also been observed in discussions of the formation of intercultural identity (Young 2001: 65–68).

Intercultural identity . . . is not a fixed psychological state . . . . As [learners] undergo adaptive changes to host communication competence (most notably, language competence), their internal conditions change from a monocultural to an increasingly multifaceted character. At the same time, the host cultural elements are increasingly incorporated into their self-concept. In this process, the [learners'] identities become more flexible. (Young 2001: 65–66)

Although this flexibility has been described above as a process within individual learners, such a process may also, by spreading through a group of learners, result in multiplicity in the recognition of language value at the level of the society and hence the state. It is also argued that the apparent lack of perfect correspondence between the official bilingual policy and the day-to-day trilingual (and, for the minorities, sometimes even multilingual) circumstances is in itself a solution not unfeasible, because the values attached to languages in a society are often, in any case, in an unavoidable state of flux and negotiation; it may even be claimed that it is the very indeterminancy surrounding the value of each language involved that allows language users and the state to trade languages on a day-to-day basis and periodically assign and re-assign value as appropriate.

The argument in the chapter proceeds as follows: first, some background information on the LEDChina project is provided; second, the negotiation of language value at the national policy level in China is outlined; third, the trilingual or multilingual experience of learners and the assignment of value to such languages by individual learners is illustrated with interview excerpts from six learners; finally, the dynamics of trading of language value by different stakeholders in language education are encapsulated in the Multi-agent Model of Language Choice (Lam 2007b).

The Language Education in China project

The Language Education in China (LEDChina) project was designed to track the impact of language policy from 1949 on learner experience in China. In addition to age as the main variable for relating the effect of policy changes to the experience of different cohorts of learners in different time periods, the learners' first dialect or language and their birthplace location ('coastal' versus 'interior') were also considered. The range of linguistic repertoires among the learners makes the findings useful for considerations of the negotiation of language value in this chapter.

There were three main types of data: policy statements, survey statistics and interview transcripts. The survey questionnaire, administered in Chinese to 415 Han Chinese respondents and 60 minority learners, included sections on biographical background and the learning of Chinese, other Chinese dialects, minority languages and foreign languages. Individual interviews aimed at eliciting language learning experiences were also conducted in Putonghua for 35 Han Chinese learners and 17 minority learners. The surveys were conducted by post and learners were interviewed face to face, each for about an hour. To ensure comparability of data from different locations, the main points of entry for investigation were the key universities (as recognized by the state) and their affiliated schools. The major limitation in the study is that all participants were university graduates; hence, the findings might not apply as well to non-university graduates. (Full project details are available in Lam 2005: 10–17.)

This chapter selects from the full LEDChina research report (Lam 2005) some data pertaining to the negotiation of language value in China for discussion. After a brief outline of the policy negotiation by the state, the discussion centres on interview excerpts from six learners: three from the majority Han Chinese group and three from the minorities, selected to provide a range of scenarios in the negotiation of language value.

Policy negotiation: between bilingualism and trilingualism

The assignment of language value is at the core of the language policy formulation in China. Part of this occurs explicitly and part of this occurs implicitly. The overt motivations are nation building, modernization and the social and cultural development of all ethnic groups in the country while the less salient motivations include understandably the twin desires for political stability and international stature.

Soon after the PRC was established in 1949, China embarked on a literacy campaign; the rationale provided then, in publicity and in reality, was the need to unify and modernize the nation. For the Han Chinese, the strategy was to standardize and propagate a national dialect, Putonghua, and a simplified script. For the minorities, to uphold a classless ideology (overtly) and to enhance political harmony (covertly), the PRC also found it necessary to respect the language and cultural rights of the minority groups in China. A major initiative to describe the minority languages was thus begun in the 1950s. In addition to the codification work on domestic languages, because China's initial strategy was to align with the Soviet Union, Russian was promoted as a foreign language. When relations with the Soviet Union did not develop as desired, from the late 1950s, China replaced the teaching of Russian with the teaching of English. All education work, however, was interrupted by the Cultural Revolution (1966–1976), during which formal education suffered a severe setback. University admissions resumed in 1978 and work on all three language policies began anew (Lam 2005: 8–10). In 1991, the disintegration of the Soviet Union provided the political space for China to navigate her way into the international arena through initiatives such as joining the World Trade Organization in 2001 and hosting the Olympics in 2008. This international orientation makes it necessary for China to include in her agenda the objective to prepare her citizens to communicate with the world, as mentioned in the latest 2003 English syllabus for the schools (Wang and Lam 2007) or the College English Curriculum Requirements at university level publicized in 2004 (Lam, Lu and Wu 2007).

The national language policy of China hinges therefore on three related motivations: to enhance literacy, to assure internal stability and to strengthen the nation with the acquisition of knowledge and economic progress so as to forestall foreign aggression. Such an agenda requires societal, if not individual, trilingualism: competence in Putonghua and English as well as a local/home Chinese dialect, if Putonghua is not normally spoken in the learner's locale/ home (for the Han Chinese) or a minority language (for the minorities). In terms of literacy, since all Chinese dialects map onto one Chinese script, Han Chinese learners only need to be biliterate (in Chinese and English) while minority learners may need to be triliterate (in Chinese, English and a minority language), if their minority language has a written form. At the moment, 44 per cent of the officially recognized minority groups (24 out of the 55 groups) still do not have officially codified scripts for their languages. While national needs seem to call for societal trilingualism, the official rhetoric tends to emphasize only bilingualism: Putonghua and English for the Han Chinese and Chinese and a minority language or, at least, a minority culture for the minorities. Perhaps the state does not wish to overtly antagonize minority communities (and, to some extent, speakers of southern Chinese dialects) by explicitly burdening them with heavier language requirements, as compared with the efforts the northern Han Chinese need to invest in their language learning because the northern Chinese dialects are closer to Putonghua, the standard Chinese dialect.

In view of the political sensitivity, the implicit trilingual and biliterate–triliterate model in China is only partially supported by explicit legislation. The *Zhonghua Renmin Gongheguo Guojia Tongyong Yuyan Wenzi Fa* (The Law on Language Use of the People's Republic of China), announced on 31 October 2000 and effective from 1 January 2001, reaffirms the official position since the mid-1950s – that Putonghua and standardized characters are the speech and the script to be used throughout the nation (Article 2) but minority groups still have the freedom to use and develop their own languages (Article 8) (Editorial Committee, China Education Yearbook 2001: 813). Although Putonghua has been required as a medium of instruction for all Han Chinese schools, the law does not forbid the use of other Chinese dialects at home or in other informal circumstances. Likewise, the teaching of English as a compulsory subject at school from around Primary 3 to both the Han Chinese and minority learners (wherever circumstances permit) is only supported by recommendations in the syllabus and various policy announcements from the Ministry of Education (Lam 2005: 191) but not required by legislation. This should not be surprising as the learning of foreign languages is not always required by law in most countries. So China is not unusual in this regard. Because the law is silent on the promotion of English, the official rhetoric concerning language learning for both the Han Chinese and the minorities can therefore emphasize bilingualism, sidestepping the problems an explicit trilingual model may entail. The Han Chinese are encouraged to become bilingual in Putonghua and English while the minorities are encouraged to become bilingual in their own minority language and Putonghua; in actual practice, most of the minorities have to learn a local Chinese dialect before they learn Putonghua and learn English as well if they wish to succeed in mainstream education.

The official policy target of bilingualism in Chinese and a minority language for the minorities is already a most significant change in policy stance from that in the 1950s and has become more overt only from around 1991 when the Soviet Union disintegrated. In the early years of the PRC, the minorities enjoyed greater cultural and linguistic autonomy; there was little systematic effort to assimilate them into the Greater Han culture then. The late 1950s and early 1960s marked a period of an unstable policy towards minority languages. During the Cultural Revolution (1966–1976), minority cultures and languages were suppressed. After the Cultural Revolution ended, the positive official policy towards minority groups was restored. But after 1991, China seemed to be more concerned that her minorities should be more integrated into the national culture so that they would not develop separatist tendencies like the ethnicities in the former Soviet Union (Lam 2005: 123–30). Hence, while the Chinese Constitution still supports minority language rights, the current realities are complex and greatly depend on the position adopted by local authorities, varying from promotion to permission or mere tolerance of such rights (Zhou, 2005). (This section has been adapted from Lam 2007a.)

This brief summary serves to illustrate the complexity of language trading at the policy level in China. It is a fine balancing act that China has been performing in its attempt to negotiate its way through various motivations by adopting an explicit policy of bilingualism in rhetoric and legislation while implementing, if but partially, an implicit model of trilingualism in practice.

Learners' negotiation of language value: trilingual or multilingual experience

While the state does not require Chinese learners to be trilingual by law, given the importance of Putonghua and English in education and career advancement, on a day-to-day basis, both the Han Chinese and the minorities are not at complete liberty to ignore the significant roles these two languages play, even though they may invest their learning energies into acquiring competence in other dialects or languages as well. These other Chinese dialects and minority languages still have cultural and/or instrumental value for learners, with regional Chinese dialects usually being better maintained than most minority languages, especially those minority languages which do not have writing scripts or which are spoken by very small populations (such as 100,000 people or fewer). This section first presents the circumstances of Han Chinese learners and then those of minority learners. Only pseudonyms are used and the age specified was that of the interviewee in the year 2000.

The Han Chinese learners

Among the Han Chinese, the use of Putonghua is now fairly prevalent in higher education and the workplace. At home and in other informal situations though, other Chinese dialects may still be used to some degree, particularly in the south (Lam 2005: 49). English is also the main foreign language learnt by most Han Chinese learners (Lam 2005: 85). These general trends are supported by the learning stories of three Han Chinese learners (Table 9.1).

Table 9.1 Languages/dialects learnt by three Han Chinese learners

Pseudonym of learner (Age)	Birthplace location	Chinese dialect(s)	Foreign language(s)	Minority language(s)
Lian (50)	Southern coastal	The Wuyi dialect [H] Putonghua Understands Baihua, the Wuhan dialect, the Sichuan dialect, the Guiliu dialect	English	None
Wei (31)	Northern interior	The Tongwei dialect [H] The Dingxi dialect Putonghua	English Russian	None
Shan (26)	Northern interior	The Shanxi dialect Putonghua [H] Tianjinhua Dongbeihua Shaanxihua Shangdonghua	English Japanese	None

Lian (Southern Coastal Chinese Interviewee 34, female, aged 50, a library administrator) (Lam 2005: 19–21).

Background. Lian was born in the city in the Wuyi county in Zhejiang in 1950. In 1958, when she was 7 or 8, she entered primary school. In 1964, she entered junior secondary school, also in the same county. After that, she enrolled in a technical college but when the Cultural Revolution began, classes were cancelled. So in 1968, she started working in a textile factory. Then from 1973, she worked in a company producing salted eggs and century eggs. In 1984, she went to Guangxi. She first worked in the Nationalities Research Institute as an information officer. In 1985, she studied political education at a university in the southern interior of China and graduated in 1988. At the time of the interview, she was working in the library of that university.

Native dialect. Her first dialect was the Wuyi dialect and she appeared well aware of its value to mark in-group solidarity. She reported, "There are 11 dialects" in Zhejiang. Every county has a different dialect. Most people can understand five or six of them . . . The dialects in that county are very special. That county was like a "dialect island". People who could speak that dialect were all in that county. There were very few speakers. Outside that county, people could not understand that dialect. My husband can also speak my dialect because he grew up in Zhejiang. My child, born in Wuyi, also learnt this dialect. Now my child is working in Wuhan. When we talk on the telephone or go out together, we speak this dialect and we can keep our conversations secret because people around us cannot understand it. When I visit my maiden home, I also speak the Wuyi dialect.'

Putonghua. Lian learnt Putonghua when she was growing up in the county because everyone spoke Putonghua in the city then. She recognized explicitly the value of Putonghua as a means of interdialectal communication in her account: 'The teachers at the school also used Putonghua because they were from different parts of China. It was like that in primary school and also in secondary school. In the technical college that I attended, Putonghua was also used as the medium of instruction because the college was for the whole province. Students came from all over the province; so they could only communicate in Putonghua.' When she started working, Putonghua was regularly used for professional communication but its value as an inter-dialectal code was retained. She reported, 'Among colleagues at my present workplace, Putonghua is spoken. Sometimes they speak Baihua [the dialect spoken in her present location in Guangxi] with each other but when there are visitors from another place coming here to discuss something, they will use Putonghua.' Likewise, Putonghua could help her communicate with her husband's family; she explained, 'My husband's family is in Wuhan. When we visit them, I speak Putonghua. They can understand me. When they speak the Wuhan dialect, I can understand them too though I cannot speak it well.'

Other Chinese dialects. Lian could speak other Chinese dialects but mostly for instrumental reasons. She admitted, 'I can understand Baihua because when the locals chat with each other, they speak Baihua. I cannot speak Baihua well and do not enjoy speaking it. . . . I also understand the Sichuan dialect and the Guiliu dialect a little because I often go to villages to do research. In the villages, if you do not understand their dialects, it is very hard to collect information.'

English. She learnt English from junior secondary school. After that, she learnt on her own through the correspondence course supported by television broadcasts. She studied at a television university for two years from 1989 to 1990. She mentioned that learning English was just to meet an educational or occupational requirement. 'My English was good for examinations. . . . We are assessed very often, for example, for promotion at our workplace. If you do not study, it will not do. I was already assessed twice for promotion, five years between each assessment. If you want to be promoted again, then you need to be assessed again. If you do not want promotion, then you will not be assessed. On the mainland, a lot of us study for the purpose of assessment.'

Using English in Hong Kong and France. Although Lian learnt English mainly for assessment, she did eventually use it for communication in some way. 'I was in Hong Kong once. I was on an exchange programme at the Chinese University in April 2000. When I met students, they all spoke Cantonese or English. Since I could not speak Cantonese well, when I had to ask them questions about certain matters, I could only use English. My English was rather rusty but under those circumstances, I was forced to use it. After a period of time, I was better and felt there was much improvement. When I meet a foreigner, we must speak English. So even if I cannot speak English well, I must still speak it. . . . In September 2000, I was also in France to do research on the Yao and Miao ethnic groups [ethnic minorities from China] living in France. The first generation of these groups there could still speak some Chinese but their second generation could only speak French and some of them could speak a little English. Since I could not speak French, we could only communicate in English. I could also buy things and ask for directions in English. The environment forced me to improve. I was very happy about it. Language could help me solve problems. If you are travelling and do not speak English at all, you will not dare to go and buy things. You are like a dumb person. Some of the people who went with me were older and could not speak English. They did not even dare to buy anything. So I could only be brave and went to shop for them. They were very grateful to me.' Because Lian could use English for communication, though mostly to 'solve problems', or instrumentally, she still derived pleasure in the interaction involved.

Wei (Northern Interior Chinese Interviewee 31, male, aged 38, a mathematics and philosophy teacher) (Lam 2005: 21–23)

Background. Wei was born in Tongwei in Gansu in 1962. He grew up in a rural area and completed his primary and secondary education there. In 1979, he enrolled in a teacher training university in the provincial capital and graduated in 1983. Upon graduation, he taught mathematics in a teachers' training college in Dingxi, a small city, for 5 years. In 1988, he went to a university in the north-western region to do his Masters, graduating in 1991. At the time of the interview, he was teaching mathematics and philosophy at that university.

The Tongwei dialect. Wei was less articulate about the value he attached to his native dialect, the Tongwei dialect. He mentioned that he learnt it well from his parents because it was spoken all around him. (Dingxi was near his home so he could speak the Dingxi dialect too, which was similar to the Tongwei dialect.)

Putonghua. His learning of Putonghua was less easy because he did not use it for interaction until he went to university when Putonghua became useful as an interdialectal means of communication. He reported, 'I did not learn Putonghua very well. I also learnt it from my parents but all along, I could not speak it well. The teachers in my primary and secondary schools did not use Putonghua to teach, not even in Chinese lessons. My classmates and I did not use Putonghua for interaction. Only when I went to university at the provincial capital in 1988 did I learn Putonghua. That was because the students came from all over the country and they could not understand my dialect.' But even then, he did not achieve perfect competence in Putonghua because he did not feel he needed to do so. 'Because I teach mathematics and philosophy . . ., the teaching involves the disciplinary knowledge more. So even if my Putonghua is not so good, the effect is not so great.'

English. In contrast to his learning of Putonghua which appeared quite instrumentally motivated, Wei's learning of English seemed to have a mixture of instrumental as well as intrinsic motivation. He recounted, 'A few days ago, some visitors from overseas came to visit our department and basically we could communicate about academic matters, not very well, but we could interact. My father at first did not know any English. He was a farmer. But my grandfather was a *ju³ren²* [a person who passed the local qualifying examination in the civil service examinations in imperial China] in the Qing dynasty. So my father studied a lot under my grandfather. Later, my father studied English by himself. He could read English books but could not pronounce the words. So from a young age, I liked English because I was influenced by my father. At university, I liked English particularly. Perhaps that was why I spent more time on it. I relied on self-study because, in those days, the standard of English teaching was rather low. At university, we were using a series of books produced by Nankai University but those were more suitable for developing professional English. At that time, I wanted to learn English more widely. So I studied the set of books by Xu Guozhang by myself. In my third year at university, I became interested in English literature and read a series on English literature. I also read a poetry anthology including the poetry of Byron. That was the first book I read in English by myself. Now I have basically no problem in reading English but writing is very difficult, very difficult. I am still continuing to learn. I hope I can write academic papers in English and publish internationally. That would be best.' To Wei, English carried a host of values: communicative, intrinsic and literary.

Russian. Although Wei also studied Russian, he reported that he had forgotten almost all of it but if he used a dictionary, he could still use it to read some Russian books. To him, Russian was therefore merely a tool, and not a very useful one, because of his limited competence in it.

Shan (Northern Interior Chinese Interviewee 11, female, aged 26, a Chinese language teacher) (Lam 2005: 26–28)

Background. From the time Shan was born in 1974 till she entered university, she was living in Huhehaote [or Hohhot], the capital of Inner Mongolia. In 1980, she entered primary school. In 1986, she went to junior secondary school and in 1989, senior secondary school. In 1992, when she was 18, she went to Beijing for her university education. She did a double degree in biomedical engineering and scientific editing for five years. At the time of the interview, she was studying for her Master's programme in economics part-time and teaching Chinese part-time at a university in Beijing.

The Shanxi dialect. Although Shan was born in Inner Mongolia, her parents were originally from Shanxi. So they spoke the Shanxi dialect at home. Usually, they spoke the Shanxi dialect and Shan spoke Putonghua at home. Like Lian, Shan recognized the value of her native dialect for dialectal cohesion and reported, 'if we have a visitor from Shanxi, then I will try to speak the Shanxi dialect because the visitor will then recognize that we are very close.'

Putonghua. Since she spoke Putonghua even at home and her teachers at school used Putonghua as a medium of instruction, her best language was Putonghua. But she expressed an intrinsic interest in learning dialects. 'I have a strong wish to learn dialects. I am very surprised I have this interest. I just feel China is so vast and the southern dialects are so different from the northern dialects. I am very curious about other people's dialects.' She ended up learning Tianjinhua, Dongbeihua and some other northern dialects and enjoyed being able to communicate with her friends in those dialects.

English. She started learning English in Junior Secondary 1. Her reading and writing in English were good. She confessed, 'This might . . . be related to the fact that in the university entrance examination in 1992 only reading and writing were assessed. For people like us coming from a small and faraway place, the only route to leave that place and have any advancement is to enter university. It seemed as if we only had one thought in our brains – to learn the answers to all the questions that might appear in the examination.' So for Shan, the instrumental value of English was undeniable. Yet later, she went beyond trying to pass examinations and 'paid attention to listening and speaking English from [her] university days for the purpose of interacting with other people. Before that, it was only to study it as an examination subject. In many "small places [i.e. not big cities]" in the northern part of China, it is like this, probably all like this.' Her observation that most Chinese learners outside the big cities were only motivated by the examinations could well be true because of the lack of opportunity to use English for genuine interaction.

Japanese. Shan also learnt Japanese at university for about a month but there was a time clash with something else she had to do. So she gave it up. She mentioned, "It was also because there were too many people in the class – about 40-odd students. So it was rather tiring. We learnt from zero level but it was very repetitive. I already knew something, and we had to say it over and over again. The course was free of charge. You had to pay a deposit but, if you passed the examination, it would be refunded to you. I lost my refund. It was not a requirement and you could choose to learn Japanese, French, German or even Russian.' Unlike English, Japanese was understandably less valued because it was not a requirement.

The minority ethnic groups

While Han Chinese learners may learn more Chinese dialects, they tend not to learn minority languages. In contrast, minority learners almost inevitably learn one or more Chinese dialects, usually as a precursor to learning Putonghua (Table 9.2). The repertoires of minority learners tend therefore to be greater, as a comparison of Table 9.1 and Table 9.2 reveals. (For more examples of minority learners' repertoires, see Lam 2005: 170.)

Table 9.2 Languages/dialects learnt by three minority learners

Pseudonym of learner (Age)	Ethnic group	Minority language(s)	Chinese dialect(s)	Foreign language(s)
Mei (37)	Yao	The Yao language[H] The Zhuang language	Putonghua The Guilin dialect Baihua	English Japanese
He (29)	Hui	Arabic	A local northern dialect[H] Putonghua	English
Ma (25)	Dong	The Dong language[H] The Zhuang language	The Guiliu dialect Putonghua	English Japanese German

[H] Home language as a child.
Source: Adapted from Lam 2005: 170.

Mei (Yao Interviewee 4, female, aged 37, a minority language teacher) (Lam 2005: 160–61)

Background. Mei was born in Lingui in Guangxi in 1963. She went there [a city in the southern interior] in 1989. After graduation, she left to teach in a secondary school for four years. Then she was transferred back there to establish Yao studies. At the time of the interview, she was teaching nationalities studies, linguistic theory and the Yao language at that university [in the southern interior].

The Yao language. She started learning the Yao language at home from the time she was born. Everyone in her home spoke the Yao language. She grew up in the Yao region and went to a primary school in a village where some Han Chinese lived. She did not have any Yao language classes in primary school, secondary school or university. She only learnt the written form of the Yao language when she started working. In primary school, some of the lessons for other subjects were taught in the Yao language. During primary school, she often used the Yao language to speak with her classmates; in secondary school, she still did so sometimes. But at university, she did not use the Yao language with her classmates because her classmates came from several different regions. So it was easier for all of them to communicate in Chinese.

Ethnic pride. Although she used mostly Chinese for the instrumental purposes of education and communication, she still felt ethnic pride in her Yao language. She reported, 'Ever since I was young, I have felt very proud that I can speak my own language. Though I have been outside [my village] studying or working for 20 or 30 years by now, I still feel the same. If I meet my friends from my ethnic group, or my relatives, there is no occasion when I have the opportunity to use the Yao language that I do not. I am not like some people who have this attitude – if they speak the Yao language, they are afraid other people will laugh at them. I do not have this feeling. I feel very proud I know my language. After I started working, I found that there are also Yao people residing in countries outside China. I can communicate with them using our language. I often do interpretation. So I feel my language can cross national boundaries. I feel very proud. I do not feel any pressure.' The pride she felt in her Yao language could also be partly attributed to the fact that the Yao minority has a large population of 2.6 million (Lam 2005: 155) and there are also Yaos in other parts of the world outside China. Hence, in Mei's case, the Yao language has both cultural and instrumental values.

Hanyu in primary school. At the time when Mei was growing up, there was very little opportunity for them to be exposed to Hanyu [Chinese]. She reported,

'Unlike nowadays, there was no television and no radio. Now, children in my home village are much better. At two or three years old, they know Hanyu. When I started primary school, I did not know Hanyu. I only knew my own ethnic language.' During her Primary 1 and Primary 2, her teacher was from her ethnic group. The teacher taught them bilingually using the Yao language and Hanyu but she did not teach them the Yao script. 'She only taught us how to say "Have a meal" and other phrases in Hanyu and in the Yao language. In that way, we could understand what she was saying. Even Hanyu lessons were taught partly in the Yao language and partly in Putonghua.' As a member from a minority language group, learning Hanyu was quite difficult for Mei. 'I remember the first week when I went to primary school, my grandmother gave me ten cents. In those days, ten cents could buy four pieces of candy. I did not know how to speak Hanyu. When I went to the shop, the woman there could not understand my Yao language. I did not know how to speak with her. So for a whole week, I did not succeed in buying candy. Later, another student from a higher grade, who was also from my village, told me, "Let me buy the candy for you. I know how to speak Hanyu." So she went to buy it. After she bought it, I gave her half of it. I only got to eat half of it.' Soon as Mei spent more time with Han Chinese classmates, she could speak Chinese. But they were speaking in the Guilin dialect though the teacher was speaking Putonghua in class. It is obvious that minority learners like Mei need both the local dialect as well as Putonghua to survive.

Putonghua at a later age. In primary and secondary school, Mei had about eight lessons per week for Chinese and at university, she still had six Chinese lessons per week. By secondary school, only Putonghua was used to teach Chinese and other subjects. But she and her classmates still responded largely in the Guilin dialect. Only at university did they really use Putonghua to respond to the teacher and talk with each other. When she started working, she used mostly Putonghua. In the Yao language classes she later taught, she used both the Yao language and Putonghua. But for all other subjects she taught, she only used Putonghua to teach. They were required to do so at that university.

Other minority languages or Chinese dialects. Mei could also say a few sentences in the Zhuang language because there were some Zhuang people living in her region. When she was a child, they played together. She also knew some Chinese dialects like Baihua [Cantonese] because she studied and worked at different places.

English. Only in the last year of her senior secondary school did her teacher talk to her about learning English because she had to take an examination in English. Mei reported, 'I really learnt English only when I went to university. It was a requirement. We had 6 lessons of English per week for 2 years. We only managed to go through Books 1 and 2 of Xu Guozhang's series. The lessons were partly taught in Putonghua. I never used English to speak with my class-mates. Very few people in my region used English. So I did not learn it well and I was already rather old when I started learning it. I spent a lot of time pur-posely to memorize the vocabulary but I am not pleased with the results. I do not use English at all now.' In Mei's case, English eventually lost its value because she had no use for it any more after she passed her examination.

Japanese. Mei also began to learn Japanese because she had to pass her promo-tion assessment. That knowledge of a foreign language is needed for promotion in some occupations in China is a contentious issue with most learners in China finding it an unreasonable requirement.

He (Hui Interviewee 3, male, aged 29, a computer scientist) (Lam 2005: 164–65)

Background. He came from the Hui minority group and was born in a village in the Ningxia Autonomous Region in 1972. He only attended one-and-a-half years of Primary 1 and 2. He did not go to Primary 3 because the school was closed at that time. Only after the Gang of Four was destroyed [a term to signify the end of the Cultural Revolution when four influential members lost their power] did he go to school again. He went straight into Primary 4. He completed his primary and secondary education in Ningxia. In 1989, when he was 17, he moved to Lanzhou to study mechanical engineering. He was the only one from his birthplace who could go to university. Upon graduation in 1993, he started working in the Computer Centre of a key university in the northern interior.

Arabic and Islam. Before he went to school, he learnt a little Arabic at home and mostly at the 'Muslim temple'. He reported, 'All the Hui children went to the temple to learn Arabic. It was one big class, with 10 to 20 children altogether. The master would give us individual work according to our levels. We memorized extracts from the Koran. When I started school, I learnt Arabic at the "temple" only intermittently. I learnt to write a little Arabic too but I have forgotten all of it. However, Islam is still my religion. The Hui people have adopted the Chinese language but language is language and religion is religion.' To He, the Arabic language had religious and related cultural value.

Chinese dialect at home and Putonghua at school. At home, most of the time, he spoke the local northern Chinese dialect with his family members. He also spoke it with his friends and classmates or when buying things. He started learning Putonghua only when he went to school at nine or ten. He reported, 'In secondary school, the yu^3 wen^2 [Chinese] teacher would play tapes to us to train us to speak Putonghua. Almost all the teachers taught in Putonghua but the influence of the Chinese teacher was the greatest. He was always carrying the tape recorder just to play tapes to us. After school, I did not practise much because my family conditions were not so good. We could not afford a tape recorder or receive broadcasts. My classmates were in a better position. They had tape recorders, could receive broadcasts and had more books at home.'

From Chinese words to stories. He had great difficulty learning Putonghua. He analysed his difficulty in this way, 'I felt my Chinese dialectal pronunciation was a hindrance to my learning of Putonghua; because my pronunciation was not accurate, I could not figure out the words. By Primary Three, my classmates already knew many words. I knew very few. Learning Chinese was very, very painful for me in my primary and junior secondary schooldays. I often failed my Chinese. In junior secondary school, I spent about two years reading books of folktales and fairytales in our town library. Then I could link up the words into sentences and the sentences into texts. That was how I learnt Chinese – from memorizing words and from reading those stories. I did not consciously try to practise speaking Putonghua to learn it better. When I went to university, my Chinese dialect became Putonghua by and by though we had no Chinese lessons then. My best language now is Chinese.' He is an obvious example of how minority learners have to choose to learn Chinese for the purpose of education, no matter how difficult it may be.

English. English is also not easy for minority learners to acquire. He reported, 'I started learning English only in senior secondary school so I was weaker than other students in English when I went to university. They had learnt it for six years by that time but I had only studied it for three years. Outside class in my schooldays, sometimes I would do some exercises in English but not often. At university, studying English was also rather strenuous for me. The classes were very big. The teacher talked. A lot of people listened together. Outside class, there were some English activities, like the English Corner. Some people went to them but I did not because I felt my English was not good. I did pass the Band 4 Exam [a national English examination for university students]. I think my English is just average now. Reading and listening – I am okay. But speaking and writing – I cannot handle them. . . . Before 1995 or 1996, we were not connected to the Internet. When we became connected, what we first did was to send emails. We did so in English. Now every day, I go onto the Internet.

Sometimes, I come across some web sites in English. I am not afraid of reading web sites in English. I can read through them slowly.' Difficult though it was for He to learn English, like some other minority learners, he realized its usefulness or value and so persevered.

Ma (Dong Interviewee 1, male, aged 25, a foreign languages graduate student) (Lam 2005: 167–69)

Background. Ma was born in a mountain village in Guangxi in 1975. At the age of 7, from Primary 1 to Primary 4, he studied in the village school. After that, he went to the school in the *zhen*[4] [town] to study for one year. In those days, primary school only consisted of five years. Then in 1988, he went to the city in the *xian*[4] [county] to enter junior secondary school. In 1991, he went to Liuzhou for his senior secondary school education. In 1994, he entered the Guangxi Normal University to study English and graduated in 1998. In 1998, he went to a key university in the northern interior to do his Masters in English.

The Dong language and the Zhuang language. Ma's first language was the Dong language. It was spoken at home. He also learnt the Zhuang language because the next village was a Zhuang village. He reported, 'When we went over to play, whatever they said, we just tried to speak the way they did. I cannot write the Zhuang script because I did not study it formally. It is a new script, artificially created after Liberation [establishment of the present Chinese government]. I cannot write the Dong language either.' A Roman alphabetic script was actually designed for the Dong language but it might not have been widely propagated.

The Guiliu dialect. From Primary 1 to Primary 4, Ma was taught in the Guiliu dialect. He reported, 'We also spoke it outside class. When I went to the school in the town for Primary 5, because there were people from different minority groups in the town, we needed a common language. The Guiliu dialect was used for interacting with people from different minority groups. It was also used in class by the teacher. Sometimes Putonghua was also used by the teacher.'

Putonghua. When Ma went to the junior secondary school in the *xian*[4], Putonghua was used as the medium of instruction. He reported, 'Outside class, the teacher would also use the Guiliu dialect sometimes, for example, during meetings for the class. In the English lesson, he would also use Putonghua to teach. The *yu*[3]*wen*[2] [Chinese] teacher would use Putonghua to teach

Other teachers sometimes used Putonghua and sometimes the Guiliu dialect. During my junior secondary school years, my Putonghua was still not passable. When I went to senior secondary school in Liuzhou, all the teachers used Putonghua to teach. By then, I was able to interact with others in Putonghua. But it was at university that I really used Putonghua frequently outside class because the classmates came from several different places in Guangxi. When I was learning Putonghua, I did not purposely listen to tapes. So sometimes, my pronunciation is not very accurate. Only at university did I watch television or listen to broadcasts in Putonghua. Sometimes, I found it difficult to differentiate between Putonghua and the Guiliu dialect. So I tend to use the Guiliu dialect when I am speaking more colloquially. But when I need to be more literary, then I speak Putonghua. I am now best at Putonghua and my Dong language. Both are just as good.' Like He, Ma also had some difficulty learning Putonghua, also partly because he first learnt another Chinese dialect (the Guiliu dialect), not Putonghua. But this could not be helped because in that region, the Guiliu dialect was used for communication. So his switch from a regional dialect to the standard one had to be negotiated as he progressed in his studies.

English. Ma started learning English from Junior Secondary 1 in the *xian*[4]. He reported, 'I learnt it well mainly because I was very interested. At that time, I did not think I wanted to become an interpreter or something instrumental like that. I just felt it was good to learn so I wanted to learn it well. For example, when I read the books and there were some pictures and I wondered, "Why does this person have yellow hair?" So I became interested and wanted to learn their language. In junior secondary school, the teachers sometimes played tapes to us. I also did some reading in English outside class. There was also an English Corner that I sometimes went to in senior secondary school. At university, I also went to the English Corner. In class at university, the teacher required us to only use English. So we did. Outside class, sometimes I watched television or listened to broadcasts. Because they were native speakers, their pronunciation was purer. So I kept wanting to imitate them, even their facial expressions. My Dong language has affected my pronunciation of both Putonghua and of English. But sometimes, I found some similarities between English and the Dong language. For example, the word for "door" in the Dong language is *duo*, similar to English. So it was easy for me to remember.' At the beginning of his learning of English, it seemed to have intrinsic value for Ma; he wanted to learn it for the sake of learning it. Yet, it would be difficult to argue that that was the only value English carried for Ma because he later chose to specialize in English and even to do a Master's degree in English. So eventually, English acquired occupational value for Ma as well.

Japanese and German. Ma's second foreign language [of secondary importance] was Japanese and he also learnt a little German. Second foreign languages tend to have only the value of meeting course requirements for English majors in China. Only about a third of them may still use these additional foreign languages in their work upon graduation (Lam 2005: 101).

Summary observations: implicit trilingualism and value assignment

Three main observations can be made with reference to the individual learning stories presented above. First, most learners in China have to negotiate among more than two languages or dialects. The minorities, in particular, have the greatest number of languages or dialects to trade with. The implicit language education model in China is therefore at least trilingual, perhaps even multilingual. The other observation is that learner assignment of language value, while in line with the policy circumscribed by the state, tends to go beyond that. For example, although Putonghua has been promoted for inter-dialectal communication and is used for such, learners may still learn other Chinese dialects for in-group solidarity or merely out of interest or as an intermediary code before they learn Putonghua, this being particularly true of the learning experience of minority learners. Likewise, while the state prescribes the learning of English as having instrumental value, learners may, like Ma, ascribe to it some intrinsic value and may learn it for the sake of learning it. For a foreign language like English in China, where opportunities to practise the language are not always available, to have intrinsic motivation, which may enhance learner responsibility, may be a more enjoyable path to learning success. Similarly, while the learning of minority languages has been publicized by the State as a way to maintain the cultural roots of the minorities, such a learning goal seems to have engendered mixed feelings among the minorities. On the one hand, they may wish to keep their minority languages or cultures; on the other, they need English and Putonghua for education and subsequent advancement. It is almost as if the state has passed on a most difficult decision for minorities themselves to make – that of whether they should invest more of their energy into learning Putonghua and English rather than their own minority language. Yet, this state of affairs is probably still more pedagogically desirable than forcing minorities by legislation to shift to Putonghua without any leeway whatsoever for alternative learning pathways. The third observation is that learners often assign more than one value to a language in their repertoire. Mei's use of the Yao language, for example, was at once cultural and instrumental as she was able to even use it to communicate with Yao people outside China. This complexity in value assignment also underpins the language policy motivations of the state. For example, the propagation of Putonghua does not only have the cultural value of integrating the various dialect groups but also have the instrumental value of enhancing literacy and hence economic and national development.

The Multi-agent Model: interactive negotiation by agents

From the policy analysis and the learner interviews discussed above, it can be seen that each of the languages carries value for the state as well as the learners. The negotiation of values can be conceptualized as language choice at several levels of decision making, involving a number of agents of choice interacting with each other.

The term 'language choice' can conjure up a host of phenomena ranging from language planning made by the state to individual language choices made by language learners or users. There has been relatively little discussion in the research literature to directly connect these two phenomena or other related phenomena, which is unfortunate as this makes it difficult for some stakeholders in language education to see how the choices they make can have educational consequences for language learning. To synthesize the several dimensions of language choice in the research literature, Lam (2007b) proposed the Multi-agent Model (Table 9.3) involving agents such as: policy makers in the government, educators, parents (and other family members), learners and other language users.

In making policy decisions, policy makers are not only influenced by the patterns of language use in the society at the time of policy making but also by their hopes for the national future, taking into account language use around the world. Likewise, all agents in the model take account of the *status quo* at their level and make choices, overtly or covertly, to 'engineer' (Spolsky 1998: 66) some desirable linguistic future in view of the value(s) of the languages involved in daily interaction, in education, in career advancement, regionally, nationally and globally. All choices involve conscious and active investment of resources such as time, energy and money to optimize learning

Table 9.3 The Multi-agent Model

Agents	Language choices	Phenomena
Policy makers in the government	What language(s) or dialect(s) to promote in government, education and the public media.	Language planning. Linguistic imperialism (if enforced by a foreign power).
Educators (principals, teachers)	What language(s) or dialect(s) to use as the medium/media of interaction or instruction in and outside the classroom, in what proportion and under what circumstances.	Models of bilingual or multilingual education.
Parents (and other family members)	What language(s) or dialect(s) to speak to each other and the child in and what medium/media of school instruction to choose for the child.	Language use in mixed marriages and international families. Interface between the home and the school.
Learners	What language(s) or dialect(s) to use with others or invest learning energy/time in while growing up and also in study plans in adulthood.	Language acquisition and learning. Adult language learning.
Competent language users	What language(s) or dialect(s) to use in everyday interaction (for example, the workplace) and cultural or literary expression.	Code-switching/code-mixing. Workplace interaction. Interculturality and negotiation of cultural identity.

Source: Lam (2007b).

or language-use conditions such as learning materials, teaching input and language-use opportunities. Any investment of resources is inevitably linked to value assignment, conscious or sub-conscious, explicit or implicit. The more valuable a language is to a government, a team of educators, parents or learners, the more investment will be made into the teaching or learning of that language. Investments made by agents at one level inevitably affect the investments made by other agents. The learner is but one agent in this interactive language investment or trading process. The very interactive nature of such a process gives rise to a certain indeterminancy in the assignment and re-assignment of language value; and it is this very indefiniteness that allows a state, such as the Chinese government, to officially argue for bilingualism while, in reality, to expect or at least encourage learners to be trilingual. (This section is adapted from Lam 2007b.)

Conclusion

This chapter has shown that while the Chinese government seems to emphasize bilingualism in its policy statements, learners are often at least trilingual in day-to-day language use. It is argued that this apparent paradox is actually not an unrealistic solution to an otherwise politically difficult set of language circumstances to negotiate. The Chinese government will find it difficult to enforce an officially trilingual model as that will seem to lay too heavy a learning burden on native speakers of Southern Chinese dialects and especially on the learners from minority ethnic groups. It is more politically expedient to therefore promote bilingualism officially and leave the emergence of trilingualism to the interaction of choices among different stakeholders in the language education process. What the state lacks in legal provision, the language investments made by intermediary agents at various levels of the language education process such as educators, parents and other competent language users in the society, will provide the impetus for learners to choose to become trilingual if they wish to participate in the mainstream life of the nation. This state of language trading can occur in China, and perhaps even in other countries, because the values attached to languages in any community are often in an unending state of flux and negotiation. One can even go so far as to state that it is the very indefiniteness surrounding the value of each language involved that permits governments and the language users in the realms they govern to trade languages from time to time and assign and re-assign value as they adjust to the changing market values of the languages involved both nationally and globally.

Note

1 This chapter draws upon the findings in the Language Education in China project which was fully supported by a grant from the Research Grants Council of the Hong Kong Special Administrative Region, China (Project No. HKU7175/98H). The permission from Hong Kong University Press to adapt some case reports from Lam (2005) for this chapter is gratefully acknowledged.

References

Dornyei, Z., and Skehan, P. (2003), 'Individual differences in second language learning' in C. J. Doughty and M. H. Long (eds), *The Handbook of Second Language Acquisition* (Malden, MA: Blackwell), pp. 589–630.

Editorial Committee (2001), *China Education Yearbook 2001* (Beijing: People's Education Press).

Gao, Y.-H. (ed.) (2004), *Zhongguo daxuesheng yingyu xuexi shehui xinli: Xuexi dongji yu ziwo rentong yanjiu* [The social psychology of English learning by Chinese college students: Motivation and learners' self-identities] (Beijing: Foreign Language Teaching and Research Press).

Gardner, R. C., and Lambert, W. E. (1972), *Attitudes and Motivation in Second Language Learning* (Rowley, MA: Newbury House).

Huang, H.-H. (1987), *Hanyu fangyanxue* [Chinese Dialectology] (Xiamen: Xiamen University Press).

Kramsch, C. (2001), 'Intercultural communication' in R. Carter and D. Nunan (eds), *The Cambridge Guide to Teaching English to Speakers of Other Languages* (Cambridge: Cambridge University Press), pp. 201–06.

Lam, A. S. L. (2005), *Language Education in China: Policy and Experience from 1949* (Hong Kong: Hong Kong University Press).

Lam, A. S. L. (2007a), 'Bilingual or multilingual education in China: Policy and learner experience' in A. Feng (ed.), *Bilingual Education in China* (Clevedon: Multilingual Matters), pp. 13–33.

Lam, A. S. L. (2007b), 'The multi-agent model of language choice: National planning and individual volition in China', *Cambridge Journal of Education* 37(1): 67–87.

Lam, A. S. L., Lu, Z.-S., and Wu, Y.-A. (2007), English-medium instruction in higher education in China: Two case studies. Manuscript in preparation.

National Bureau of Statistics of the People's Republic of China (2001), *Communique on major figures of the 2000 population census (No. 1)*, Retrieved 11 October 2003, http://www.stats.gov.cn/english/newrelease/statisticalreports/200204230084.htm

Spolsky, B. (1998), *Sociolinguistics* (Oxford: Oxford University Press).

State Language Commission (1995), *Yuyan wenzi gongzuo baiti* [100 Questions in Language Orthography Work]. (Beijing: Yuwen Chubanshe).

Wang, W-F, and Lam, A. S. L. (2007). The English language curriculum for secondary school in China from 1949. Manuscript in preparation.

Young, Y. K. (2001), *Becoming Intercultural: An Integrative Theory of Communication and Cross-Cultural Adaptation* (Thousand Oaks, CA: Sage Publications).

Zhou, M.-L. (2003), *Multilingualism in China: The Politics of Writing Reforms for Minority Languages 1949–2002* (Berlin: Mouton de Gruyter).

Zhou, M.-L. (2005), 'Legislating literacy for linguistic and ethnic minorities in contemporary China', *Current Issues in Language Planning* 6(2): 102–21.

Language Policy, Vernacular Education and Language Economics in Postcolonial Africa

10

Nkonko M. Kamwangamalu

Over the past 40 years language-in-education policies in post-colonial Africa have been dominated by two ideologies: the ideology of decolonization of education on the one hand, which requires replacing former colonial languages (French, Portuguese, English and Spanish) with indigenous languages as media of instruction, hence vernacular education; and the ideology of development, which requires continual use of colonial languages in the education system because, it is believed, development is possible only through the medium of European languages. This chapter revisits the debate surrounding these two ideologies. It points out that although colonialism ended years ago, its legacy (now reincarnated as globalization) continues to impact the language policies of most African states. Drawing on recent theoretical developments in the economics of language, the chapter discusses ways in which equity can be achieved between African languages and former colonial languages in the education system. It highlights the consequences of language policy failure for the indigenous African languages, with a focus on language shift that is currently taking place in Africa's urban communities; and calls for language policies that not only consider the development and use of the indigenous African languages in education and other higher domains as an integral part of Africa's economic development programme, but also ensure that former colonial languages function in addition to rather than at the expense of African languages and the majority of their speakers.

Introduction

Vernacular education, defined here as education that uses an indigenous language as the medium of instruction throughout the entire education system, has been the locus of the debate on language-in-education policies in Africa since the early 1960s. Soon after they liberated themselves from Western colonialism, African countries were faced with two ideologies concerning the medium of instruction in public schools: the ideology of decolonization of education on the one hand, and the ideology of development on the other. The former requires replacing economically dominant ex-colonial languages such as English, French, Portuguese and Spanish with demographically majority indigenous languages as media of instruction, hence *vernacular education*; while the latter requires retention of ex-colonial languages in education and other higher domains.

The issue of the medium of instruction has received considerable attention in recent literature (e.g. Ramasamy 2001; Lai and Bryan 2003; Tollefson and Tsui 2004; Lin and Martin 2005). In Africa, the debate around the medium of instruction appears to be based on a wanting dichotomy: socioeconomic development is possible only through the medium of European languages; indigenous African languages are good only for preserving African cultures and traditions. This debate is in part being rekindled by the widening gap between the elite, who overtly profess the promotion of indigenous languages as medium while sending their own offspring to schools where the medium of instruction is a former colonial language; and the masses, who are marginalized because they have no access to the latter language. Also, the renewed interest in the question of vernacular education seems to be informed by UNESCO's (1995) model of mother tongue literacy, commonly referred to as mother tongue education, reviewed recently by Tabouret-Keller, Gardner-Chloros and Varro (1997). The model, which is supported by documented findings in several studies around the world, suggests that children perform better at school when they are taught through the medium of their mother tongue rather than through the medium of a foreign language (e.g. Akinnaso 1991; Auerbach 1996; Mfum-Mensah 2005)

In this chapter, I revisit the debate around the issue of vernacular education against the background of recent developments in language economics, a field of study whose focus is on the theoretical and empirical analysis of the ways in which linguistic and economic variables influence one another (Vaillancourt and Grin 2000; Grin 2006). I argue strongly against an either (an African language)/or (a European language) perspective to the issue of the medium of instruction; and question the dichotomy between tradition and modernism, on which the ideologies of decolonization and of development appear to be subtly based. I argue further that ex-colonial languages and indigenous languages can co-exist in education as well as in other areas, provided the indigenous languages are also associated with upward social mobility, much as is the case for former colonial languages. I call for language-in-education policies that take into account not only new forces such as globalization in language policy and language management but also recognize the link between African languages and economic development if these languages are to become, like their colonial counterparts, the languages of upward social mobility.

The chapter is divided into four sections. In the next section, I review colonial language policies to provide the background against which the ideologies of decolonization and development have evolved in the postcolonial nations. Also, such a review is necessary because, as London (2003) points out, it is difficult to discuss postcoloniality without bringing colonialism into the picture. The review will be followed by an in-depth critique of postcolonial language policies to determine to what extent they differ from or are similar to the inherited colonial language policies. In the last section of the chapter, I discuss briefly the consequences of language policy failure in Africa for the indigenous African languages, with a focus on language shift from the indigenous languages to Western languages that is currently taking place especially in Africa's urban communities. I then suggest the way forward for the indigenous languages, underscoring the importance of the link, as yet to be established, between the indigenous languages and the economy. I argue that any language policy that does not take such a link into account is doomed to failure.

Language planning and policy in the colonial era

When European countries agreed at the Berlin (Germany) Conference of 15 November 1884 to 26 February 1885 to divide up and colonize Africa, they imposed not only political control but also assimilationist language policies aimed at spreading European languages, among them French, Spanish, English and Portuguese, in the newly acquired territories. The imposition of European languages in the colonies was informed by the classical ideal of the centralized nation state, which was very popular in Europe at the time and according to which, as Ager (2001) explains, a country must have 'one language, one culture, one territory, one political conception'. Against this background and in line with their *mission civilisatrice* (*civilizing mission*) in Africa, the French believed that 'the metropolitan community and the African peoples subject to their rule must share a common political destiny' (Spencer 1985: 389–93). However, this destiny could not be shared unless both the Africans and their colonial masters shared the same language, French. Comparing the attitudes of the French and the English towards the indigenous African languages, Haugen (1981: 11) puts it bluntly as follows: 'The English were tolerant of native tongues but unwilling to accept their speakers as equals. The French were willing to receive natives of all colours into the French community provided they gave up their identity and learned French.' It follows that the indigenous African languages had no place in colonial language policies, except perhaps in Bible study and translation and in lower primary education, as was the case especially in British and Belgian colonies (Fabian 1986). In other words, where the authorities made use of indigenous languages, they did so to advance their own aims, such as to proselytize the indigenous population, and train low-level manpower to provide clerical assistance in the administration of the colonies. As a matter of fact, the literature provides sufficient evidence that colonial authorities had a negative attitude towards the development of indigenous African languages, which they referred to as dialects. For instance, Sir Rivers-Smith, Director of Education in the then British colony of Tanganika, now Tanzania, claimed that

> [t]he vast majority of African dialects . . . must be looked upon as educational cul de sacs [*sic*]. From a purely educational standpoint the decent interment of the vast majority of African dialects is to be desired, as they can never give the tribal unit access to any but a very limited literature. (Whitehead 1995: 7)

Also, Sir Rivers-Smith stressed the important link between language policy and economic growth. In his view, use of the vernacular could isolate a tribe from commercial intercourse. For him,

> To limit a native to a knowledge of his tribal dialects is to burden him with an economic handicap under which he will always be at a disadvantage when compared with others who, on account of geographical distribution or by means of

education, are able to hold intercourse with Europeans or Asiatics. (Whitehead 1995: 8)

A similar view is echoed in a report by the World Bank (1980: 20) when the institution notes that 'the emphasis on local languages can diminish an individual's chances for further education and limit access of specific groups or countries to the international body of knowledge.'

The assumed functional or formal inadequacy of indigenous languages and, therefore, of indigenous mind or civilization was often alleged to justify European tutelage (Gilliam 1984: 68). It is ironic that the colonial authorities, who took pride in and associated their vernaculars with economic development and progress, could not bring themselves to see indigenous African languages in the same light. Instead, they associated African languages with economic and technological stagnation and backwardness, as is evident from the above quotes from Sir Rivers-Smith and the World Bank.

The introduction of the colonial languages into African societies and their use as media of education and as communicative instruments for the modernizing process, observes Spencer (1985: 395), froze not only the opportunities for functional development of almost all the African languages but also linguistic competition between languages for access to new domains such as modern science and technology. It is this state of affairs that African leaders sought to reverse, through post-independence language policies aimed at promoting the indigenous African languages, when the former colonies became independent states in the early 1960s. The section that follows examines some such policies in the postcolonial nations.

Language policies in the postcolonial era

In this section, I argue that in Africa language policies aimed at promoting the indigenous languages in education have failed. In order to appreciate and understand this argument better, I shall return to and review further the two ideologies mentioned in the introduction to this chapter: the ideology of development and the ideology of decolonization.

The ideology of development

In spite of the post-independence euphoria to promote the use of indigenous languages in education, it has proven difficult for emerging independent

African states to sever the ties with inherited colonial language policies, which require continual use of ex-colonial languages in education. The literature has attempted to explain this situation as follows. First, rather than promote the cultural and linguistic diversity that is characteristic of African polities, policy makers viewed then, as they do now, instruction in the language of the former colonial power as an approach that will lead to greater proficiency in that language, representing a further step towards economic development and participation in the international global economy (Mfum-Mensah 2005). This goal has, however, not been achieved. Instead, for the majority of African countries economic dependency on the West remains the norm rather than the exception.

Second, in retaining former colonial languages as media of instruction, language policy planners expected that the adopted European language would develop into a viable medium of national communication, that it would be adopted by the African population, that it would spread as a *lingua franca*, and perhaps eventually also as a first language by replacing the local languages, as was the case in large parts of Latin America (Heine 1990: 176). Contrary to these expectations, and despite the fact that European languages have been used in African education for almost 400 years, the social distribution of these languages remains very limited and restricted to a minority elite group. In other words, the majority remains on the fringe, language-based division has increased, and the illiteracy rate among the populace remains high (Alexander 1997: 88). The masses have become increasingly aware that ex-colonial languages are the catalyst for socioeconomic inequalities, and that only access to these languages can bring about a remedy to this situation.

Third, in retaining inherited colonial languages as media of instruction, African language policy makers have perpetuated the colonial myth that indigenous African languages do not have the linguistic complexity to enable them to be used in higher domains; and that these languages are good only to preserve African cultures and traditions. In doing so, language policy makers have stuck to what Wiley (2006: 143) has critiqued as 'the colonizer's model', a Western-based paradigm once used to justify colonialism and the repression of indigenous peoples and one according to which 'good things' develop in the West and then spread to the periphery. Contrary to this model, linguistic scholarship has shown conclusively that the notion that some languages inhibit intellectual or economic development is a myth. In this regard, McArthur (1983: 21) explains that all languages are equally capable of expressing whatever their users need them to express, and have equal potential, although historical events may significantly benefit or impede a particular language. Although the languages of the colonized people are typically described as subordinate and traditional, and lacking higher literary forms, Tollefson (1991) warns that these assessments of value must be understood as reflections of relationships of power and domination rather than objective linguistic or historical facts. Thus, as Woolard and Schieffelin (1994: 63) observe, the model of development is pervasive in postcolonial language planning, with paradoxical ideological implications that condemn languages, like societies, to perennial status as underdeveloped. Consequently, in the postcolonies in Africa the position of the indigenous African languages in education has remained closely linked to the inherited colonizer's model, which perpetuates the hegemony of ex-colonial languages over the indigenous African languages.

The ideology of decolonization and vernacular education

In Africa, the need for the decolonization of education, hence vernacular education, arose against the failure of inherited colonial language policies to reach the goals for which they were retained, whether in terms of national unity, national economic development or literacy; and against high rates of school failure resulting from the use of ex-colonial languages as the sole medium of instruction in African schools. The need for vernacular education was articulated by the now defunct Organization of African Unity (OAU) in what the organization called the 'Language Plan of Action for Africa', whose goals were, *inter alia*, as follows:

a. to liberate the African peoples from undue reliance on utilization of non-indigenous languages as dominant, official languages of the state in favour of the gradual takeover of appropriate and carefully selected indigenous languages in this domain.

b. to ensure that African languages by appropriate legal provision and practical promotions assume their rightful role as the means of official communication in public affairs of each Member State in replacement of European languages which have hitherto played this role. (OAU 1986)

Similar and most recent recommendations concerning the state of language policy and planning in Africa are made in the [January 2000] Asmara (Erithrea) Declaration on African Languages and Literatures, which reads as follows:

• All African children have the unalienable right to attend school and learn their mother tongues at all levels of education;

- The effective and rapid development of science and technology in Africa depends on the use of African languages;
- African languages are vital for the development of democracy based on equality and social justice;
- African languages are essential for the decolonization of African minds and for the African Renaissance. (Asmara Declaration, 2000) [http//www.queensu.ca/snid/asmara.htm]

Along these lines, Bamgbose (2006) points to what he refers to as 'laudable initiatives' in efforts to promote the status of the indigenous African languages in higher domains. Some such initiatives include terminology development, which has resulted in the publication of the *Multilingual Mathematics Dictionary* (for Grades 1–6) in all 11 official languages compiled by the National Language Service of the Department of Arts and Culture in South Africa; the ongoing translation of Nigeria's Constitution into the country's three major languages (Yoruba, Igbo, Hausa) under the auspices of the Ministry of Information in Nigeria; the translation of the 2006 Nigerian Census Questionnaire into 13 Nigerian languages by the National Population Commission; the establishment of the African Academy of Languages (ACALAN), which was approved in January 2006 as a specialized scientific institution of the African Union (AU), the successor to the Organization of African Unity (OAU); and the declaration by AU of 2006 as 'the Year of African Languages'. Let me digress briefly on each of these seeming 'achievements'.

The publication of the multilingual dictionary is indeed a step in the right direction, but more still needs to be done for African languages in South Africa 'to arrive' (Kamwangamalu 1997: 140). Likewise, the translation of the Nigerian Constitution and the Census from English into the country's major languages must be welcomed, but it does not in any way qualify as a laudable achievement. Such an activity, taking place as it does almost a half century since Nigeria obtained independence from Britain in the early 1960, is at best described as lip service intended perhaps to appease language activists. Also, it seems that Bamgbose (2006) mistakes language-related political events for progress in language planning. More specifically, the establishment (by the African Union) of the African Academy of Languages (ACALAN) and the declaration of 2006 as 'the year of African languages' are, in my view, political events rather than 'a significant development in empowerment of African languages'. When all is said and done, these policy declarations, neither the first nor the last of their kind, will ultimately be thrown into the garbage bin of policy declarations about African languages. There have been many such declarations about African languages (including the now 20-year old Language Plan of Action for Africa) in the past but all of them have come and gone, leaving no trace to remember them by.

Akin to their predecessors in the 1990s, the policy initiatives and declarations highlighted above are not matched with practical steps to use indigenous languages in education or to make them economically or politically useful to their users. In other words, no matter how laudable such initiatives are claimed to be, they do not ensure upward social mobility for the majority of Africa's population. The indigenous African languages remain confined to the cultural domains, much as they were in the colonial era. Against the background of the globalization and spread of English, it is becoming increasingly difficult for African languages to find space in domains such as education. This is even harder in former French and Portuguese colonies since here indigenous languages struggle to survive not only against French and Portuguese but also English, a language that some former French or Portuguese colonies have adopted (e.g. Rwanda) or contemplate adopting (e.g. Mozambique) as the second official language in addition to French or Portuguese, respectively. Market forces ensure that English, the golden language (Walsh 2006: 32), becomes what Bamgbose (2003) has termed 'a recurring decimal', for the language seems to turn up everywhere as a result of its global instrumental value. Thus, as Fishman (2004: 421) notes with respect to immigrant languages in the USA, African languages remain exposed to the Darwinian law of the linguistic jungle, according to which the strong survive and, in competition, if any, with the strong, the weak die off. I concur with Amy Tsui when she remarks, about the medium-of-instruction policies in Hong Kong, that

> [such] policies are shaped by an interaction between political, social and economic forces. However, among these agendas, it is always the political agenda that takes priority. Other agendas, be they social, economic, or educational, come to the fore only if they converge with the political agenda. Yet it is always these [other] agendas that will be used as public justification for policy making. (2005: 113)

A number of questions arise as a result: How can the agenda for universal literacy in indigenous languages in Africa be implemented if such an agenda is always overshadowed by the political agenda? Also, would universal literacy in indigenous languages, if it is ever achieved, facilitate upward social mobility for the language users? If not, what should be done to remedy this situation? The last section of this chapter addresses these and related questions against the background of recent developments in the field of language economics, to which I turn below. It also points to the consequences of language policy failure for the indigenous African languages, with a focus on language shift from these languages to Western languages such as English and French especially in Africa's urban communities.

Language and the economy

The main argument in this section is that for language-in-education policies to succeed, policy makers must acknowledge and establish the link between the indigenous languages and the economy. Such a link entails that an academic (i.e. school-acquired) knowledge of the indigenous languages should become one of the requirements for access to resources, much as is the case for former colonial languages. In other words, there is the need for the indigenous African languages to be associated with at least some of the privileges and perquisites that have, for centuries, been the preserve of former colonial languages only. The missing link between African languages and the economy, I argue, constitutes a major stumbling block in efforts to promote the social, political, and economic status of the languages. This argument draws on recent developments in *language economics*, a field of study which, once again, investigates the ways in which linguistic and economic variables influence one another (Grin 2006). One of the key issues in language economics is the relevance of language as a commodity in the acquisition of which individual actors may have a good reason to invest. Within the framework of language economics, linguistic products such as language, language varieties, utterances and accents are seen as goods or commodities to which the market assigns a value (Coulmas 1992). The term 'market' refers to the social context in which linguistic products are used. On a given linguistic market, some products are valued more highly than others. The market value of a linguistic product such as a vernacular language is determined in relation to other languages in the planetary economy (Coulmas 1992: 77–85). It is, as Gideon Strauss (1996: 9) notes, an index of the functional appreciation of the language by the relevant community.

The literature increasingly recognizes the importance of the relationship between language and the economy in the success or failure of language policies (Paulston 1988; Le Page 1997; Vaillancourt and Grin 2000; Kamwangamalu 2004; Canagarajah 2005; Walsh 2006). For instance, Paulston (1988: 12) remarks that language planning efforts are most likely to be successful if they are supported by economic advantage or similar social incentives for the minority groups. Canagarajah (2005) makes a similar point when he says that it is important that nations give all languages not only a place in their curriculum but also a functional status in their social and economic life. Brook-Utne (2000) concurs, noting that if Africa is to develop economically and encourage mass participation in this process, the secret lies with its languages. True development of a political, economic or social nature, say Nettle and Romaine (2000: 172), cannot take place, however, unless there is also development of a linguistic nature. Unless the population has access to information, they will be controlled by a small elite minority who have access to the dominant language – in most cases, a metropolitan European one (Nettle and Romaine 2000: 172), as is the case especially in the African context. In other words, citizens who cannot functionally communicate in the economically dominant language, in this case a former colonial language, are excluded from political participation and opportunities for social advancement (Francis and Kamanda 2001: 236). Along these lines, those who are able to exploit a former colonial language, whether to sell goods and services or ideas, not only wield a very considerable power (Halliday 2003: 416) over the masses, but they also, as Hasan (2003: 436) puts it, specialize in winning while those who are not specialize in losing: the winners specialize in fixing the rules to ensure that the losers, in this case the masses, stay where they are. It follows that one major factor impeding the promotion of African languages particularly in education is the lack of incentives for studying or using them. It is not surprising, as Bamgbose (2006) notes, that even when a language policy makes it possible for African languages to be studied in the school system, students still do not willingly opt for them because they know that a qualification in an African language does not confer as much advantage, if any advantage at all, and opportunity for upward social mobility as a qualification in a Western language such as English or French does.

The need for upward social mobility, which in most African countries can be met only if one has knowledge of a former colonial language, has contributed to language shift that is currently being observed in Africa's urban communities. For instance, in a study of the language situation in Botswana, Smieja (1998) reports that there exists a steady language shift from Setswana and other minority languages to English, for the language is seen as a powerful economic and educational tool, the language with higher social status and prestige, and one in which the elite reproduces itself. In a similar study,

Kamwangamalu (2003a: 234–36) reports that, in South Africa, Zulu-speaking pupils use both English and Zulu in the family, suggesting that language shift is indeed in progress, since bilingualism is a major precursor of language shift (Lieberson 1980). While English is welcomed with open arms into the traditional domain of the Zulu language, that is the family, Zulu is not welcomed at all in higher domains such as education, for this is perceived as the preserve of English. Attempts to promote Zulu and other official indigenous languages in education raise a lot of suspicion; and are seen as a disguise and a painful reminder of apartheid-driven Bantu Education, whose key goal was to deny the black child access to English (Kamwangamalu 2003b: 75–78). I argue that, in Africa, the observed language shift is a consequent by-product of language policy failure, and more specifically, of the failure to implement economy-driven policies aimed at promoting the indigenous languages in education and other higher domains.

It is not surprising that language shift is taking place in Africa's urban communities, nor is this unique to Africa. Research reports, summarized in Kamwangamalu (2003a: 227), indicate that individuals or language communities around the world tend to shift to an economically dominant language due to the advantages with which the language is associated. For instance, in a study of ethnic mother tongue maintenance and shift among the Maltese migrants in Ontario and British Columbia, Canada, Slavick (2001: 149) found that the strongest factor contributing to the shift from Maltese to English was the negative attitudes many Maltese hold toward the Maltese language because it has no prestige and is not economically viable in the Canadian context. Gal (1979) draws a similar conclusion concerning the shift from Hungarian to German in Oberwart, Austria; and so do Dorian (1981) and Landon (2000) concerning the shift from Gaelic to English in East Sutherland. With respect to the Hungarian case, Gal explains that the need for the Hungarians to integrate into the increasingly dominant Austrian socioeconomic community for work and social advancement contributed to the shift from Hungarian to German. As for the shift from Gaelic to English, Dorian and Landon note that Gaelic speakers have over centuries formed negative attitudes towards Gaelic because of the low status of the language, and this has contributed to the shift to English, which Gaelic parents believe is the way forward for their children. Parental ambitions for the children are also said to have contributed to what Crowley (1996) calls *pragmatic language shift* from Irish to English in Ireland; and to a shift from Tamil to English in Tamil communities in Singapore and

Malaysia (Gupta 1997). To counter language shift especially in the postcolonial nations, I argue, there must be a shift from the colonizer's model (Wiley 2006), as described earlier, to what Wee (2003, and Chapter 2 this volume) refers to as 'linguistic instrumentalism', that is, 'a view of language that justifies its existence in a community in terms of its usefulness in achieving specific utilitarian goals such as access to economic development or social mobility'. After all, as Fishman, Cooper and Conrad (1977: 115) say, languages are rarely acquired for their own sake. They are acquired as keys to other things that are desired in life, among them the desire to be able to have access to employment, which now generally requires knowledge of a Western language such as English; and the desire to move up the social ladder and identify with the power elite (Kamwangamalu 2004: 141).

Conclusion

This chapter has attempted to address the issue of vernacular education in postcolonial Africa. Unlike previous discussions of this issue, the chapter has sought to associate the promotion of indigenous languages in education with tangible outcomes for language users, such as access to resources, political participation, and upward social mobility. Drawing on recent developments in language economics, I have argued that African masses would not support or strive for an education in an indigenous language, even if it were made available, unless this education were given a real cachet in the broader political and economic context. Rather, if they can afford it parents will send their children to a school where the medium of education is a Western language, for they are aware not only of the status of both the indigenous languages and a former colonial language in society, but also of the dividends that an education in the medium of a Western language will provide for their children and their future. Put differently, the payoffs for educating one's child in the medium of a Western language far outweigh the payoffs of an education in the medium of an indigenous language. Accordingly, I argue that any language policy that seeks to promote indigenous African languages in education must demonstrate economic advantages if it is to be successful. I share the view, expressed by Ager (2001: 36–37), that without the bottom-up advantages, without an identity in which all social categories can share, language policies will remain empty, symbolic gestures, a plaything for the intellectuals. This is perhaps more so in Africa than in any other continent in the world.

References

Ager, Dennis (2001), *Motivation in Language Planning and Language Policy* (Clevedon: Multilingual Matters).

Akinnaso, F. Niyi. (1993), 'Policy and experiment in mother tongue literacy in Nigeria', *International Review of Education* 39(4): 255–85.

Alexander, Neville (1997), 'Language policy and planning in the new South Africa', *African Sociological Review* 1(1): 82–98.

Auerbach, Elsa R. (1996), 'Re-examining English-only in the ESL classroom', *Teachers of English to Speakers of Other Languages Quarterly* 27(1): 9–32.

Bamgbose, Ayo (2003), 'A recurring decimal: English in language policy and planning', *World Englishes* 22 (4): 419–31.

Bamgbose, Ayo (2006), 'Multilingualism and exclusion: policy, practice and prospects', Keynote address at the Symposium on Multilingualism and Exclusion. University of the Free State, Bloemfontein, South Africa, 24–26 April 2006.

Canagarajah, Suresh (2005), 'Conclusion to "Toward a more inclusive applied linguistics and English language teaching: A Symposium"', *Teachers of English to Speakers of Other Languages Quarterly* 39(4): 745–48.

Coulmas, Florian (1992), *Language and the Economy* (Oxford: Blackwell).

Crowley, A. (1996), *Language in History: Theories and Texts* (London: Longman).

Dorian, Nancy (1981), *Language Death: The Lifecycle of a Scottish Gaelic Dialec.* (Philadelphia, PA: University of Pennsylvania Press).

Fabian, J. (1986), *Language and Colonial Power: The Appropriation of Swahili in the Former Belgian Congo 1880-1938* (Cambridge: Cambridge University Press).

Fishman, Joshua A. (2004), 'Language maintenance, language shift, and reversing language shift' in Tej Bhatia and William Ritchie (eds), *The Handbook of Bilingualism* (New York: Blackwell), pp. 406–36.

Fishman, Joshua A; Robert L. Cooper; and Andrew W. Conrad (1977), *The Spread of English: The sociology of English as an Additional Language* (Rowly, MA: Newbury House Publishers, Inc).

Francis, David J. and Mohamed C. Kamanda (2001), 'Politics and language planning in Sierra Leone', *African Studies* 60 (2): 225–44.

Gal, S. (1979), *Language Shift: Social Determinants of Linguistic Change in Bilingual Austria* (New York: Academic Press).

Gilliam, A. M. (1984), 'Language and 'development' in Papua New Guinea', *Dialectal Anthropology* 8(4): 303–18.

Grin, Francois (2006), Economic considerations in language policy in Thomas Ricento (ed.), *An Introduction to Language Policy: Theory and Method*, (Malden, MA: Blackwell), pp. 77–94.

Gupta, Anthea F. (1997), 'When mother-tongue education is not preferred', *Journal of Multilingual and Multicultural Development* 18(6):496–506.

Halliday, Michael A. (2003), 'Written language, standard language, global language', *World Englishes* 22(4): 405–18.

Hasan, Ruqaiya. (2003), 'Globalization, literacy and ideology', *World Englishes* 22(4): 433–48.

Heine, Bernd (1990), 'Language policy in Africa' in B. Weinstein (ed.), *Language Policy and Political Development* (Norwood, N.J.: Ablex Publishing Corporation), pp. 167–84.

Haugen, Einar (1981), 'The implementation of corpus planning: Theory and practice' in J. Cobarrubias and Joshua A. Fishman (eds), *Progress in Language Planning: International Perspectives* (Berlin: Mouton), pp. 269–89.

Kamwangamalu, Nkonko M. (2004), 'Language policy/language economics interface and mother tongue education in post-apartheid South Africa' in: N. M. Kamwangamalu (ed.), *Language Problems and Language Planning, Special issue: South Africa* (Amsterdam: Benjamins) 28(2): 131–46..

Kamwangamalu, Nkonko M. (2003a), 'Social change and language shift: South Africa', *Annual Review of Applied Linguistics* 23: 225–42.

Kamwangamalu, Nkonko M. (2003b), 'Globalization of English, and language maintenance and shift in South Africa', *International Journal of the Sociology of Language* 164: 65–81.

Kamwangamalu, Nkonko M. (1997), 'Multilingualism and education policy in post-apartheid South Africa', *Language Problems and Language Planning*, 21(3): 234–53.

Lai, Pak-Sang and Bryam, Michael (2003), 'The politics of bilingualism: a reproduction analysis of the policy of mother tongue education in Hong Kong after 1997', *Compare* 33(2): 315–34.

Landon, John. (2000), 'Language policy development in primary education in Scotland', Paper presented at the ELET conference, University of Natal, Durban (September 2000).

Le Page, Robert B. (1997), 'Political and economic aspects of vernacular literacy' in Andre Tabouret-Keller, Robert Le Page, P. Gardner-Chloros and G. Varro (eds), *Vernacular Literacy: A Re-evaluation* (Oxford: Clarendon Press).

Lieberson, S. (1980), 'Procedures for improving sociolinguistic surveys of language maintenance and language shift', *International Journal of the Sociology of Language* 25: 11–27.

Lin, Angel M. Y. and Peter Martin(2005) *Decolonisation, Globalisation: Language-in-Education Policy and Practice* (Clevedon: Multilingual Matters).

London, N. (2003), 'Ideology and politics in English language education in Trinidad and Tobago; the colonial experience and a postcolonial critique', *Comparative Education Review* 47(3): 287–320.

McArthur,T. (1983), *A Foundation Course for Language Teachers* (Cambridge: Cambridge University Press).

Mfum-Mensah, Obed (2005), 'The impact of colonial and postcolonial Ghanaian language policies on vernacular use in schools in two northern Ghanaian communities', *Comparative Education* 41(1): 71–85.

Nettle, Daniel and Romaine, Suzanne (2000), *Vanishing Voices: The Extinction of the World's Languages* (Oxford: Oxford University Press).

OAU (1986), 'Language Plan of Action for Africa. Council of Ministers', Forty-Fourth Ordinary Session, July 1986. Addis-Ababa, Ethiopia.

Paulston, Christina B. (1988), *International Handbook of Bilingualism and Bilingual Education* (New York: Greenwood Press).

Ramasamy, K. (2001), 'Mother tongue and medium of instruction – a continuing battle', *Language in India* 1(6): 1–6.

Smieja, B. (1999), 'Codeswitching and language shift in Botswana: Indicators for language change and language death? A progress report', *Review of Applied Linguistics*, 123–24, 125–60.

Spencer, John (1985), 'Language and development in Africa: The unequal equation' in Wolfson, Nessa and Joan Manes (eds), *Language of Inequality*, (Berlin: Mouton), pp. 387–97.

Strauss, Gideon. (1996), 'The economics of language: diversity and development in an information economy', *The Economics of Language. Language Report* 5(2): 2–27

Tabouret-Keller, A., Gardner-Chloros, P. and Varro, G. (1997, eds) *Vernacular Literacy: A Re-Evaluation* (Oxford: Clarendon Press).

Tollefson, James (1991), *Planning Language, Planning Inequality* (New York: Longman).

Tollefson, James W. and Amy B. Tsui (2004, eds) *Medium of Instruction Policies: Which Agenda? Whose Agenda?* (Mahwah, NJ: Erlbaum).

UNESCO (1995) *The use of vernacular languages in education* (Paris: UNESCO).

Vaillancourt, F. and Grin, F. (2000), *The Choice of a Language of Instruction: The Economic Aspects. Distance Learning Course on Language Instruction in Basic Education* (Washington, DC: World Bank Institute).

Walsh, John (2006), 'Language and socio-economic development: Towards a theoretical framework', *Language Problems and Language Planning* 30(2): 127–48.

Wee, Lionel (2003), 'Linguistic instrumentalism in Singapore', *Journal of Multilingual and Multicultural Development* 24(3): 211–224.

Whitehead, Clive (1995), 'The medium of instruction in British colonial education: A case of cultural imperialism or enlightened paternalism', *History of Education* 24(1): 1–15.

Wiley, Terrence (2006), 'The lessons of historical investigations: Implications for the study of language policy and planning' in Thomas Ricento (ed.), *An Introduction to Language Policy: Theory and Method*, (Malden, MA: Blackwell), pp. 135–52.

Woolard, Kathryn A. and Bambi B. Schieffelin (1994), 'Language ideology', *Annual Review of Anthropology* 23: 55–82.

World Bank (1980), *Education Policy Paper* (Third edition) Washington, D.C.

On the Appropriateness of the Metaphor of LOSS[1]

11

David Block

In this chapter, I explore the extent to which the metaphor of LOSS (MoL) is always appropriate as a way of framing discussions of language maintenance and shift in the lives of individuals. I begin with a brief discussion of loss in existing literature on language endangerment. I then consider three London-based case studies which show how in different ways individuals are relatively ambivalent about what some would view as the loss of languages in their lives. I conclude with a call for a more nuanced approach to the research of language maintenance and shift contexts.

Introduction

'Do Not Cut My Tongue, Let me Live and Die With MY Language.' A Comment on English and Other Languages in relation to Linguistic Human Rights

(The title of an article by Tove Skutnabb-Kangas, 2004)

Dolça Catalunya,	Sweet Catalonia.
pàtria del meu cor,	homeland of my heart,
quan de tu s'allunya	to be far from you
d'enyorança es mor.	is to die of longing.
…	…
Adéu, germans;	Good-bye, brothers and sisters;
adéu-siau, mon pare,	farewell, my father,
no us veuré més!	I shan't see you again!
Oh, si al fossar	Oh, if in the graveyard
on jau ma dolça mare	where my sweet mother lies
jo el llit tingués!	I had my bed!
Oh mariners,	Oh mariners,
el vent que me'n desterra,	the wind that banishes me,
que em fa sofrir!	that makes me suffer!
Estic malalt, més ai!,	I am sick, and more!,
torneu-me a terra,	return me to land,
que hi vull morir!	for I want to die there!

(Verses 1 and 3 of 'L'emigrant' by Mossèn Jacint Verdgauer, 1888;
translation from Catalan into English by the author)

These are two fragments from my day-to-day life, the first arising from my reading of academic journals and the second arising from my exposure to a nineteenth-century poem, which I first read nearly 30 years ago. Though different in origin, and separated by a good many years, they have in common their framing of experiences involving change in one's linguistic and cultural environment emotively and in terms of great loss. In the first fragment, Skutnabb-Kangas's title indicates that in the article that follows she will be defending her position that a failure to maintain one's first language and an attendant shift to another language (probably one deemed to be dominant in the world, such as French or English) can have dramatic consequences for one's sense of self over a lifetime. In her work over the years, she has argued passionately against the loss of languages to groups of speakers and in favour of the rights of individuals to be able to live their lives fully (most importantly, to be educated) in their first languages. The second fragment contains the first and last verses of the Catalan poet Mossèn Jacint Verdaguer's ode to the emigrant who leaves behind all of his childhood points of reference, such as homeland, family, landscape and climate. The poem captures the sense of loss felt by those who yearn for a past to which they cannot return.

The theme of loss conveyed in these two fragments is central to this chapter. In particular, I wish to adopt a critical stance towards what we might call the metaphor of LOSS (MoL) that runs through them and is a constant in much current literature on language maintenance and shift. Following Donald Schön's classic work on problem framing, in this chapter I understand metaphor to be

> central to the task of accounting for our perspectives on the world: how we think about things, make sense of reality, and set the problems we later try to solve. In this second sense, 'metaphor' refers both to a certain kind of product – a perspective or frame, a way of looking at things – and to a certain kind of process – a process by which new perspectives on the world come into existence. (Schön, 1979: 254)

My aim is to reflect on whether or not the MoL is always appropriate as a way of framing discussions of language maintenance and shift in the lives of individuals. I begin by looking at some current literature which critiques some of the notions associated with the MoL before examining briefly how informants in three studies of bilingualism frame their experiences of language maintenance and shift in their lifetimes.

This chapter differs from other contributions to this volume in that it critiques the view that languages are repositories of cultures inextricably linked with national and ethnic identities and it does not deal with languages in terms of Heller's (1999: 5) 'new pragmatic position', whereby languages are viewed instrumentally as skills to be traded on as resources in local and global job markets. Indeed, the main thrust of this volume seems to rest on the assumption that the former view of language has been superseded by the latter view and that this has led to different ways of approaching language policy in many parts of the world. Here, I do not intend to contest this portrayal of recent history, as I agree that matters seem to have evolved in this way in many different language policy contexts. However, the point I wish to make here is that it is important to examine what has been behind discussions of languages as cultural and identity markers as I believe that such discussions have been based – and continue to be based – rather uncritically on the assumption that languages defined variably as 'mother tongue', 'home' or 'community' are necessarily the most important identity markers for individuals.

Language endangerment and loss

There is a by now a well-established academic literature on the interrelated issues of language rights and language endangerment which frames language maintenance and shift in terms of the MoL (e.g. Fishman, 1991; 2001;

Crystal, 2000; Skutnabb-Kangas, 2000; May, 2001; 2005; Patrick and Freeland, 2004; Duchêne and Heller, 2007). In addition, as authors such as Jaffe (2007) and Cameron (2007) observe, pronouncements about language endangerment are increasingly coming from government and supra-government organizations and agencies (Jaffe cites as examples the National Science Foundation, a funding agency in the USA, and UNESCO) as well as in the popular media (Cameron cites a story about the 'extinction' of languages on the website of the global news channel CNN). Examining a sample of sources focusing on language endangerment, Jaffe notes a constellation of accepted views on the matter. First, language is framed as the main vehicle through which cultures are constructed, maintained and passed on from one generation to another. This being the case, the loss of a language is seen as synonymous with the loss of a culture. In addition, the loss of a culture is seen as the loss of another unique part of the mosaic that is humanity in all its diversity. Important here is the relative unquestioning acceptance of the ecological metaphor as appropriate for language survival and endangerment among those who disseminate such thinking. Thus, just as it is good to conserve animal species and wildlife in general, it is good to preserve languages. Finally, languages are seen as the single most important aspect of both collective and individual identities and the loss of a language is seen as necessarily damaging to the individual's ongoing life narrative.

Elsewhere, Cameron examines and critiques the growing tendency among sociolinguists and lay people to frame discussions of language maintenance, shift and vitality in terms of emotive and moralistic terms. She notes that particularly when this topic appears in the mass media, it takes on some of the characteristics of what is known as 'moral panic'. Thus, there is 'the presupposition of a dire and rapidly deteriorating situation, . . ., the repeated expression of alarm about the scale of the problem, and the use of emotively, loaded terms to describe it (e.g. *death, endangerment, extinction, threat*)' (Cameron, 2007: 269). In addition, like Jaffe, Cameron is critical of the growing tendency to see languages as part of a global ecology, their existence and survival going hand in hand with the existence and survival of the physical environment. Cameron sees in this 'ecologized' framing of language a return to views that the biological takes precedence over the social. She also notes that there is a problem in the metaphor of LANGUAGES ARE BIOLOGICAL SPECIES: while biological species are genetically defined, languages are not. Thus to liken the disappearance of a language, such as Saami, to the disappearance of a bird species, such as the Kirkland's Warbler, is to adopt what she terms an 'organicist view of language' that most linguists would today reject. Ultimately, however, the big problem with discourses of endangerment is how they too often essentialize the inter-connections and interrelationships between language, culture and identity. As both Cameron and Jaffe suggest, matters are not as mechanistic as so many who are concerned about the languages of the world would have us believe.

Alastair Pennycook (e.g. 2004) has also devoted a good deal of attention to the problematicity of the 'language ecology terminology'. Among other things, he suggests that sociologists and language policy scholars drink from the waters of the biological at their own peril because in doing so, they may easily find themselves defending contradictory and simultaneously oppositional positions. Thus, they are for the high minded and liberal notion of diversity in a 'natural' world ecosystem that includes not only plants and animals, but also languages; however, in taking this position, they find themselves aligned philosophically with politically conservative evolutionary biologists who eschew social constructivism in favour of hard-core determinist or teleological scientism.

A further problem with the MoL is how in so many discussions about loss and preservation, language is framed as a stable ontological reality. If languages are under threat or can die or be killed, the presumption is that they exist as freestanding entities, both definable and describable by linguists and pro-tectable by, for example, government authorities. Some two decades ago, Roy Harris (e.g. 1990) wrote about the 'myth' of linguistics, questioning, among other things, the idea that linguistics as a discipline must have language as the chief unit of analysis and that languages, as postulated by linguists, actually have any empirical validity. More recently, Harris's ideas have been taken forward forcefully by authors such as Blommaert (2006) and Makoni and Pennycook (2006), as part of a general rethinking of how language, as emergent in social activities and practices, is to be made sense of. Thus, many applied linguists are now questioning the traditional idea that languages are self-contained entities with lives of their own, or 'artefacts' in Blommaert's terms, independent of users and analysts. The new emergent view of languages is summed up well by Pennycook: 'Languages are not organisms that interact with the environment, or fixed, static systems, but rather shifting changing cultural artefacts' (Pennycook, 2004: 231). It is therefore hard for those draw-ing on the MoL in their discussions of languages to reconcile a realist take on languages, which posits an existence prior to and independent of human contact, with a (sometimes critical) poststructuralist view of the world which accommodates, among other things, the social construction of reality as a foundational notion.

While Jaffe, Cameron, Makoni, Pennycook and others are making their comments with reference to debates which are generally about the survival of languages and cultures that are indigenous to particular geographical spaces, what they say also applies to discussions of language maintenance and shift among people who have migrated from one country to another. In these contexts as well, the interrelationships between language, culture and identity are not as simple as they are often perceived and presented and in my view, the MoL is not always the most appropriate way of framing matters. One way of making the latter point is to listen to the stories told by people who have experienced, either directly or indirectly, migration in their lifetimes. I refer here to individuals classified as 'immigrants', but perhaps more importantly, their children. As I hope to show with admittedly selective examples, the MoL is often either not a part of the story of many migrants and their children, or it is considerably nuanced in the stories told by them.

The MoL and young Londoners from South Asian backgrounds

The MoL is closely linked to a tendency among educators in London (and Britain who talk about bilingualism and bilinguals to engage in what Roxy Harris calls 'romantic bilingualism'. Harris defines romantic bilingualism as 'the widespread practice, in British schools and other educational contexts, based on little or no analysis or enquiry, of attributing to pupils drawn from visible ethnic minority groups an expertise in and allegiance to any community languages with which they have some acquaintance' (Harris 1997: 14). In Harris (2006) we see just how ill-judged such attributions can be as well as the often exaggerated nature of suggestions that the children of immigrants feel a great sense of loss if they are not able to maintain strong links with the languages and cultures of their parents. Drawing on a questionnaire, written accounts, self-made audio recordings and in-depth interviews, Harris explored the language use patterns and characteristics of 31 secondary school students in London, calling his cohort the 'Blackhill youth'. The students were for the most part the children of immigrants from South Asia and Harris was interested in exploring issues around race, ethnicity and national identity, all mediated by language use as acts of identity (LePage and Tabouret-Keller, 1985).

Relevant to the discussion here, Harris found a great deal of ambivalence about the maintenance of home language, cultural and religious practices. On the one hand, the students talked about the importance of 'my' language and professed an interest in learning and being able to speak it. However, many made statements in which they admitted to having very little knowledge of the languages of their parents. In the following excerpt, Narjot, a young man from a Punjabi Sikh background, describes his relationship with Punjabi:

> My language I don't really know all of it because I was just when they were raising me they were just speaking English all the time and I just learned English I never really learned . . . (Harris, 2006: 117; transcription modified by this author to aid readability)

Harris sees comments like this one as indicative of 'an apparent paradox between . . . [his informants'] propriety claims and their simultaneous disavowal of a high level of expertise' (p. 117). Exploring further, he discovered that unlike Narjot, many of his informants attributed their lack of knowledge of home languages not to the dominance of English in their lives but to their lack of interest in learning it in community language classes that their parents sent them to as children. The following exchange between Gurshanti (G), a young woman from a Punjabi Sikh background, and Harris (R) shows quite clearly the former's ambivalent attitude towards learning Punjabi:

> G: It's just I don't know what to do because I can't speak it.
> R: Does it worry you or
> G: Yeah sometimes like erm one of my friends she takes lessons but . . . I can't be bothered to do that. I wouldn't want to do it.
> R: What why don't you want to do it?
> G: I mean I have taken lessons like . . . my mum sent me to them sometimes but I didn't learn anything . . . I'd practise the same thing over and over again and still not learn it.
> R: So how long did you do it for?
> G: I did it for a little while . . . when I was young.
> (Harris, 2006: 120; transcription modified by this author to aid readability)

Harris sees such passivity in the face of the potential loss of languages such as Punjabi as part and parcel of a natural tendency towards language shift (here, the near-total shift to various forms of English) as new ethnicities arise in his informants' day-to-day lives in London. Exposed to a wide variety of English-mediated school, work and leisure activities, these adolescents would have to make an extraordinary effort if they truly desired to achieve a good working competence in home languages. The latter come to be associated with family life, and in many cases only partially so. Above all, they cannot compete with the seduction of English and the symbolic capital (Bourdieu, 1991) associated with it both in informal peer group contexts and in wider society in education and work environments. Ultimately, the informants in Harris' study were most expert in and affiliated to what they termed 'slang' English, the all purpose emergent London 'yoof-speak', which is characterized by an amalgam of features drawn from traditional Cockney, revived Jamaican Creole and American and Australian Englishes, along with some elements traceable to South Asian forms of English. Their speech was thus characterized by the extensive use of glottal stops (e.g. /ʔ/ for /t/); dental fricatives for labiodentals (e.g. /ð/ replaced by /v/ as in 'bruver' for 'brother'; /θ/ replaced by /f/ as in 'fing' for 'thing'); the 'be + like' quotative (e.g. 'He's like . . . and I'm like . . .'); uptalking (i.e. the use of rising intonation at the end of statements); and finally, the all purpose tag question 'innit' (e.g. 'You live in London, innit?'). Taking into account his informants' exposure to the different language varieties that make up the linguistic map of London, Harris describes their home language ethnolinguistic status as follows:

> The condition of the Blackhill youth, with respect to community language expertise, looks predictable and does not require undue melancholia on the part of grandparents, parents or sympathetic observers. The young people are, here, clearly subject to larger social structural forces, which defy voluntarism. In other words, there is something in their British ethnicity which constrains the utility of the community languages and reduces them gradually to the kind of symbolic status which accommodates the continued use of phrases like 'my language' and 'my culture'. It should be emphasised that the Blackhill youth did not show any particular discomfort about these circumstances. (Harris, 2006: 123)

Crucial in this quote is the last sentence where Harris notes a lack of deeply felt loss among his informants. Nevertheless, we might ask if the Blackhill youth are typical of London youth from South Asian backgrounds. Shifting to a different part of London and dealing with a slightly older cohort, Siân Preece (2006) found some of the same self-positionings as Harris in her study of the language practices of students at a new university in London. One such student was Tahir, who was born and raised in a London household in which both Urdu and Punjabi were spoken by his Pakistani-born parents. Tahir also had access to Arabic when he attended Koran reading classes as a child. In university records, Tahir was classified as bilingual, as an English, Urdu and Punjabi speaker. However, when asked by Preece to talk about his expertise in the latter two languages, he responded as follows:

> Me and the little ones, my sisters and brothers, we [speak] mixed innit? . . . My mum and dad they can speak Punjabi and Urdu, they understand both. . . . They're

> quite similar . . . Urdu and Punjabi . . . have words . . . that mean the same in both
> languages . . . My mum and dad . . . can understand both Punjabi and Urdu. They
> can speak Punjabi [and] Urdu and read it whereas we can't. We just pick up a little
> bit here, pick up a little bit there [and] just speak as we go along. My parents don't
> mind . . . [but] I think relatives do sometimes. Relatives think [we] should speak
> proper Urdu or Punjabi. . . . When I speak in front of my mum and dad I say what
> I want but when I speak in front of relatives and they're speaking Urdu or Punjabi,
> in that case I just don't talk. (Tahir, 7/11/01) (Preece, 2006: 183)

There are several issues arising in this quote that relate to Tahir's status as
a bilingual Londoner. First, as Preece notes, he does not distinguish between
Urdu and Punjabi very clearly, seemingly grouping them together as basically
the same language. This failure to distinguish perhaps does not speak very
highly of Tahir's expertise in either language and it certainly runs against language surveys in Britain which deal with them separately (e.g. Alladina and
Edwards 1991; Baker and Eversley, 2000); however, in fairness to Tahir, such
conflation is not uncommon among the children of immigrants who speak
these languages at home. It is also, as Canagarajah notes, characteristic of the
linguistic diversity of South Asia, where 'people are so multilingual, interacting
with many languages group . . . that it is difficult to say where one language/
group begins and the other ends' (Canagarajah, 2007: 234). Second, Tahir
makes reference to a kind of family idiolect, drawing on English, Urdu and
Punjabi, which has arisen due to varying degrees of expertise in all three languages among family members. Such code mixing is common in such situations: it has been documented extensively over the years by sociolinguists such
as Milroy and Muysken (1995) and Myers-Scotton (2002), and it is reported
by some of Harris's informants as well. Third, Urdu and Punjabi are clearly
positioned by Tahir as languages for use in very specific circumstances, primarily with members of the extended family, a tendency also observed in Harris's
study. Thus, for most of his daily activities, Tahir does not use these languages
and for the most part, he does not show a strong emotional tie to them.
Ultimately, the bilingual story that he relates to Preece is one of English as his
dominant language and Urdu and Punjabi, the source of his putative bilingual
status, very much as secondary communicative resources in his life. Tahir sums
up the languages in his life, and his relative affiliation to them, as follows:

> When I speak Urdu I think of my parents . . . when I speak Punjabi for some reason
> I think of Sikh people, the language belongs to them . . . When I speak English
> I don't think of English people, I think of me. I think of me in England. When I
> think of Arabic I think of religion because that's what I was there for. I went [to]

Saudi Arabia and MAN it's . . . just like 24-7 religion out there. (Tahir, 7/11/01)
(Preece, 2006: 171)

As regards Tahir's bilingual identity, he is similar to Harris's informants as he shows a high level of expertise in and affiliation to his 'slang' London English. Commenting on the masculine subject positions that he adopts, Preece describes Tahir as follows:

> With his peers and while talking about his peers in the interviews, Tahir frequently enacts laddish masculinity that is rooted in London as a global city, a setting in which aspects of 'cool' cultures from around the world can become fused with British popular youth culture. In contrast, he appears more ambivalent about doing 'acceptable' masculinity in the setting of his family, frequently discussing this in terms of family obligations and duties . . . Tahir only really seems at 'home' with his London laddish self . . . [and] shows little inclination to use the networks of his family and community to develop his own links with Pakistan. (Preece, 2006: 190)

If Tahir feels at home in London as an English speaker, does he feel any sense of loss as regards his relative rudimentary knowledge of Punjabi and Urdu? In general, it would appear that he does not, acting much like Harris's informants who seemed to go through the motions of lamenting their wasted opportunities to learn home languages when they were young children. If Tahir does feel loss, it would appear to be motivated by discomfort experienced in the here and now, specifically how he frames as problematic his inability to speak Punjabi and Urdu well in family encounters both in Britain and when he has visited Pakistan. Thus, for Tahir, any sense of loss is defensive in nature: it would make his life easier if he could speak Punjabi and Urdu better on certain occasions, but he does not show any strong affiliation or emotional ties to what might be considered his first languages. Rather, like Harris's informants, he moves more in the world of the here and now, as he affiliates to and inhabits London situated and inflected subject positions.

Leaving the Anglophone world

One noteworthy characteristic of MoL dominated discussions of language loss and maintenance among immigrant populations is its Anglo-centric nature. It seems that while the putative loss of language in immigrant populations is a much discussed topic in the Anglophone world (i.e. countries such as the USA Canada, Australia and the United Kingdom), it is not as significant a part of public debate elsewhere. From this perspective it is perhaps a good idea to listen not only to voices of immigrants in places like the USA and Britain but also to those who have migrated to countries where English is not the principal language of communication. Recently an MA student at the Institute of Education, Elena Soriano, carried out a small-scale study of two immigrants to Barcelona, which provides some further food for thought alongside that provided by Harris and Preece.[2]

Soriano interviewed a sister and a brother (whom I will here refer to as J and L), both Spanish citizens of Gambian descent, who had moved to London at the ages of 15 and 17. J and L were born and raised in Barcelona and in a sense can be seen as early pioneers and part of the first wave of the massive immigration of people from Sub-Saharan Africa, North Africa, South America and Eastern Europe to Catalonia and Spain, which began in the early 1990s. The two recall growing up with a strong Gambian culture at home in terms of language (they spoke Mandika with their mother), religion (they were practising Muslims), food and eating habits, festivals and so on. However, at the same time they recall interacting with children from a variety of different backgrounds in their neighbourhood in Barcelona. In this environment, they appear to have embraced the emergent Catalan culture of their neighbourhood as their own.[3]

Their father was an English teacher, educated in Gambia and the United Kingdom, who worked in a private school where the siblings studied until their departure from Barcelona, a school which they described as '*un colegio católico sin religión*' ('a catholic school without religion'). The two were educated in Catalan, although they reported that the vast majority of their friendships were established in Spanish. They recall that they were the first black and Muslim students to attend the school and that they did note differences between themselves and their white classmates, as regards certain customs such as eating norms. However, in their interview, they recounted a positive narrative of acceptance by their classmates and of becoming Spanish during their formal education in Barcelona. When asked how he preferred to identify himself, L framed his response in terms of *jus sanguinis* (rooted in one's blood) and *jus solis* (rooted in the land where one is born) versions of national identity, showing a preference for the latter approach:

> To tell you the truth I probably identify more as Spanish because for me saying that I am Spanish is more about nationality not skin colour. (L)
>
> *Yo si quieres que te diga la verdad [me identifico] a lo mejor más como español porque para mí . . . decir que soy español va más con la nacionalidad no viene a colores. (L)*

The siblings move to London came about because their parents believed that, as people of colour, they would have more opportunities to prosper in the United Kingdom. L explained matters as follows:

> [A]ctually our parents pushed us a little . . . (Laughter) but it's also because of where we grew up and stuff. I don't know. To tell you the truth perhaps a lot of people don't think so but I believe that in England – I spent months here on holiday before coming to live – and I believe that there are more opportunities for people of colour than in Spain . . . for me there are more opportunities here than in Spain. (L)

> . . . *la verdad es que los padres nos empujaron un poco . . . (risas) pero es porque también donde nos hemos criado y eso. No se. Si quieres que te diga la verdad a lo mejor mucha gente no lo piensa pero yo creo que en Inglaterra– he estado meses de vacaciones antes de vivir– y yo creo que hay mas salida para gente de color que en España . . . para mi hay más salida aquí que en España.* (L)

Here L presents colour as more important than nationality as regards how he would be treated in Barcelona. Despite having been born and raised in Barcelona, he would encounter discrimination as he moved from formal education to the job market. The notion of going to London for greater opportunities is interesting in how it simultaneously presents Barcelona/Catalonia as racist and London as not racist.

At the time of their interview, the two siblings had been in London for three years. Although they had adapted to English-mediated education and appeared ready to stay in London for the foreseeable future, they still self-identified as Spanish. Without denying their Gambian roots, they had rather matter-of-factly flowed with changes in their lives in terms of culture and language. Ultimately, the language and culture that had most impacted them was their form of Spanish culture lived in Barcelona. Interestingly, in their interview-elicited narratives, there is no mention of loss. They present a picture of having achieved a healthy balance between their heritage language and culture and the languages and cultures of Barcelona. Thus, while their relationship with their parents and extended family amounted to a stabilized feeling of Gambian identity, the overwhelming presence of Catalan and Spanish languages and Catalan culture in the street and school, as well as their Spanish citizenship, meant that 'Spanish' was their predominant reference point when they explained to others who they were.

Conclusion

After critiquing some of the assumptions behind current literature on language endangerment and loss, in this chapter I have considered different contexts in which language loss takes place in different ways and to varying degrees. My main point has been that across different language maintenance and shift contexts – and specifically with reference to individuals with migrant experience – there need to be more nuanced approaches that move away from the overly emotive and romantic tendencies of the quotes produced at the beginning of this paper and the MoL. However, I hasten to emphasize here that my aim has not been to say that those who adopt emotive and even romanticized stances towards particular languages are *wrong*. Neither is it my view that language shift, when it does occur, is somehow necessarily and always a good thing (see Creese and Martin, 2006, for convincing examples in favour of efforts to maintain languages among ethnic minority populations in Britain). And, I do not embrace an overarching evolutionary argument whereby shifts from minority to majority languages are inevitable and that individuals and collectives should just let currently dominant discourses such as neo-liberalism and American cultural imperialism wash over them. Indeed, my own personal experience of having immersed myself in Catalan language and culture for the virtual entirety of my adult life has taught me the importance of the links between language and collective and individual identities. After living 11 years in London, I still use Catalan every day and I am acutely aware of its symbolic value for me as part and parcel of an identity I have fought to maintain for nearly 30 years.

Nevertheless, I believe it imperative for researchers to resist tendencies I often find in the popular media and in academic writing towards exaggeration as regards what it means for a language to disappear from the repertoire of individuals or entire collectives. Above all, it is not enough to use throwaway lines, such as the following ones, which I have heard at conferences over the years:

> [with reference to bilingualism] And apart from all of the arguments in favour, it's just a good thing.
>
> Bilingualism is good for the soul.
>
> I feel sorry for monolinguals.

Those of us who are interested in linguistic and cultural diversity surely need to make our case better, and in a more sanguine manner.

Obviously, every context is different and above all, every context is lived differently by individuals within. In my view, we would do better to listen a little more to the stories of individuals actually living through language maintenance and shift and a little less to those who pronounce on such matters from outside of such contexts, often basing what they say on the assumed validity of ecological analogies and the MoL. The kind of research I have reviewed here, albeit briefly, can help to move us away from more extreme views towards the adoption of calmer approaches. Thus, from Harris's and Preece's research, we learn that the 'loss' of home languages among many young people of South Asian backgrounds in London is often less traumatic than many might imagine or assume. And from Soriano's interview with the brother and sister from Barcelona, we see that some individuals seem to flow with their surroundings. Thus while individuals in such contexts do not reject or repudiate their pasts, they also do not romanticize them or feel a sense of loss if they slowly fade to a less significant role in their lives. Indeed, as I suggest elsewhere (Block, 2006), they live their multilingualism and multiculturalism as prosaic, ordinary, commonplace, a fact of life and even banal: it is what it is, and it is certainly not much to get excited about, as academics so often do.

I am also bothered by how discussions of language maintenance and loss can carry with them a degree of condescension towards the affected parties, who are typically the politically and economically less powerful of the world. This tendency is mentioned and criticized by some scholars. For example, Pennycook cites Glynn Williams (1992) who wrote long ago about the 'overriding desire to support the underdog, accompanied by a sociological perspective which reflects the power of the dominant' (Williams, 1992: 226; cited in Pennycook, 2004: 221) that is manifest in the work of many sociolinguists. Meanwhile, John Edwards cites George Orwell's barb that 'this business about the moral superiority of the poor is one of the deadliest forms of escapism the ruling class have evolved' (Orwell, 1970: 208 and 230; cited in Edwards, 2008: 8). Once again, the MoL as a dominant frame in discussions of language maintenance and loss can put proponents in the company of unwelcome travelling companions, in this case practitioners of a modern form of *noblesse oblige.*

As I suggested previously, the MoL seems to be much more a centrepiece of debates taking place in English than it is in debates taking place in other languages. In a well-articulated critique of academic imperialism, Bourdieu and Wacquant (2005) decry the way in which 'numerous topics directly issuing from the intellectual confrontations relating to the social particularity of American society and its universities have been imposed, in patently dehistoricized form, upon the entire planet' (Bourdieu and Wacquant, 2005: 178). The authors go on to explore how debates about race and multiculturalism have been Americanized in different parts of the world, citing as an example attempts by some US funding agencies to persuade Brazilians to frame their country's particular racial diversity in American black-and-white terms.

The MoL is not an American invention, even if it does find a home very easily in liberal American academic thought. It is, on the other hand, a metaphorical frame which is progressively becoming 'planetarized or globalized', to use Bourdieu and Wacquant's terminology, via English-mediated academia around the world. And the point to be made here is one that comes up in the critiques of Pennycook and Edwards, namely that those who frame their discussions of language maintenance and loss according to the MoL, may well be practising a kind of academic imperialism akin to the one described by Bourdieu and Wacquant, a political stance that they would surely not be comfortable with.

To conclude, it is my view that we need to think more about matters related to language maintenance and loss at a conceptual and theoretical level, so as to avoid some of the inconsistencies and contradictions I have noted in this chapter. In addition, we need to listen to the voices of those who have actually lived through language maintenance and loss, so as to avoid romantic depictions of such experiences. Finally, as regards a general theme of this book, Heller's (1999) pragmatic turn in language policy, I close with a thought. While the view of languages as cultural repositories may have given way to the view of languages as commodities in many parts of the world, what are we to make of the possibility that the former view was never representative of the feelings of the masses of people it was purported to be representative of? Perhaps it is a widespread ambivalence about the MoL which has led language policy makers to find new ways of framing and promoting languages. This is not to say that the pragmatic turn has not been part and parcel of the general marketization of our day-to-day lives in the new global economic order. Neither does it imply cynicism on the part of those dedicated to the elaboration of language policies. Rather, it is to suggest that there may be other factors besides broader structural changes that come into play in such developments, factors which have to do with the complexity of language-mediated activity at the local level, as described in the research cited in this chapter. Indeed, what ultimately galvanizes people around a language is probably not a question of either/or: *either* the more emotive cultural/national identification with the language *or* the more practical instrumental uses of language. Both are more linked to one another than has hitherto been argued explicitly. Certainly, Harris's and Preece's informants would suggest as much, as they affiliate strongly to their varieties of English both in affective and instrumental terms.

Notes

1 I am grateful to Jan Blommaert, Melanie Cooke, Peter Martin, Tim McNamara, Håvard Skaar, Cathie Wallace and the editors of this volume for their helpful comments on earlier drafts of this chapter.

2 I am grateful to Elena Soriano and her two informants for granting me permission to use extracts from their interviews in this chapter.

3 NB I refer here to a notion of Catalan culture, not in terms of language – J and L self-present as predominantly Spanish speakers educated in Catalan medium schools – but in terms of cultures emergent in present-day Catalonia.

References

Alladina, S. and Edwards, V. (eds) (1991), *Multilingualism in the British Isles*, volume 2 (London: Longman).

Baker, P. and Eversley, J. (eds) (2000), *Multilingual Capital* (London: Battlebridge Publications).

Block, D. (2004), 'Globalisation, transnational communication and the internet', *International Journal on Multicultural Societies* 6(1): 13–28.

Block, D. (2006), *Multilingual Identities in a Global City: London Stories* (London: Palgrave).

Blommaert, J. (2006), 'Language ideology', in K. Brown (ed.), *Encyclopaedia of Language and Linguistics, Volume 6*, 2nd edition (Oxford: Elsevier), pp. 510–22.

Bourdieu, P. (1991), *Language and Symbolic Power* (Oxford: Polity).

Bourdieu, P. and Wacquant, L. (2005), 'The cunning of imperialist reasoning', in L. Wacquant (ed.), *Pierre Bourdieu and Democratic Politics*, pp. 178–98.

Cameron, D. (2007), 'Language endangerment and verbal hygiene: history, morality and politics', in A. Duchêne and M. Heller (eds), *Discourses of Endangerment* (London: Continuum), pp. 268–85.

Canagarajah, S. A. (2007), 'After disinvention: possibilities for communication, community and practice', in S. Makoni and A. Pennycook (eds), *Disinventing and Reconstituting Languages* (Clevedon, UK: Multilingual Matters), pp. 233–39.

Creese, A. and Martin, P. W. (eds) (2006), Special Issues of *Language and Education* on 'Interaction in Complementary School Contexts. Developing Identities of Choice', *Language and Education* 20/1.

Crystal, D. (2000), *Language Death* (Cambridge: Cambridge University Press).

Duchêne, A. and Heller, M. (eds) (2007), *Discourses of Endangerment* (London: Continuum).

Edwards, J. (2008), 'The ecology of language: insight and illusion', in A. Creese, P. Martin and N. H. Hornberger (eds), *Encyclopedia of Language Education, 2nd edition, Volume 9: Ecology of Language* (New York: Springer), pp. 1–11.

Fishman, J. (1991), *Reversing Language Shift* (Clevedon, UK: Multilingual Matters).

Fishman, J. (ed.) (2001), *Reversing Language Shift* (Clevedon, UK: Multilingual Matters).

Harris, Roxy (1997), 'Romantic bilingualism: time for a change?', in C. Leung and C. Cable (eds), *English as an Additional Language: Changing Perspectives* (Watford: NALDIC), pp. 14–27.

Harris, Roxy (2006), *New Ethnicities and Language Use* (London: Palgrave).

Harris, Roy (1990), 'On redefining linguistics', in H. Davis and T. Taylor (eds), *Redefining Linguistics* (London: Routledge), pp. 18–52.

Heller, M. (1999), *Linguistic Minorities and Modernity: A Sociolinguistic Ethnography* (London: Longman).

Jaffe, A. (2007), 'Discourses of endangerment: contexts and consequences of essentializing discourses', in A. Duchêne and M. Heller (eds), *Discourses of Endangerment* (London: Continuum), pp. 57–75.

LePage, R. B. and Tabouret-Keller, A. (1985), *Acts of Identity: Creole-based Approaches to Language and Ethnicity* (Cambridge: Cambridge University Press).

Makoni, S. and Pennycook, A. (2006), 'Disinventing and reconstituting languages', in S. Makoni and A. Pennycook (eds), *Disinventing and Reconstituting Language* (Clevedon, UK: Multilingual Matters), pp. 1–41.

May, S. (2001), *Language and Minority Rights* (London: Longman).

May, S. (ed.) (2005), Special Issue on Language Rights, *Journal of Sociolinguistics* 9(3).

Milroy, L. and Muysken, P. (eds) (1995), *One Speaker, Two Languages: Cross-disciplinary Perspectives on Code-switching* (Cambridge: Cambridge University Press).

Myers-Scotton, C. (2002), *Contact Linguistics: Bilingual Encounters and Grammatical Outcomes* (Oxford: Oxford University Press).

Orwell, G. (1970 [1944]), As I please (*Tribune*, 30 June and 28 July, 1944). *The Collected Essays, Journalism and Letters of George Orwell, Volume 3*, pp. 208 and 230.

Patrick, D. and Freeland, J. (eds) (2004), *Language Rights and Language Survival: Sociolinguistic and Sociocultural Perspectives* (Manchester: St. Jerome).

Pennycook, A. (2004), 'Language policy and the ecological turn', *Language Policy* 3(3): 212–39.

Preece, S. (2006), 'British Asian undergraduate students in London', Chapter 8 in D. Block. *Multilingual Identities in a Global City: London Stories* (London: Palgrave), pp. 171–99.

Schön, D. (1979), 'Generative metaphor: A perspective on problem-setting in social policy', in A. Ortony (ed.), *Metaphor and Thought* (Cambridge: Cambridge University Press), pp. 253–83.

Skutnabb-Kangas, T. (2000), *Linguistic Genocide in Education or Worldwide Diversity and Human Rights?* (Mahwah, NJ: Lawrence Erlbaum).

Skutnabb-Kangas, T. (2004), '"Do not cut my tongue, let me live and die with MY language." A comment on English and other languages in relation to linguistic human rights', *Journal of Language Identity and Education* 3: 127–34.

Verdaguer, M. J. (1888), l'Emigrant, Retrieved 30.10.2006, : http://www.geocities.com/poesiasantcugat/verdaguer.htm.

Warschauer, M. (2003), *Technology and Social Inclusion* (Cambridge, MA: MIT Press).

Williams, G. (1992), *Sociolinguistics: A Sociological Critique* (London: Routledge).

12 The Commoditization of English and the Bologna Process: Global Products and Services, Exchange Mechanisms and Trans-national Labour

Michael Singh and Jinghe Han

Chapter Outline

As a commodity English is constituted as global products and services; it facilitates various forms of exchange and is an integral aspect of the skills-base of trans-national labour. English itself is now sold in various guises by small-to-medium businesses. Further, English facilitates the exchanges necessary to effecting trade between people, including those who otherwise have no common language. Third, workers who are proficient in English enhance the trans-national trade in labour. The internationalization of education, especially the globalization of the Bologna Process, is playing a role in the commoditization of English. Using evidence about teacher education, this chapter explores tensions between the desire for the Bologna Process to lower the informational barriers necessary for securing trans-national student and labour mobility, and the need to form multicultural subjects by respecting linguistic diversity. In this way it captures some of the complexities, if not the unpredictable and chaotic features of language as commodity.

Introduction

In the world's multilingual knowledge economies, the English language plays multi-dimensional functions as a commodity, and it has done so for a long time. The interdependent dimensions of language as commodity come together through the internationalization of education markets, in particular developments spurred by the Bologna Process. Started in the late 1990s ostensibly as a European initiative the Bologna Process sought to create a continent-wide system of comparable undergraduate and postgraduate degrees; establish a common credit transfer system; and promote a cooperative approach to quality assurance (Witte 2004). At the same time, the Bologna Process is committed to respecting the diversity of cultures, languages and national education systems. However, it obliges higher education institutions in Europe 'to certify foreign language competence in Masters level courses, and in most case this . . . means English' (Coleman 2006: 6). Despite the Bologna Process guaranteeing provision for linguistic diversity, the European Diploma Supplement, used to describe graduates' knowledge and competences, is issued in English, or the language of instruction and English.

In response to deliberations about the impact of the Bologna Process beyond Europe, the Australian Government developed an Australian Higher Education (AHEGS) to secure better recognition of Australian qualifications overseas and increase the trans-national mobility of its students and graduate labour (Bishop 2007). More specifically, an Australian Government inquiry into teacher education also argued for national accreditation of courses in this field to ensure harmony with the Bologna Process via international mutual recognition arrangements (Hartsuyker 2007: 30).

The internationalization of education promotes the commodity value of English, a process that has been intensifying since at least the 18th century. As argued by Singh, Kell and Pandian (2002), apart from its printed form this international language continues to diversify, expanding the mass of speakers of World Englishes rather than a single standardized version. Increasingly, World English Speakers (WES) are developing capabilities for appreciating this international language's diverse functions and to proactively engage in both-ways communication with those who speak its different varieties, as well as acknowledging the need for capabilities in other languages, especially given the acceleration and scale of language loss in the world today. Here the term

'World English' and its derivatives are used as an inclusive category, and thus includes speakers of 'Anglophone English.' The Bologna Process is both a part of, and a contribution to international efforts to standardize higher education, just as much as English (Singh and Han 2007). On the one hand, it seeks to lower the informational barriers necessary for securing trans-national student and labour mobility, and in doing so is promoting the use of English in this work of documentation. On the other hand, the Bologna Process itself advocates respect for linguistic diversity in recognition of the need to form multicultural graduates.

By drawing on evidence from teacher education, this chapter explores tensions between efforts to reduce informational barriers and non-documentary restrictions that affect the trans-national mobility of WES student-teachers. Specifically, it analyses the results of interviews with Ajit, Darshan, Surra, Guli, Harsha, Jigar Anbu, Abha, Fareen and Barbur, all pseudonyms for participants in the study (Singh and Han 2007). The first section of this chapter summarizes evidence indicating the commodity value of English in corporatized education in Australia. The sale of English language products and services is integral to the formation of trans-national knowledge workers, the new generation of local/global subjects. The second section addresses the uses of World Englishes in facilitating trans-national communicative exchanges associated with the flows of multilingual populations. It indicates reasons for the demand for workers with multicultural skills. The final section of this chapter presents an analysis of the relationship between the trade in English and the transnational labour market for knowledge workers. To begin with we situate the commoditization of English in terms of its development as a product or service. In doing so, we hope to represent a little of the complications, contradictions and chaos inherent in language as commodity.

English as product and service

Among the multi-dimensional roles played by English as a commodity in the world's multilingual knowledge economies, one of its key roles is as a product and service. These are sold by a range of English language providers to mostly eager consumers throughout the world. For instance, Australia's education export industry focuses on English as a tradable product and service to be sold in the local/global marketplace (Singh, Kell and Pandian 2002). Recruiting international students is driven by the globalization of higher education and English, practices now being stimulated further by the internationalization of

Europe's Bologna Process (Foude 2005). For example, both Australia and China, among others, have a stake in international education, World Englishes and the Bologna Process (DEST 2006). The Bologna Process began as an ambitious effort to create a European Higher Education Area for 16 million students studying across some 4,000 higher education institutions. As a vehicle for the harmonization or standardization of Europe's Higher Education systems, it seeks to better position them in the global competition for international fee-paying students from outside Europe.

However, the marginalization of other varieties of English does cause problems of economic inequality and social injustice. One solution to these problems has been to expand and improve opportunities for international students and newly arrived immigrants to gain literacy and skills in an acceptable form of standardized English. Of course, this creates and furthers opportunities for the marketing of English language products and services. All student-teachers from countries where English is not the primary language and who plan to teach in schools in Australia must sit for an English proficiency test (Institute of Language UNSW, n.d.), for which a substantial fee is charged. As Ajit explained the test applies irrespective of their English language proficiency or teaching experience in English:

> All the immigrant teachers [from non-English speaking countries] have to take the English test after immigration. The Department should make sure whether the teacher really needs to go to the English test or not. They cannot simply say that everyone has to do the test just because you are from a non-English speaking country. In Fiji, we teach students in English from primary to university. Why should they still test our English language?

The English test functions as a formal constraint on these teachers who had migrated to Australia from Fiji or similar countries. However, Ajit could not see any necessity for this test since English was the language in which he successfully completed all levels of education. Despite his objections, which were based on his assumptions about the acceptability of Fijian English, it is not clear how prospective employers in Australia could know the level of his proficiency without such a test. Even so, Darshan shared a similar view:

> I taught English in India for nearly ten years in university. After I came here, they asked me to take the English language test. It is ridiculous. You cannot just group them and say, 'Ok. You are from another country so have to do the language test.' The English test is not of a high standard. It does not test your real English ability. It simply tests the basics.

After a decade of English teaching experience in India, Darshan still had to take the English test before becoming a teacher in an Australian school. His English had the tempo and shape of Tamil. He questioned this formal barrier, but had to follow the regulations that imposed this constraint on him. Although it might be reasonable to consider these teachers' claims to proficiency in English, it is a problem to assume they can teach in English without demonstrating their proficiency. Further these tests are not surprising, if one accepts Phillipson's (2006: 16) observation that education is 'increasingly considered a service that can be traded, under the aegis of the World Trade Organization (WTO), and more specifically, of the General Agreement on Trade in Services (GATS).' Like the Bologna Process, these teachers are caught between lowering informational barriers; the encouragement of international trade in all areas of education and respecting linguistic diversity, including presumably the diversity of World Englishes (Singh and Han 2007). The provision of English language products and services is a large contributor to Australia's foreign earnings.

Discussion

Foreign students studying English in Australia contribute substantially to spending on education and associated costs. In 2005 the total economic impact of international student enrolments was 1,082 million Australian dollars, an increase of 16 per cent over the previous year (English Australia 2007: 4). For over 20 years, Australia's public education institutions have been driven to develop exports in English language products and services. By reducing funds to its higher education institutions, Australian government education policies created the economic drivers and the administrative surveillance mechanisms to stimulate the international marketing of English. The situation is similar in New Zealand, Canada, the USA and the UK; in the UK the

> English-language industry is a vital pillar of the British economy, with over half-a-million people travelling to the UK for language courses, and a massive export of publications and know-how, with the British Council in a key integrative [i.e. marketing] role worldwide. (Phillipson 2006: 20)

Neoliberal globalism, the political move for the commoditization of almost everything, has driven government policies in this direction. Consider for a moment the Australian English Language Intensive Courses for Overseas Students (ELICOS) Association. It was established in the 1970s with five member schools being responsible for teaching English to migrants. By 1985, the number of ELICOS schools had grown to just ten. Within the next 4 years, the number had increased to 107. The number of students enrolled in ELICOS centres rose from 4,000 in 1986 to 24,000 in 1988. Attracted by the world's growing 12-billion-Australian-dollar English language industry, Australia's Government encouraged the establishment of ELICOS centres (Kendall 2004: 26). In 2001, 189 ELICOS institutions in universities, technical institutes, private colleges and secondary schools were registered with the National English Accreditation Scheme (NEAS). By 2004, there were 226 such institutions. Australian providers of ELICOS products and services operate as commercial enterprises. Mostly these are small to medium public and private enterprises, rather than big businesses (Singh, Kell and Pandian 2002). Enrolment increased markedly from 78,338 in 2003 to 101,087 in 2005 (English Australia 2007).

In 2005, the ELT market produced an income for Australia of over 1 billion Australian dollars in student enrolment fees and spending. Eighty per cent of the ELICOS enrolments in 2005 were Asian students. Nearly half of the 230,000 overseas students studying in Australia that year were enrolled in ELICOS courses (Froude 2005: 13). Short-term English courses have become an effective and an important way of up-selling other areas of Australian higher education. The diversity of ELICOS providers allows them to compete in various niche markets, such as research for second-language learners and teaching English language test-taking skills. They target the international offshore and onshore markets throughout Asia and beyond. This suggests why the Australian Government is worried. If Asian countries choose to align with the Bologna Process, as China (China Youth 2005) is considering, then students from Asia may be more attracted to Europe than Australia (Department of Education, Science and Training 2006).

English sells. The demand for English language products and services is growing in China where there is a large demand for native English speakers to work in this industry (*China Daily* 2002). Many public and private schools in China have developed various programmes for students to learn English. It is sold as a means of connecting its consumers with symbols of openness; overseas educational opportunities; trans-national communication and participation in the local/global economy. This brings benefits to most of those who learn or sell it (Pegrum 2004: 3–9). The demand is so great, people in China are prepared to pay to learn Indian- or Malaysian-English; countries where there is increasing commoditization of English. While BBC and especially VOA English may not have a monopoly in the English language market, broadcast standard American English is privileged. Being highly prized it fetches a premium. English is an asset for native speakers.

English products and services are marketed worldwide through images and imaginings of modernization, globalization, self-development and the enjoyment of a cosmopolitan life. Marketing has strengthened and reinforced the dominant position of VOA English, which is the unchallenged market leader (Coulmas 2005: 9–10). This influences students' attitudes towards others varieties of English. Even so, English language education around the globe has experienced an upward economic movement. English is now a functional tool for effecting exchanges internationally as much as the trans-national exchanges that occur in school classrooms.

World Englishes and the structuring of exchange

English is a vehicle for promoting exchanges using mechanisms for standardizing what is held to be common in the language. These include dictionaries and teaching prescriptions. Tireless guardians keep the borders of Anglophone English under surveillance watching for errors of diction, intonation, syntax and pronunciation (Coulmas 2005: 11). Struggles over the latter are represented and expressed in the varieties of World Englishes immediately present in so many disparate localities (Singh and Han 2006). A pertinent example of which can be found on the pull-down menu of Microsoft Word, in the 'language' option under 'tools'. This variety of World Englishes listed there plays an important role in facilitating exchanges in commodities, including the expression of identities. Graddol (2000: 56) argues that there is no need to worry about this trend towards a diversity of World Englishes, as it will not threaten the role of Anglophone English. Modern technologies such as broadcasting and computer media are helping to contain the gap between Anglophone English and the other Englishes of the world. However, trends in cultural hybridization are evident in the acknowledgement of World Englishes. Questions are also being asked about whether it can be taken for granted that native speakers are authorities on many aspects of the language. Anglophone English-speaking countries are recruiting lecturers who studied English as a foreign language to teach native-speaking student-teachers its grammar. These trends are a challenge to the educational and other cultural institutions charged with standardizing English nationally.

Through its encouragement of trans-national mobility the Bologna Process raises questions beyond reforms to degree structures, credit transfer and recognition of qualifications (Wächter 2004). There are also constraints on student and graduate mobility derived from the national grounding of the education cultures and knowledge that immigrant teachers and student-teachers bring to their teaching career in their new homeland. For instance, the character of teacher/student relationships in Australian schools puzzles and even horrifies them (Han 2006). In the education cultures of Asia, teachers are said to be respected. A student who interrupts her/his teacher by asking a question without first getting permission to do so is regarded as rude. Throughout Asia, teachers are said to be a powerful presence before their students. However, in Australian schools teacher/student relationships are markedly different, popularly imagined to be egalitarian. Whatever the character of the English they speak, these immigrant teachers and student-teachers are constrained by the new teaching environment and the educational culture of Australian schools. Not only is recognition of their qualifications and other informational barriers a challenge, but their different knowledge of education, schooling and teaching is also a hurdle to jump in becoming 'Australian teachers'.

These immigrant teachers gained the impression that students in Australian schools seem to have more rights, while teachers apparently have relatively less substantive power. Surra said that it looked as though the students and their teacher treat each other equally:

> In my country, the teacher is like a god. The kids respect their teacher very much. While the teacher is teaching, they keep quiet and never talk. The students respect their teacher a lot, but here the relationship between teacher and students equal.

Surra spoke English. However, the model of teacher/student exchange she had learned in her home country was like an invisible shadow that clung to her. Typical Australian teacher/student relationships provided her with a limited model of a 'good teacher'. She was very excited when explaining teacher/student exchanges in Afghanistan, where she was respected as a teacher, and proud that her students did so. She was also happy with the explicitness of the hierarchical power relations between teachers and their students in her former homeland. Another student-teacher, Guli was more direct in his comments on the constraints he faced in Australian schools:

> If the kids are naughty in class, the teacher here cannot punish them. You have to be very patient to be a teacher here. In China, the teacher can pat the kid on the

> head to show encouragement, but here we are not allowed to touch the
> students. You will be in trouble if you do. I found that the students have too many
> rights here.

Guli's choice of the words 'cannot punish' and 'have to be patient,' indicate
his disappointment with the constraints on Australian teachers' exercise of
(physical) power. He used 'cannot, have to, not allowed' to construct a (questionable) sense of teachers' power as limited and helpless. Knowing this did
not make it easy for Harsha to adjust to the behaviour of Australian students:

> I was surprised to see the students were given prestige. For example, they would
> talk back. Their language use was really a big difference to me. Oh, my God! In
> Fiji, the students even won't look at teachers, eye to eye.

As an immigrant student-teacher Harsha was surprised that Australian
school students seemed to be given a status apparently comparable to their
teachers whose power was more constrained. She was not used to this behaviour, expecting respect as a student-teacher, at least in so far as the students
would be quiet and not talk back. Harsha had long imbibed this view of
teacher/student exchange and so it was a challenge for her to change. These
accounts of teacher/student power relation provide a glimpse of the national
grounding of educational cultures. This poses challenges for trans-national
mobility for such knowledge workers. While they spoke English, their communicative exchanges were constrained by the different educational cultures.
They could teach in English, but they were constrained by a lack of substantive
knowledge about the Australian teaching environment. While trying to sell their
capacity to engage in exchanges in English, this sale was limited by the nationally grounded cultural framing of Australian schools (Singh and Han 2007).
These were beyond the formal accreditation of their English language proficiency or the recognition of their academic qualifications that the Bologna
Process is addressing, even as it defends cultural diversity. They were not free
to teach what or how they use to teach in their former homeland.

Discussion

English has diversified into various local forms via shifts from being a foreign
language through to being a second then to being a first language. Anglophone
English speakers are worried about whether they will continue to have the
power or authority to prescribe the standardized use for English worldwide.
There is speculation that maybe one or another English variety could overtake
Anglophone English for the purposes of international communication and

teaching (Graddol 2000: 56). This is unlikely in the near future. However, for countries such as India, Fiji and Sri Lanka, the curriculum, instructional materials and teaching methods bring non-native models of English into competition with Anglophone varieties.

There are good linguistic reasons for even more Asian Englishes to be accepted into the family of World Englishes (Niu and Wolff, n.d.). However, some are facing rejection. For instance, novelist Hsu-Ming Teo (2000: 3), a Singaporean immigrant looks at these different varieties from the perspective of a character who has carefully acquired Australian English. The character brings to Australia from Singapore her sense of 'superior disgust' in response to these other varieties of English. The World English speakers' incorporation of vocabulary from multiple languages and 'chopped' or 'wrenched' syntax causes these speakers and their ideas to be rejected by this character in the novel. However, this character also disdains the elocution lessons purchased to help Anglophile Asians to efface their local patois. Having bought a veneer of BBC English, this character sees them as carefully cultivating and maintaining this pseudo-dialect to the point of caricature (Teo 2000: 62).

Consider for a moment the ways universities in Britain have capitalized on the structuring of exchanges in World Englishes in the context of the Bologna Process. For instance, Furlong (2005: 60) argues that because English is the international *lingua franca*, the UK has a fortuitous advantage in the Bologna Process over other European countries in the international competition over education. Phillipson (2006: 21) observes that 'the international linguistic marketplace gives unfair advantages to native speakers of English, not only in cross-cultural interaction but also in the workings of the market.' This remains so, even though countries such as the Netherlands have been able to secure a share of the international market in English language education as well as education in English (Dow 2006: 10). Rather provocatively Neave (2005: 19) contends that the worldview of British universities is nation-centred, being defensive, self-interested and narrow-minded. Because of the English language's international status, he says that the responses of these institutions to the Bologna Process include expressions of superiority, complacency and neocolonial paternalism. Because of this prejudice, the (multilingual) knowledge and knowledge networks of international students tend to be ignored. Australia shares a similar complacency, albeit compounded by the guilt this pleasure induces.

English is today's international language because its exchange value; symbolically expressing modernity and a resource for trading technological knowledge. Consequently, English will maintain its role as the world's *lingua franca* for some time (Baumgardner 2006). Moreover, American VOA English is still the sun around which other varieties of English revolve. For many, an education in English, as much as English names can be exchanged for their advancement and prosperity. However, they might find that these exchanges involve more than they anticipated when they are labelled as persons of 'non-English speaking background' (NESB). In Australia, this label serves to justify the prevailing monolingual, Anglophone control systems that reproduce the uneven distribution of linguistic power in ways that take English-only pedagogies as given. Globally, the dominance of English gives rise to 'anglocentrism', a form of ethnocentrism that causes people to act as if their own group's language provided the 'appropriate' guidelines against which all other people's English should be tested. Our preference for the term World English Speakers (WES) echoes the disagreements about different ways of interpreting these issues (Han 2006).

The colonial and postcolonial spread of English worldwide has created many varieties of World English Speakers, albeit stratified according to different historical, sociolinguistic and literary contexts. World English Speakers include the native English speakers of Australia, New Zealand, the USA, the UK and Canada; those from countries colonized by the former; those from the rest of the world, and those engaged in interactions between the latter two. The increased mobility of the world's English speakers is multiplying the diversity of Englishes with which native speakers of the language have to engage in exchanges. However, while immigrants, international students and foreign visitors learn to communicate with Anglophone English speakers, the latter hardly have begun to acquire the necessary communicative skills for appropriate exchanges with the increasing diversity of World English Speakers (Kubota, 2001). Both listeners and speakers share responsibilities so that communicative exchanges can take place. The presence of diverse World English Speakers is influencing daily exchanges among people within Anglophone English speaking countries. Anglophone English speakers cause communication difficulties through their intolerance of (speakers of) other varieties of World Englishes. Unfortunately, the latter are then blamed for this miscommunication (Kubota, 2001). Interactions composed of shallow gestures make it easier not to go deep, or to enter into anything requiring the negotiation of intricate communications. These informal, cultural constraints on communicative exchanges in English are compounded by the different education knowledge carried by these various English-speaking constituencies. This results in the economic devaluation of these speakers of other Englishes in Anglophone countries. Added to this, the symbolic and instrumental functions of English are integral constituents in the skills-base of trans-national knowledge workers.

Trading English speaking knowledge workers

Speaking English with a non-Australian accent is a reason that immigrant teachers and student-teachers are devalued and their teaching constrained. For instance, Jigar was concerned about the affects of his Indian English on his teaching:

> I came to this new school and gained a permanent position here. English is my main language in my 35 years of teaching. I wasn't too bad. But the first year was a nightmare. My accent was making too many problems. But again I had to change and to learn. Like 'Hello' and 'hallo' are different. I have taught a few student-teachers [who speak different varieties of English] to get over this accent problem, simple pronunciations like, "What 'work' [uə:] are you doing? or What 'work' [uə:r] are you doing?" Saying New Zealand or New Źealand makes a big difference. We can actually teach people to come close to what is acceptable pronunciation. It does make a difference. As soon as you open your mouth, kids say, 'It's not just the colour of your skin. You cannot speak my language.' You don't worry about an article in India, but here they would say you cannot speak their language.

Jigar had many years of experience teaching in English. However, his Indian English troubled his first year of teaching in Australia. These constraints were not due to government policy or regulations but part of the rules governing Australia's educational culture. These student-teachers had to learn to change their particular variety of English to make it acceptably Australian. Diverse accents, lexical differences or grammatical variations could devalue their English and teaching. Anbu had such an experience:

> The students do tend to tease you by imitating the accent you are talking. They do things they are not supposed to be doing in class. But all of a sudden when another teacher from an Australian English speaking background comes in, they all sit up and listen. As soon as that teacher walks out, again the behaviour problems start.

Anbu's Indian English became a target for her students, constraining her capacity to teach. She observed that the students misbehaved in her class even though they were well-behaved for Anglo-Australian teachers. This attributed to her Indian English. One of the student-teachers Anbu supervised also spoke Indian-English:

> I had supervised a student-teacher last semester. He is from India. He did pretty well except for his accent. The students were shocked when they heard somebody speak like that. He did face some difficulties there. Otherwise his subject was fantastic.

The major difficulties these student-teachers experienced during the practicum were to do with the variety of World English they spoke. This difficulty was compounded by their lack of knowledge of the local educational culture. The devaluing of their English was evident in their students' responses to them. This may explain in part their frustrations in securing job opportunities. They did not seem to have the same opportunities when accessing permanent teaching positions as their Anglophone peers:

> After you go through all these studies, it is going to take you a few years to get a permanent job. Many local teachers get permanent positions straight away, but as a migrant teacher, although you have the experience and qualifications, you won't have the same status. (Abha)

Abha observed that migrant teachers' knowledge of education was not given the same status as that of the local teachers. Despite their educational capital, these teachers were disadvantaged in the labour market where they were not valued as much as Anglophone teachers. Darshan made a similar observation:

> They teach maths and I teach science. Maybe because of the shortage of maths teacher, immigrant maths teachers can get a permanent job ahead of me, a science teacher. My observation is that before local Anglo-Australian student-teachers complete their practicum, they are often offered a permanent job. For us from other English speaking backgrounds, we have to wait for a permanent position.

While open to question, a few of these interviewees were of the view that Anglo-Australian student-teachers were more likely to be employed permanently before themselves. Even so, among these immigrant teachers, those with expertise in mathematics education quickly gained permanent jobs relative to teachers in other subject areas, reflecting the skills mismatch affecting these fields (Santoro, Kamler and Reid 2001). Anglo-Australian student-teachers were thought to more likely to get a job offer while doing their teaching practicum whereas student-teachers who spoke other varieties of English had to wait much longer for such opportunities. Fareen told of her experience of being a casual teacher:

> I migrated here from Fiji seven years ago . . . . I did casual teaching as a 'mobile permanent'. They moved me around schools. In 1999, I started here. It took time to get a permanent job. I was a teacher of accounting in Fiji for ten years in a high school. I found it was hard to fit into somebody else's schedules as a casual teacher. I didn't have my own room. I had to teach one class there, and one class here. I was running around every lesson. If you are a casual teacher, you don't have authority. You are here for one day and you are in another school the next. You can't give them detention. I hated the job. I don't like it. If I go into the classroom as a teacher, I want to teach. If I am in my own department, that might be alright. So I know the subject, I may be able to teach. If I am just a casual teacher, I am there baby-sitting the kids. You know I am not being used properly.

Fareen was an experienced teacher in Fiji but only employed as a casual teacher after migrating to Australia. She found doing casual teaching a difficulty. Moving around different schools and classes to 'baby sit' students gave her no authority and many challenges. She hated this, but had to do it while waiting for the opportunity to gain a permanent position. Like other immigrant teachers, she tended to attribute the reason for having difficulties in finding a permanent job to the lack of proficiency in Australian English, and thus issues of communicative competence. However, Abha explained that this was one of many factors that influenced their job searches:

> Here you don't have fixed textbooks as we do in India, so you have to know the curriculum and no one is going to teach you the curriculum. After you get the approval, the system is totally different here in Australia compared to India. There should be an orientation at the Department level. There is absolutely no proper communication between the teachers and the Department. The Department does not tell you what you are going to teach and what you are going to do. There should be an orientation for migrant teachers to observe in school class. In our context to know the expectation in class is more important for us.

Abha did not confront any difficulties in gaining recognition for his Masters degree from India; and he was given permission to seek employment as a teacher in Australia. However, even with the formal recognition of his qualifications he could not sell the labour this qualification represented in the market for Australian school teachers. Because of the apparent absence of any induction or mentoring programme at the time of his recruitment, he had no systematic knowledge of Australian curriculum and therefore no idea of how and what to teach. This was among the reasons that some of these immigrant teachers were less valued and thus experienced difficulties in securing jobs. The Department concerned now does much more to address these issues. Babur explained that the constraints derived from a lack of familiarity with the taken-for-granted ideas, practices and relationships embedded in such a nation-bound workplace as schools. This usually takes immigrant teachers a few years of very hard work to overcome:

> I had been teaching for six years in Fiji before migration. The first difficulty I had was the education system. Nobody taught me how exactly the system works. Even though I have been teaching for two and half years in Australia, I still don't know some of the procedures followed in this school. I am still learning how to manage the students' behaviour and what policies and procedures employed for this. You have no direction. You don't really know where to get yourself into.

Babur was overwhelmed by the difficulty of learning and understanding the Australian education culture, its system, policies and procedures. The recognition of his Fijian qualifications was relatively easy. For him and the other immigrant teachers we interviewed, 'learning the ropes', the nationally-grounded educational culture, took much longer and considerable effort.

The Bologna Process aims to promote the trans-national mobility of students and graduate knowledge workers by removing obstacles to the recognition of qualifications. Trans-national mobility of human capital is a key reason the Australian Government (DEST 2006) is interested in engaging with and responding to it. These teachers who had migrated to Australia followed the requisite procedures to gain formal recognition of their qualifications (Han 2006). However, the gap between their knowledge of Australia's educational culture and that of their former home country could not be bridged solely by formally attesting to the comparability of their qualifications. Unfortunately, at the time of the recruitment of these particular teachers there were no mentors to guide them to bridge their 'gap' in knowledge about nationally-grounded education cultures. These cultural constraints saw them learning by 'trial and error' to follow the nation-centred policies and procedures. This typically occurred only after they were 'shocked' into doing so by being confronted with the challenges of managing their students and the curriculum. Their difficulty was not in the informational constraints posed by the trans-national recognition of qualifications, important as these are, but in the knowledge constraints borne of the different education cultures (Singh and Han 2007). If Australia is interested in aligning with Bologna Process, this raises the question of how is it going to address tensions due to the differences in the education cultures between countries. This is because the capacity of knowledge workers to trade on their English language competence differs between immigrant and native English speakers.

Discussion

To illustrate this point, consider the following examples. First, the *China TEFL Network* (2006) provided a list of the 71 foreign teachers it employed to work as English language teachers in China. The qualification of these Anglophone speakers of English had the following features. All were from Anglophone English speaking countries except for one from Argentina and another from Egypt. Eleven people had no degree but had short-term TESOL training; five had degrees with English majors; and seven had a degree in education. The rest (n=47) had degrees in areas such as law, psychology, medicine or information technology. None of the latter had teaching qualifications or experience. Apparently, one so-called 'teacher' was nineteen years old and had only five years of education himself. Second, examine the following advertisement.

Project:	Teaching English in China
Start dates:	1st and 3rd Mondays of each month
Departure and End Point:	Beijing International Airport
Language Need:	Fluency in English
Accommodation and meals:	Host family and school accommodation, Chinese foods 3 times a day by host
Activities:	Teaching English to public and private school children
Working hours:	20-30 hours per week
Qualification:	No qualification is needed

(Source: Global Crossroad, 2006)

In India, English is no longer an instrument in the struggle to assert anti-colonial identities. It is now used to testify workers' worldly status as speakers of accent-neutral English, which is seen as appropriate for doing local/global business via internet telephony (Kachru 2006). In this way, English is having a profound influence on Australian business, commerce and labour through the outsourcing of work to India. 'Cheap' English speaking labour from India and elsewhere in Asia is being used to sell premium products and services in the Minority World (McIlveen 2006).

In some places native English speakers are recruited to teach the language, sometimes without any relevant educational or linguistic qualifications. The recruitment of unqualified and inexperienced Anglophone speakers as English language teachers is a sign of the market value of this variety of the language. In terms of its commodity value the English of native speakers is regarded as superior, despite them speaking a diversity of dialects (Singh, Kell and Pandian, 2002: 182–183). Often no academic qualifications in language studies or education are required. At best, there is an expectation that Anglophone speakers might have some English teaching experience, or at least experience working with students. These differences extend to the accumulation of financial capital by immigrant and native English speakers. In a pioneering study Borjas (1994) found that in the USA native English speakers have higher earnings than those who are not. In other words there is a link between English language proficiency and the rate of wage convergence, with native English speakers gaining higher wages than their equally qualified peers who spoke other varieties of the world's Englishes.

Students who do not speak the local version of standardized English are at a disadvantage when competing in the labour market with those who do. This is true for Anglophone students who speak different dialects of English as it is for speakers of other World Englishes (Tollefson 1991). In the USA, English language programmes are mainly designed to lead newly arrived World English Speakers into particular types of jobs. Tollefson's (1991) ground-breaking research found that the teaching of English as a second language served to channel them into jobs in the marginal economy, such as milk bar attendants or taxi drivers. Where these speakers of other varieties of English have been unable to acquire fluent, standardized English, they end up working in poorly paid, casual employment with little opportunity for socioeconomic advancement. Linguistic marginalization has negative consequences on the socioeconomic benefits these workers may gain:

> Language policies requiring widespread second language acquisition may help to sustain a system in which language is a key marker of socioeconomic class and power. When such a system is sustained over time, individuals whose economic advance is blocked may increasingly support revolutionary changes in language policy. (Tollefson 1991: 136)

Following World War II, Australia's immigration policy changed from favouring English speakers and their rapid assimilation in the 1950s, through integration in the 1960s, to multiculturalism from the 1970s until the 1990s. In the late 1990s, these policies began to be reversed under nation-centred protectionism. Even so this latter policy paints a pleasing portrait of respecting cultural, linguistic and religious differences, as does the Bologna Process. Over this time Australia's language policy has not devalued English as the national language; it is the country's common language. Australian English is the language of advanced education, business, the highest-paying jobs and entitlement to citizenship:

> Lack of proficiency in standard[ised] English correlated closely with occupancy of lower paid employment and, to a great degree, occupational mobility in Australia depends on skills in the English language. (Lo Bianco cited in Tollefson, 1991: 181)

English is not just an income-generating product or service, as well as a means of facilitating the exchange of the knowledge integral to the 'new' economy (Wächter 2004). In the world's trans-national labour market, English plays multidimensional symbolical and instrumental functions as a commodity (Coulmas 2005). For instance, the Bologna Process for harmonizing European higher education sees English as constituting an integral aspect of the trans-national mobility of students and graduate knowledge workers (Coleman 2006). As a key driver in the current phase in the internationalization of higher education, the Bologna Process is influencing the local/global structuring of the trans-national labour market. For example, the Bologna Process for enhancing mobility has affected the structure and content of higher education courses in Iceland, encouraging their teaching in English (Hilmarsson-Dunn 2006). The labour that goes into producing textbooks, examinations, lectures, subjects, PhD theses and research publications increasingly works in English. In order to position themselves internationally, in the competition for foreign students and international labour, Iceland's higher education institutions are moving to targeting the marketing of their English language courses abroad. The trans-national labour force being created through higher education sees English exerting pressures across all domains and the corpus of the Icelandic language. Phillipson (2006: 16) contends that, in the Bologna Process, the formation of a trans-national knowledge workers means 'English medium higher education'. The currency of other Englishes and other languages is being deflated.

Conclusion

In the world's multilingual knowledge economies, the English language plays multidimensional roles as a commodity. English in itself is sold as a product or service. It is a means for facilitating exchange. Further, it constitutes an integral aspect of the skills-base of trans-national labour. The immigrant teachers and student-teachers whose experiences have been reported in this chapter spoke a variety of Englishes. However, these were not valued as much as Australian English for the purpose of communication in Australian schools; or in the international market for teachers' labour, or as marketable products and services in themselves. This is not just a language issue. The reasons for this situation are partly because the carriers of these particular varieties of the world's Englishes were from different national education systems and cultures, with all that this means for differences in educational policies, philosophies and pedagogies.

Added to this, the globalization of Europe's Bologna Process is challenging countries such as Australia to take the next step in responding to the intensification of competition in the international market for education, including its trade in English language products and services. The promotion of trans-national mobility among students and graduates is integral to this journey. English is an important cultural constraint in the harmonization of a European Higher Education Area as aspired to under the Bologna Process. Despite formal recognition of qualifications, as governed by explicit policies and procedures, it puts English-speaking countries in the advantageous situation in the Process. Australia has already begun to consider the formal constraints on cross-border student and graduate movement, through reviewing its policies, rules and regulations, to produce an Australian Higher Education Graduate Statement. The evidence presented in this chapter suggests that in the quest for innovative solutions to this threat due regard might also be given to the cultural constraints that are necessarily created by nationally grounded professions, such as teaching. It may be that these barriers are as important as the informational barriers being addressed through the globalization of the Bologna Process.

Acknowledgement

Michael Singh acknowledges the support of the University of Western Sydney's Professional Development Programme for time to work on this chapter. Jinghe Han's contribution to this chapter was made possible by a Write-up Award from Charles Sturt University.

References

Baumgardner, R. (2006), 'The appeal of English in Mexican commerce', *World Englishes* 25 (2) 251–66.

Bishop, J. (10 January 2007), Towards a world-leading skills passport for Australian students (Media release), Retrieved 29 January 2007, http://www.dest.gov.au/Ministers/media/Bishop/2007/01/B001100107.asp

Borjas, G. (1994), 'The economics of immigration', *Journal of Economic Literature* 32: 1667–717.

China Daily (5 October 2002), Government encourages public to learn English.

China TEFL Network (2006), Wai jiao zhao pin. Retrieved 13 August 2006, http://cn.chinatefl.com/wjzp/teachershow.asp

China Youth (2005), Europe commits to building 'aircraft carrier' for Higher Education. Retrieved 15 November 2006 http://news.xinhuanet.com/world/2005-04/27/content_2882665.htm

Coleman, J. (2006), 'English medium teaching in European higher education', *Language Teaching* 39: 1–14.

Coulmas, F. (2005), 'Changing language regimes in globalising environments', *International Journal of the Sociology of Language* 175/176: 3–15.

Department of Education, Science and Training (2006), *The Bologna Process and Australia* (Canberra: The Department).

Dow, E. (2006), 'Britannia meets Bologna', *Perspective* 10(1): 9–14.

English Australia (2007), *English Australia Survey of Major ELICOS Regional Markets* (Surry Hill (NSW): English Australia).

Foude, A. (2005), 'Meeting the needs of international students in schools', *Independent Education* 35(3): 13–14.

Furlong, P. (2005), 'Doing politics', *Politics* 25(1): 53–61.

Global Crossroad (2006), Volunteer English teaching in China. Retrieved 13 August 2006, http://www.globalcrossroad.com/china/teaching_in_china.php

Graddol, D. (2000), *The Future of English* (London: The British Council).

Han, J. (2006), *The Retention of 'World English Speaking' Student-Teachers.* PhD thesis (Sydney: University of Western Sydney).

Hilmarsson-Dunn, A. (2006), 'Protectionist language policies in the face of the forces of English', *Language Policy* 5: 293–312.

Institute of Language UNSW (n.d.), *Professional English Assessment for Teachers* (Sydney: Institute of Language UNSW).

Kachru, Y. (2006), 'Mixer lyricing in Hinglish', *World Englishes* 25 (2): 223–33.

Kendall, T. (2004), 'Exporting Australian educational services to China', *Journal of Higher Education Policy and Management* 26 (1): 23–33.

Kubota, R. (2001), 'Teaching world Englishes to native speakers of English in the USA', *World Englishes* 20(1): 47–64.

McIlveen, L. (2006), 'Finding their calling', *The Daily Telegraph.* Retrieved 14 October 2006, www.news.com.au/dailytelegraph Saturday, 67

Neave, G. (2005), 'The supermarketed university', *Perspectives* 9(1): 17–22.

Niu, Q. and Wolff (n.d.), English or Chinglish? Retrieved 18 October 2000, http://www.usingenglish.com/esl-in-china/english-or-chinglish.pdf

Pegrum, M. (2004), 'Selling English: Advertising and the discourses of ELT', *English Today* 20(1): 3–10.

Phillipson, R. (2006), 'English, a cuckoo in the European higher education nest of languages?', *European Journal of English Studies* 10(1): 13–32.

Santoro, N., Kamler, B. and Reid, J. (2001), 'Teachers talking difference', *Teaching Education* 12(2): 191–212.

Singh, M. and Han, J. (2006), 'Global English', *Mosaic* 13(1): 34–36.

Singh, M. and Han, J. (2008), 'Trans-national mobility and World English Speaking student-teachers: Bologna's interruption of absences in teacher education' in Phelan, A. and Sumsion, J. (ed.), *Critical Readings in Teacher Education: Provoking Absences* (Rotterdam, The Netherlands: Sense Publishers).

Singh, M., Kell, P. and Pandian, A. (2002), *Appropriating English* (New York: Peter Lang).

Teo, H. (2000), *Love and Vertigo* (St Leonards, NSW: Allen & Unwin).

Tollefson, J. (1991), *Planning Language, Planning Inequality* (London: Longman).

Wächter, B. (2004), 'The Bologna Process', *European Journal of Education* 39(3): 265–73.

Witte, J. (2004), 'The introduction of two-tiered study structures in the context of the Bologna Process', *Higher Education Policy* 17: 405–25.

Index